Designing Information Systems

Stanley G. Blethyn BSc, MSc

Carys Y. Parker BSc

Butterworth–Heinemann
London Boston Singapore Sydney Toronto Wellington

PART OF REED INTERNATIONAL P.L.C.

First published 1990

© **Butterworth–Heinemann Ltd, 1990**

British Library Cataloguing in Publication Data

Blethyn, Stanley G.
  Designing information systems.
  1. Information systems. Design
  I. Title   II. Parker, Carys Y.
  004.21

ISBN 0-750-61038-7

Library of Congress Cataloging in Publication Data

Blethyn, Stanley G.
  Designing information systems/Stanley G. Blethyn,
    Carys Y. Parker.
    p.   cm.
  Includes bibliographical references and index.
  ISBN 0-750-61038-7
  1. Management information systems. I. Parker, Carys Y.
II. Title.
T58.6.B518   1990   90-2179
658.4'038--dc20   CIP

Phototypeset by Scribe Design, Gillingham, Kent
Printed and bound in Great Britain by Courier International Ltd, Tiptree, Essex

Preface

As system designers we learned our art slowly and painfully by working with good designers and by making mistakes. As teachers, we hoped that we could help our students to find a shorter learning path. Generally, we were disappointed.

There are many splendid texts describing data flow diagrams, data modelling and the problems of implementing design solutions and of project management. There are other texts which explore system concepts such as boundary, purpose, feedback and control within businesses. Yet more tell us about human problems in industry. What we couldn't find was something which brought these threads together into a coherent structured pattern. We believe that this is what we have now done.

The book is divided into five parts. Part 1 presents some concepts of the system approach, related to a number of human activity systems. We have used the opportunity to introduce some basic methods of describing systems.

Part 2 describes the mechanics of structured design. It is the longest segment, but that is what must be expected. We have used the project life cycle framework for the design activity, and have emphasized the key documents and products which constitute progress milestones for structured design.

Design must be managed, and Part 3 relates to issues of planning, control and maintenance. Necessarily, we must ensure that the purposes of the design are achieved; that this is done within the budgeted resource limits allowed for a project; and that the completed system can be successfully maintained. In Part 3 we have written about the use of data dictionaries. We believe that rigorous use of words and symbols is an essential part of design. It isn't enough by itself. We can't gainsay the need for the spark of creativity, and for being clear about what we are trying to do. We do assert that sloppy description makes for sloppy design.

Design is for the benefit of people, and designed systems are built by and used by people. The more successfully the real needs of people are met, the more successful the design. A designed system which did not serve human needs would be a nonsense. Part 4 is dedicated to those human needs. Why do people do the things they do? What can all the various constituencies expect to gain from any system that they are part of? How does the system designer fit into all this?

We suggest that Part 1 can be taken in at a first reading. Come back to it for more wealth of detail, but start there for the foundation of what we mean by human activity systems.

Within Part 2, Chapter 4 gives the broad view. Chapters 5 and 6 on functional analysis, and Chapter 7 on data analysis, are the basis of the hard work you will have to do. Work through them slowly, and make all the use you can of the examples we give. Chapters 8 and 9 can be read in your own time. They are important, but you won't need to have mastered data analysis and functional analysis to get value from them.

We suspect that Part 3 deserves to be read again before you finally put the book down. Only when you have an idea of how complex design is, can you appreciate the problems of attempting to control and manage it.

We have not assumed specialized prior knowledge. We anticipate that the material would be taught on undergraduate and diploma courses for students of information system design, business studies and accountancy and on professional courses. It would be suitable for postgraduate students not specializing in information system design. We include case study material and discussion points which make it suitable as a course text in these areas.

Quite deliberately, we have avoided specific reference to any particular computer hardware or software. We believe that there is a robustness of design principles which transcends the current hardware or software flavour of the month. Above all, we offer this book as a book to be read. We have tried to write it in English. Jargon hinders both design and learning.

The material has been tested. We have used it on several degree and diploma courses at Bristol Polytechnic; on courses leading to the award of the National Computing Centre Basic Certificate in Systems Analysis; and for courses designed for staff from Rolls-Royce PLC.

The methodology is not unique. It has commonality with many of the current approaches to system design. In particular, we applaud the greater awareness of structure brought about by the use of SSADM (Structured Systems Analysis and Design Methods).

If you enjoy reading this book but have some suggestions or

criticisms that can improve it, we should like to hear from you. We should still like to hear from you if you don't enjoy it, to tell us why not!

Thanks are due to Frank Maddix for the authorship of Chapter 12 dealing with Human–Computer Interaction. This develops in much more detail some of the ideas we introduce in Chapter 8.

We are grateful to the many people who have been willing to talk ideas through and who have given constructive criticism. Thanks are due especially to our students. There are so many people that a full list of names is impossible, but we are grateful to Sue Saunders who did some of the typing, and Chris Makepeace who took the photographs. We appreciate the help and support of Butterworth Scientific Ltd, especially Ann Berne and Nick Bliss. We also wish to acknowledge the extremely helpful comments of the referees. Finally, we acknowledge the support of family and friends without which nothing would get done: Tony, Huw, Jan, Beryl, Goronwy, Elizabeth, Sheila and Aggy.

Contents

Part 1
Human organization

Chapter 1

System basics

1.1 What is a system?

Right at the beginning, we need a few definitions. Let's list them. We need to know what we mean by 'a system'; by 'information'; and by 'systems analysis'. Later we'll also need to be clear what we mean by 'a business system' and 'a computer system': but they can wait for the moment.

When we describe systems we'll also be introducing some of the charting conventions of systems analysis. The earlier we start using them, the easier the whole business of describing things is going to be.

We're going to illustrate what we have to say with many examples, so let's start right away. A *system* has been described as a whole 'thing' (it's helpful to use the word 'entity' rather than 'thing'!) consisting of parts. In that sense we see that a *family* is a system. It is a single entity, and it consists of the members of the family. Unfortunately, this definition takes the world as it is, and there is no way that we can try to improve that world. If we are interested in doing things better, we have to suppose that our systems have some kind of purpose.

Let's try the definition again. A system is an entity *having a purpose* and consisting of *functional parts* all helping to achieve that purpose. We'll illustrate this definition by describing a sailboard; or perhaps it would be better if we called it a board-sailing system!

The real purpose of our system is the joy of sailing very fast over water. Unfortunately 'joy' is rather hard to define. For simplicity, we'll say that the purpose is to sail a board as fast as it can be made to go in the prevailing conditions. A board-sailing system is a rather good illustration of a system having parts, because at the end of a day's board-sailing we'll have to disassemble those parts and load them separately onto a car to drive home!

We'll start with the obvious parts; sailboards have a board and a sail. The sail reacts with the wind to provide forward thrust.

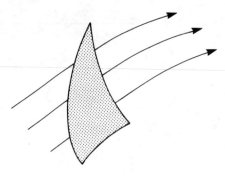

But unless there is a board as well, the sail won't be much use. The board provides a platform for the person who is sailing, and has a shape which allows it to skim over the surface of the water.

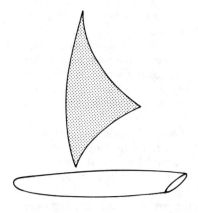

We need a mast to hold up the sail and a 'wishbone' boom, both to keep the sail taut and to give the person sailing a handle to move the sail about. When you sail a board all the direction and speed control has to come from movement of the sail mast. Necessarily, then, our board-sailing system has to have a flexible mast foot to join the mast to the board.

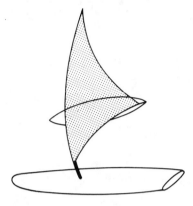

We're still not going to make much progress with our board. Unless there is some way of preventing the board from being blown sideways we'll never sail with anything except a following wind. We need a dagger board.

But it's still not a board-sailing system! We must have lots of rope, lines and cleats, as well as some more obvious omissions. For a board-sailing system we need a person standing on the board, the water and the wind. With all these the person on the board can sail!

There are some important things that we need to know about any system, apart from its purpose. If we are to understand what the system is doing we need to know its *boundary*; that is, what is included in the system (which also means what is left out!).

If we are going board-sailing we will probably need a car with a roof-rack on top and a road to drive it on. Are those included in our board-sailing system? The answer isn't obvious.

Whatever we leave out of our system is a part of the *environment* of the system. We have included the wind and the water in the board-sailing system, but there are forces of sun and moon, oceans and landmasses, atmosphere and stratosphere, which have a vital effect on the weather in which we sail. If those forces are not part of the system they are certainly part of the system's environment.

Somewhere there are undoubtedly groups of people working away designing ever-better sail-boards. They are a part of the environment, too, with a very obvious effect on board-sailing systems.

Necessarily then, there will be flows of material, of influence, of ideas, of information, across any system boundary. The boundary is *arbitrary*, we have chosen it ourselves; and it is *permeable*.

Everything within the boundary is a part of the system. Everything else is the environment. The parts within the boundary can be seen as having a purpose. The environment affects the system (and sometimes the system changes the environment) by exchanges across the boundary. The system we have described is an *open system*. If there were no exchanges across the boundary we would have a *closed system*. (But can a closed system exist? It's surely more a concept than a reality!)

If we are to achieve the purpose of our board-sailing system we need to monitor what is happening to the board and detect when anything is not going according to plan. If a board-sailor is sailing towards a distant point, and the board goes off course, then it must be brought back onto course. If the environment changes and the wind freshens or veers, then the board-sailor must be ready to adapt the system. He may sail ashore and change to smaller sails; or he may adjourn to the club bar (is that part of the system?). The purpose may still be to seek joy, but it has been adapted to seek joy in an entirely different way.

There are broadly two levels of control involved here. There is the process of monitoring deviations from a plan and taking corrective action. This is usually described as *feedback control*, and is designed to *maintain* the system doing what it is currently doing. The second level of control is the process of monitoring the environment and being ready to *adapt* the system or even to modify the purpose of the system.

1.2 Information

For both processes we need to obtain *information* to help us decide what action is required. Ideas about information tend to get mixed up with ideas about control, but although information is necessary for control, they are not the same thing. It was said of one bankrupt company that the management confused commissioning reports on the state of the company with taking corrective action. They had an information system of a sort but failed to use it effectively to control the company.

What information does our board-sailor need? As far as maintenance is concerned, he needs to see where he is trying to sail to, and by how much he is missing it. He needs to see or feel changes in the wind relative to the sail board. He needs to see what other water travellers are doing, and how this affects him.

For changes in the environment he will be looking for the pattern of the wind on the water before it hits his sail, the message of the clouds and the nature of the waves; or the arrival of so many people in the sailing area that sailing for pleasure is not possible. He may also have listened to the weather forecast before putting his board on the water.

Then he will need to monitor the environment to find what new boards are on the market, and what new and more exciting board-sailing skills are being developed.

If we pull together some of the ideas on information:

1. It must have a *surprise* content; it must tell us something that we didn't already know.
2. The information must be *action* oriented. It must cause or make more likely some action that wouldn't otherwise have been taken.
3. The action taken must be perceived as *helping us to achieve a purpose*.

The information we seek may be:

1. Feedback information, telling us about the effectiveness of past actions. The feedback may be *negative feedback*, reporting deviation from some desired standard, or *positive feedback*, which tends to encourage any existing tendency. If, for example, our board-sailor has won the last three club competitions in a season he may feel encouraged that he will win the fourth as well.
2. Information from the environment which will cause us to adapt the system, or to alter the purpose of the system.
3. Information from the environment and from our own stored experience which affects the range of actions we can take.

1.3 What we mean by systems analysis

We have outlined systems and information (whether we describe it thus or more grandly as an *information system*). We have not yet mentioned systems analysis.

Once we say that a system has a purpose it is feasible to analyse that system to find out how well it is achieving that purpose, and why it isn't doing it better. But if we are going to hang a definition of systems analysis so squarely on system purpose it is time we looked more closely at purpose.

It is wrong to suppose that all systems are alike; there is no single world view. It is also a little dangerous to classify systems, since this tempts us to exaggerate the similarities within one class. Accepting this danger, we can gain some insight by using Peter Checkland's[1] classification of systems as:

Natural systems
Designed physical systems (artefacts)
Designed conceptual systems
Human activity systems

Some *natural systems* can be regarded as having a purpose in the sense that they are *for* something; they have a *use*. Thus a human respiratory system enables an individual person to live; it is for respiration. Most other natural systems simply *exist*. Following Checkland's argument, to postulate a purpose for a whole person, or for the Baltic Sea, is to lapse into theological speculation.

A *designed physical system* exists because it is needed as a tool within a human activity system. It has a *use*, just as a respiratory system has a use. But it doesn't have any purpose of its own outside that use. It is a functional part of a human activity system. A bridge has a use within a transport system. A sailboard (or the mast or sails) has a use within a board-sailing system.

A *designed conceptual system* (for example, a method of calculating square roots, an information system or a control system) is in exactly the same situation. It exists because it is needed within some human activity system.

It is only of a *human activity system* that we can say that it can have purpose in the sense of a direction or a goal to be achieved (although the onset of artificial intelligence may alter this). We have to say that in most cases the purpose is something attributed to the system by systems analysts, or imposed on the system by a forceful manager. It is not a God-given intrinisic part of the system waiting to be discovered. We can only improve a board-sailing system by making an assumption about what the system is trying to do. If it is sailing very fast, then a certain system design will emerge; if it is performing tricks and stunts (hot-dogging!) then the design will be different.

Systems analysis, then, can be described as a process by which we attribute purposes, or goals, to a human activity system; determine how well those purposes are being achieved (if the system already exists); and specify the requirements of the various tools and techniques which are to be used within the system if the desired system performance is to be achieved. The tool with which systems analysis has traditionally concerned itself is the information system. *System design* is the whole process, including system analysis, by which an initial user requirement is turned into a working system.

In the next chapter we will use the ideas we've introduced to discuss some human activity systems. The first will be the organization of a cub-scouts sports day. The second will be a medium-sized manufacturing business. The third will be a knowledge-based system. In each case our principal concern will be the information system. We will introduce various charting conventions which will help us to describe these systems.

1.4 Summary

- Possible system definitions:

  An entity having parts;
  An entity having a purpose and functional parts to achieve that purpose.

- System boundary:

  What is included and what is excluded.

- Environment:

  Outside the system boundary; but with flows of material, of influence, of ideas, and of information across that boundary.

- Information:

  Has a surprise content;
  Is action oriented;
  The action must be perceived as helping to achieve our purpose.

- Feedback information is of two types:

  Negative feedback – helping to maintain a steady state;
  Positive feedback – encouraging any existing tendency.

- Information from the environment helps us to *adapt the system.*
- Information from the environment, and from our own stored experience, influences the range of actions we are able to take.
- Systems can be classified:

  Natural systems;
  Designed physical systems;
  Designed conceptual systems;
  Human activity systems.

- Systems analysis:

  Analysing and specifying the requirements of the information system for a human activity system.

Discussion points

1.1 Consider a family bakery business as a system.
   What is the *purpose* of the system?
   What *parts* or components does the system have?
   Describe the system boundary, and the reasons for including

some 'things' in the system and putting other 'things' in the environment.

What feedback mechanisms might operate?

What adaptive mechanisms might operate? How do these differ from maintenance mechanisms?

What information about the environment should be monitored?

1.2 There is a village called Tresaith, near the coast of Wales.

Describe the village as a system in terms of purpose, boundary, steady state, feedback, open systems, and maintenance and adaptive mechanisms.

1.3 'Only human activity systems have purpose.' Discuss.

1.4 Some writers[2] have distinguished between a *purposive* system, as being a system which pursues set purposes, and a *purposeful* system, as being a system which can generate its own purposes, and adapt not just its behaviour but also its purposes. A purposeful system 'selects ends as well as means and thus displays will'. Do you regard this distinction as helpful?

1.5 'An information system is a tool for use within a human activity system.' Discuss.

1.6 Do you consider that the systems approach provides a useful framework for analysis?

References

1 Peter Checkland, 'A systems map of the universe', in *System Concepts*, edited by Beishon and Peters, Open University Press, Milton Keynes (1972)
2 Russell L. Ackoff, 'Towards a system of system concepts', *Ibid.*

Chapter 2

Describing systems

2.1 Data flow diagrams and data dictionaries

If a picture is worth a thousand words, then we shouldn't waste time with verbal descriptions. Figure 2.1 is a data flow diagram (DFD) describing the stages in planning, organizing and executing a cub-scout sports day. We have largely used the conventions suggested by Tom de Marco[1] in drawing DFDs. The system outlined is designed to solicit entries from the cub-scout leaders, assemble all the interested people on the chosen day of the sports, complete the programme with despatch and efficiency, select the winning cub-scout pack and give them a prize, and send all cub-scouts who are winners of final races on their way with certificates.

We assume that the sports consists entirely of track events, and that for each event there are several heats and a final race. Points for calculating the winning cub-scout pack are awarded on the final race only.

The diagram has four elements:

(a) Field booking

A *data flow*. The names written against it is descriptive, but it is also a unique indentify-ing label. The data flow is a pipeline through which defined packets of data flow.

(b) Record the results

A *function*. It is less important to put a descriptive label on a function than on a data flow. It would be quite sensible, for example, to describe function 1 on our diagram as 'the function which generates the logistic details'.

(c) Sports programme

A *data store*. Any data which must be stored away for subsequent retrieval are given an identifying name and represented like this. There is usually no need to label data flows

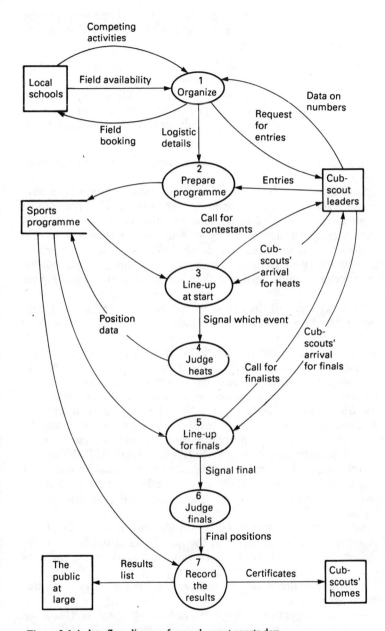

Figure 2.1 A data flow diagram for a cub-scout sports day

into or out of a data store. The content of the flows is implied by the description of the store.

(d)

Cub- scout leaders

A *source* or *sink*. This is any source of data outside the system we are describing, or any destination of data outside our system. We shall also refer to sources and sinks as *external entities*, outside our system boundary.

Each of these shapes is easy to sketch freehand on an A4 sheet of paper.

In each case any occurrence of a data flow, a function, a data store or a sink or source is given a *name* or label. That name must be *unique*. It is helpful to use a descriptive name, but the main purpose is identification. If you want an explanation of the meaning of a name, then you should look in the data dictionary; that way, everyone understands the same meaning of data. We've shown some possible entries in the Cub-Scout dictionary in Figure 2.2.

The background of the cub-scout sports day is that the organizer must first find out from cub-scout leaders how many contestants he is likely to get. He must then find a local school where the sports can be held. To do this he will check whether there are any other sports days being held which could keep the cub-scouts away on the chosen day. When all these data on *cub-scout numbers*, *sports field availability* and *competing activities* are assembled the organizer makes a *booking for a field*. He also sends a letter to cub-scout leaders telling them the day, the time and the place the sports are being held, and inviting them to *send in their entries*.

All these data are put into a SPORTS PROGRAMME, so that when the sports day arrives, contestants can be called for each heat and for each final race. Each race must be judged, so that the heat-winners can progress to finals and final winners can be chosen.

One serious limitation of DFDs should now be clear. The DFD doesn't tell us in what sequence the data flows into a function are handled. Functions 3 and 4 will be repeated many times, and may indeed be interspersed with functions 5 and 6. The DFD doesn't tell us whether the *data on numbers* must occur before or after *request for entries*.

There are alternative ways of describing systems (National Computing Centre system flowcharts, for example [2], or Jackson structure diagrams [3]) which do define the processing sequence.

DATA FLOW DESCRIPTION		
Name Of Data Flow	Explanation	Timing, Volume And Frequency
call for contestants	PA call for the contestants to come to the starting line	On the sports day, once per race
competing activities	What other events have been arranged to take place on the same day, and at the same time ?	One message for each competing activity
data on numbers	How many cub-scouts will be entered from each cub-scout pack ?	One message for each cub-scout pack
entries	Names of all potential contestants for, each event, from each cub-scout pack	One message for each cub-scout pack
cub-scouts arrival for heats	All cub-scouts due to run in a heat present themselves to the Starter	Once for every scheduled race, before the race can begin

FUNCTION DESCRIPTION				
Function Code	Name Of Function	Explanation	Trigger	Timing And Frequency
4	JUDGE HEATS	Judge the positions of contestants at the end of the race	Crossing the finishing line	Once per race
3	LINE UP AT START	Assemble the contestants on the starting line	Cub-scout's arrival for heats	Once per race
1	ORGANISE	Make all the arrangements for the sports day	Scheduled date on the calender	Once

SINK/SOURCE DESCRIPTION	
Name Of Sink/Source	Description
CUB-SCOUTS' HOMES	Where the certificates will be displayed
CUB-SCOUT LEADERS	One leader for each cub-scout pack
LOCAL SCHOOLS	Any school possessing a suitable sports field

Figure 2.2 Some possible data dictionary entries for the cub-scout sports day

Unfortunately, if we show temporal sequence on a chart it becomes difficult to represent the whole system on one simple chart.

Two data flows need particular comment. *Cubs' arrival for heats* and *cubs' arrival for finals* are both actual *events* rather than data flows about events. These events, though, are the triggers for activities 3 and 4 to start. We believe that the events carry information to the starter, and that we must put them on our data flow diagram if we want a picture of what the whole system does.

The DFD doesn't put any particular emphasis on any output reports or documents, or on the input data. The *concentration is on the data flows of all kinds,* and the way that data flows relate to other data flows. Data flows are always from or to functions. In this case we have included all relevant flows of data on one single chart.

Let us be very clear from the outset. The driving force that we represent in DFDs is flow of data. Function 5 in the cub-scout DFD, 'Judge finals', could suitably be described as the function which converts the signal that a final race is to be run into the data flow recording the final positions in the race. The DFD is a *data viewpoint* of the system, not the viewpoint of any object or person in the system, or of any process which is going to handle the data.

At present, we have only introduced the idea of representing data flows on DFDs. The story will be fleshed out as we progress.

2.2 Data models

The data store SPORTS PROGRAMME needs some more explanation. To say simply that it's stored on A4-sized sheets of paper doesn't get us very far. We want to portray the cub-scout sports data storage needs as a set of very simple tables (Figure 2.3). Each table contains data about one particular group of real-world entities. Let's call such a group an entity type, and give it an entity type name. We have used these names in the Figure 2.3 table headings.

In Figure 2.3 there is a one-line table, SPORTS, containing the basic sports day data; another table telling us about each SCHEDULED RACE on the programme; another listing the CONTESTANTS in each race; a table that for each CUB-SCOUT shows to which cub-scout pack he belongs; and finally a table recording the number of first, second and third positions won by each PACK. Obviously, this table can't be filled in until function 7 is reached. Study these tables. We believe that you will find that they are organized so that:

All the data that are needed are shown;
There is a minimum of repetition of data;
The way in which one table relates to another is clear: thus it is easy to see which cub-scout packs are competing in race number 2;
Each row in any one table is unique, and is clearly identified by the values of one or more key columns.

SPORTS TABLE					
Venue	Date	Start Time	Points For A First Position	Points For A Second Position	Points For A Third Position
Southdown school	5-Jun-90	2.00pm	3	2	1

SCHEDULED RACE TABLE			
Race Number	Event Name	Heat Number	Estimated Start Time
1	under 9, 80m	heat 1	2.10pm
2	under 9, 80m	heat 2	2.15pm
3	under 9, 80m	heat 3	2.20pm
4	under 9, 80m	heat 4	2.25pm
5	under 10, 3-legged	heat 1	2.30pm

CONTESTANT TABLE		
Race Number	Cub-Scout Name	Position
1	John Bates	second
1	Simon Jones	-
1	David Fox	first
1	Charles Wright	-
1	Rohit Patel	third
1	Simon Birch	-
2	Jason Hewitt	second
2	Simon West	first

CUB-SCOUT TABLE		
Cub-Scout Name	Date Of Birth	Pack Name
John Bates	3-Apr-82	2nd. bath
Simon Birch	12-Sep-81	2nd. bath
James Cumming	5-Dec-80	15th. bath
Jason Hewitt	12-Jan-82	25th. bath

PACK TABLE				
Pack Name	Firsts	Seconds	Thirds	Total Points
2nd.Bath	2	0	2	8
15th.Bath	3	2	0	11
25th.Bath	0	2	2	6
8th.Bath	1	1	3	8
9th.Bath	1	2	0	7

Figure 2.3 Data tables for the cub-scout sports day

The SPORTS table doesn't really describe an entity type. Rather, it is telling us something about one single entity. The entity is the cub-scout sports day system itself. In all the other tables the table heading is, in essence, the name of the entity type. The column headings are the names of attributes of the entity type. The way in which tables are linked together shows that there is a relationship between different entity types.

The structure of the data is represented symbolically in Figure 2.4. A diagram like this is variously known as a data model diagram, an entity type/relationship/attribute (ERA) diagram, or a schema. ('Schema' is defined in *Chambers' Dictionary* as a 'diagrammatic outline, or plan'.) We'll call it a 'data model diagram', because we intend to use the term 'data model' to describe the designer's perception of the relevant 'things' in the real world, and the way those things relate to each other.

The relationships between the different entity types are indicated by the connecting lines on the data model diagram. Each line in Figure 2.4 shows a one-to-many relationship. The lines do not imply a flow of data. The crow's foot at the end of a line shows a 'many' end of a relationship. Thus one row in the SCHEDULED RACE table relates to many rows in the CONTESTANT table; but one row in the CONTESTANT table relates to exactly one row in the SCHEDULED RACE table.

The 'has' and 'is entered as' relationship lines in Figure 2.4 have been drawn between attribute names which link two entity types. We are only trying to make the link clear; there is no need to see this as a charting convention. The attribute at the 'one' end of the relationship uniquely identifies single entities, and is known as a *primary key*. The attribute at the 'many' end is known as a *foreign key*, pointing away to the primary key of another, or 'foreign', entity type.

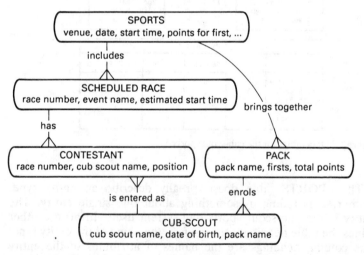

Figure 2.4 A diagrammatic representation of a data model for the cub-scout sports day

Each relationship has been given a name such that the structure of the data can be described by an English sentence:

One SPORTS includes many SCHEDULED RACES.
One SCHEDULED RACE has many CONTESTANTS.
One CUB-SCOUT is entered as many CONTESTANTS.
One SPORTS bring together many PACKS.
One PACK enrols many CUB-SCOUTS.

The entity type names are all nouns (either subject or object of the sentence), while the relationships are verbs or qualified verbs. Each relationship indicates that there is a cross reference between two tables. If there is name which common sense says should be a table heading, then it's an entity type name. If common sense says if should be a column heading, then it's an attribute name. Finally, it should be possible to link the data names together into simple English sentences.

We have listed the attribute names in any one entity type box in a horizontal row. There is not the least objection to writing them in a vertical list if that makes the presentation clearer.

The process of developing a data model is usually called data analysis. The data names that are developed as a result of this analysis must all be defined in the data dictionary. We shall be using the cub-scout sports day as the basis for the discussion on the data dictionary in Chapter 10.

2.3 Function mini-specs or structure rules

So far, we have said nothing about the *function* element in the Figure 2.1 data flow diagram. The function bubbles are all numbered, so we can pick out number 3, 'line up at start'. One way of describing this function is by a series of *structured English* statements. De Marco[1] has called these function descriptions *mini-specs* (for mini specification). We'll use that term, but prefer *structure rules*, defining what the system has to do.

When we discussed data flows in Section 2.1 we noted that the DFD doesn't tell us in what sequence data flows are processed. *The structure rule in Figure 2.5 does tell us exactly this about the data flows which relate to one function bubble.*

Although the completion of one function may require access to a data store it doesn't necessarily require access to the whole data store. As far as function 3 is concerned, it is adequate for the starter to know the name of the next race and the names of the contestants in that race. These data are the *view* of the data

For each race:

1. The sports marshall calls for contestants.
2. The contestants arrive at the start.
3. The Starter calls the contestants together.
4. For each contestant on the list of contestants:
   4.1 The starter calls the contestant's name.
   4.2 If the contestant is present

   Then
   4.2.1 The starter ticks the name on his list
   4.2.2 The starter allocates a lane to the contestant

   Else
   4.2.3 The starter puts a cross against the name.
   4.2.4 Processing for this contestant stops.

5. The starter lines up the contestants on the start line.
6. The starter informs the sports marshall that he is ready.
7. The starter writes the programme number of the race on his display board.
8. The sports marshall announces the race on the PA system.
9. The starter tells the contestants to get ready.
10. The starter fires the start pistol.
11. If the start is not good:

   Then
   11.1 The starter fires the pistol to recall contestants.
   11.2 The starter lines up the contestants on the start line.
   11.3 The starter tells the contestants to get ready.
   11.4 The starter fires the start pistol.

Figure 2.5 A Structure rule

required by function 3. 'Views' of data stores are very useful devices to which we shall be returning later.

Like the data stores on the DFD, mini-specs need more explanation than that given above. We shall meet that need in Chapter 6. Any function exists to convert data flows into different data flows. The analysis of the whole system of data flows is called *functional analysis*. We shall explore that in Chapter 5.

2.4 A business system description, partitioning and levelling

There are many more complicated human activity systems than a cub-scout sports day, and our charting conventions should help us to describe them. There are also one or two other concepts which we want to introduce.

Figure 2.6 describes a pre-cast concrete manufacturing business. The Coquotte Co Ltd makes cladding panels for buildings. The panels are custom designed for each contract and are made by assembling a wooden mould around steel reinforcing bars, pouring concrete into the mould, removing the mould, and finally applying some finishing treatment to the panel. Several panels may be made from one mould, and with alterations to the mould, some small variations in panel design can be achieved from a single mould.

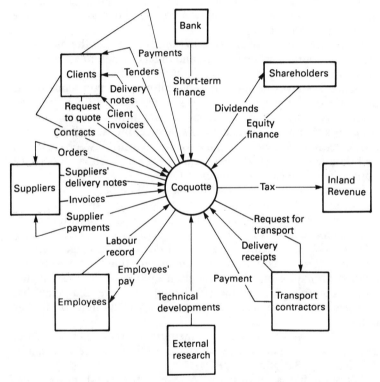

Figure 2.6 A context diagram for the Coquotte production system (After de Marco [1])

Contracts are obtained by sending tenders to clients after the clients have requested Coquotte to make a quotation. The clients will normally award the contract to the manufacturer who quotes the most favourable terms. After a contract is awarded, the Coquotte Design Office will produce detailed designs both of the cladding panels and of the moulds in which they are to be made.

Casting of panels cannot start until the moulds have been manufactured.

Once moulds have been manufactured, the Production Controller can produce *casting schedules*, *finishing schedules* and *delivery schedules*, specifying the various tasks which must be completed before the panels are delivered to the clients. The necessary stores must be purchased to allow the panels to be manufactured, and clients must be invoiced for payment for the cladding panels they have received.

All data flows are into or out of the Coquotte system. We are not interested in any data flows between sinks and sources. *They are outside the system boundary.*

Figure 2.6 is called a *context diagram*. It identifies the data flows into or out of the chosen system, and in fact by defining what these flows are it actually defines the *boundary* of the system.

Figure 2.7 gives us the same difficulty as the cub-scout sports day. A *supplier payment* is an *event*, not a data flow about an event. We can certainly describe a data flow consisting of the supplier's cheque and the supplier's invoice; but we believe it's not always either easy or necessary to distinguish between an event and data about an event. Both can trigger a function. Where it's appropriate, we show events on a DFD.

If the system is large and complex it will be helpful to *partition* it. Figure 2.8 divides our total system into the component functions. Figures 2.9 and 2.10 continue this partitioning by creating more *levels* of partitioning. Figure 2.7 is sometimes called a *level 0 diagram*; Figure 2.8 is a *level 1 diagram*; and Figure 2.9 is a *level 2 diagram*. You will see immediately that each succeeding level is an explosion of one function bubble on the next higher level. A simple guide is that (for example) a level 2 diagram has two places after the decimal point in each of its function bubble codes.

Each time we go down a level, the number of diagrams increases exponentially. Figure 2.9 shows the '3.2 DFD'. There will also be 3.1, 3.3, 3.4, 3.5 and 3.6 DFDs.

It's really like a set of maps. A map of the world shows where Europe is in relation to America and Asia. London might be marked on the map, but that isn't very much use for finding your way from Westminster to Ealing. For that, you need a map of London, which explodes a very small portion of the map of the world.

Figures 2.6–2.9 display the very important principle of *balance*. All the data flows which are seen to be flowing into or out of a function bubble in any DFD *must be present in any partitioning of*

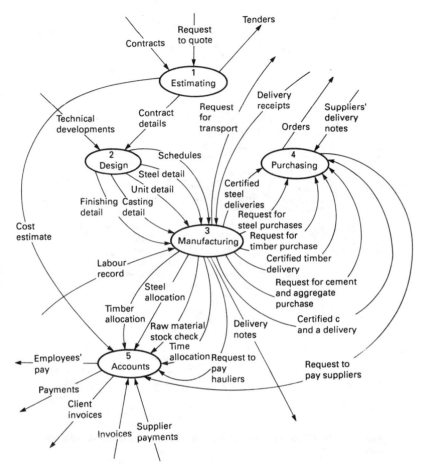

Figure 2.7 Level 0 DFD showing major partitioning of the Coquotte system

that bubble in a lower-level DFD. Not only that; *the names used for the same data flow in the two DFDs must be identical.*

Figure 2.9 isn't the only possible partitioning of the Mould Shop. Figure 2.10 gives an alternative in which the functions are differently defined. Figure 2.9 defines the functions carried out by specified people in terms of the data flow to and from these functions. We could perhaps describe this as *role analysis.* Figure 2.9 is a *physical DFD* describing what has actually been seen to happen. Figure 2.10 is a *logical DFD* describing the system which we logically need in order to achieve the system purpose.

We sometimes write 'MOULD FOREMAN', 'JOINERS' or

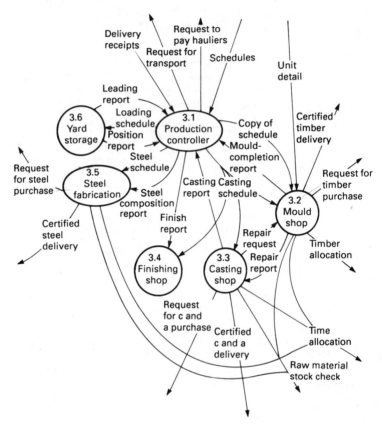

Figure 2.8 Level 1, number 3 DFD showing a partitioning of the Manufacturing function

'JANE' as the names of functions on a physical DFD. We intend these names to mean 'What the foreman does', or 'What the joiners do' or 'What Jane does'. We would never write names of people or of departments in an organization on a logical DFD!

It isn't until we come to Figure 2.10 that we show any data stores. There are none on the higher-level DFDs because there must always be a clear relationship between the content of a data store and any function which uses that data store. Above level 2 the data stores are buried inside the function bubbles. Since the nature of the data store is clear from its name, there is not necessarily any need to label the data flows into or out of a data store.

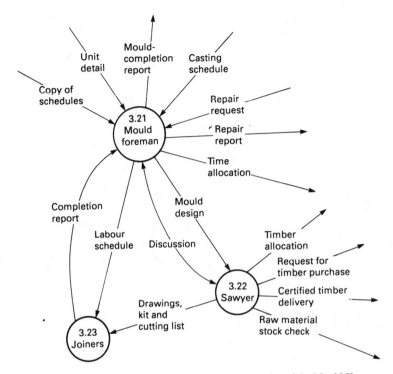

Figure 2.9 Level 2, number 3.2 DFD showing a partitioning of the Mould Shop function

The TIMBER STOCK data store illustrates our old dilemma about events and data flows. Two of the flows into or out of the data store can relate to actual timber. The Sawyer could be 'checking stock' either by examining stock record cards or by counting the actual timber pieces! All that matters is that stock is replenished because the quantity held has fallen below some acceptable minimum level.

The 'unit detail' data flow exhibits a feature which we have shown on previous diagrams but haven't noted. Data flows can split, and indeed can join, provided only that the definition of a data flow remains constant.

We have not included 'control' in any of the DFDs. The '3.23* manufacture of moulds' function may include Quality Assurance inspection and an 'acceptance report'. This is extremely important, but would cloud the perception of 'flow' given by the DFD.

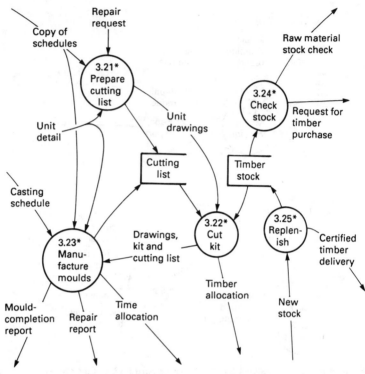

Figure 2.10 Logical level 2 DFD showing a partitioning of the Mould Shop functions

Control features are not shown on a DFD. Conversely, *control features must be included in a structure rule.*

We've summarized the 'functional decomposition' of Coquotte in Figure 2.11. 'Partitioning' and 'functional decomposition' are synonyms. 'Partitioning' puts the emphasis on what we are doing. 'Functional decomposition' emphasizes that when we decompose functions we still have functions.

Clearly, there are many more branches in the decomposition tree than those we have shown. Each of the branches in Figure 2.11 represents a clearly understandable function, with clear interfaces with other functions, data stores, or sinks and sources.

Partitioning at any one level should follow the rule 'seven plus or minus two'[1] . Many more bubbles than seven is confusing; two fewer bubbles suggests that redundant partitioning levels are being introduced.

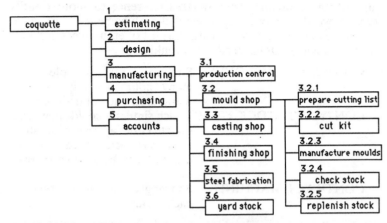

Figure 2.11 Part of the functional decomposition of Coquotte

Partitioning should continue until either you can write a reasonably short structural rule for each function at the lowest level or function conversion is *simple*. This could mean that one input data flow is converted into one, two or three output data flows; or that one, two or three input data flows are converted into one output data flow.

One last point about the DFDs; they do commit a cardinal sin. The data flow lines cross! Whenever possible, you should avoid this.

We aren't going to do a full data analysis or functional analysis of Coquotte at this stage. However, we will point the way ahead by making a first guess at what 'things' (or entity types) are important for Coquotte to keep track of.

CUSTOMER	Who keeps the company in business
CONTRACT	Presumably one customer can offer many contracts
PANEL TYPE	One group of similar panels
MOULD TYPE	One group of similar moulds
PANEL	One particular concrete unit
MOULD	One particular mould
STOCK ITEM	For example, 10 mm round steel bar, 100 mm × 150 mm timber, etc
EMPLOYEE	Without whom nothing would be produced
MACHINE	Which is also necessary for production

Only CUSTOMER, STOCK ITEM, EMPLOYEE and MACHINE can be seen as simple entity types which don't contain any attributes linking them by cross reference to another entity type. Nevertheless, it's easy to see that each name in the list could be the heading for a table of data. The list of entity types certainly isn't exhaustive. Other candidates could be:

CONTRACT-EMPLOYEE	Showing, for example, how many hours an employee has worked on one contract, or
CONTRACT-STOCK ITEM	Which similarly could show what quantity of a particular stock item has been used on one contract and how much it costs, or
CONTRACT-MACHINE	Showing the machining time for each contract

Each of these potential entity types is derived from a relationship between two entity types in the previous list.

We won't explore the other possible attributes of these entity types or the relationships between them. It is enough to remind you that a test on whether you have made a sensible selection of entity types is whether or not you could visualize data about that entity type collected into a table, with the entity type names as a table heading and attribute names as column headings.

2.5 A knowledge-based system

Many human activity systems exist simply to store, to retrieve and to apply knowledge to some useful purpose. Examples could be a solicitor's practice, a travel agency, a theatre booking office or a medical diagnosis system. It is likely that the data flow between separate functions will be small or absent, and that most functions will be concerned only with data flows into or out of the system and into or out of the knowledge store (data store).

Figure 2.12 shows a context diagram for an estate agent. It is unlikely that further partitioning into lower-level diagrams is justified because each data flow can be seen as directly destined for or originating from the data store. The whole mode of operation of the system consists of updating and consulting the data store.

Note that in Figure 2.12 there is no data flow shown between 'LOCAL PRESS' and 'POTENTIAL BUYERS'. Both of these are in the environment of our system. We are *not* concerned with describing data flows between entities which we have chosen to put outside our system boundary.

One very important point should be made here which is not solely applicable to knowledge-based systems. The tables or entity types described in Sections 2.2 and 2.4 are only a part of the *knowledge base* which a system requires. The tables could be described as *formatted data.*

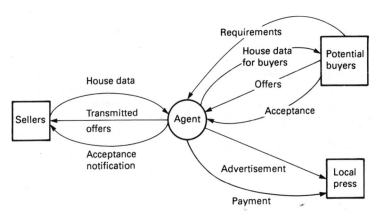

Figure 2.12 Data flows for an estate agent

Generally, we view a database as consisting only of formatted data. In a knowledge base we could expect to find charts; drawings; free text descriptions and specifications; program documentation and program back-up copies; reports and analyses; and indeed anything which is capable of being stored and which has an information content. The secret of our knowledge base planning is to ensure that the unformatted data can not only be stored but can also be updated and retrieved.

2.6 Summary of the descriptive models

2.6.1 Data flow diagrams

We have based this summary very closely on de Marco[1].

- The system description identifies *data flows*, data stores and *functions*. Additionally, outside the system being described, *sinks* and *sources* are identified:

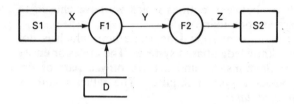

X's arrive from source S1 and are transformed into Y's by
function F1, after retrieving data from data store D. Y's are
subsequently transformed into Z's by function F2 and are
delivered to sink S2.

- The DFD presents a *data viewpoint* of the system, not the
  viewpoint of any person or of any object in the system, nor that
  of any processor which is going to handle the data.
- Data flows are always from or to functions and also link data
  stores and sinks or sources to functions. They constitute
  pipelines through which defined packets of data flow:

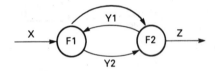

Data flows Y1 and Y2 don't constitute either one pipeline or
one packet. They never travel together; they have different
uses; and they may be produced by different people.

- Data flows are named; no two data flows have the same name;
  names are descriptive, and tell us something about the data
  flow.
- It may not be necessary to name data flows into or out of named
  and defined data stores.
- Data flows may diverge and converge, provided that all the
  branches handle the same data packages. This is very unlikely
  for converging data packages!

- Try to avoid crossing data flows.
- The DFD is for the analyst's convenience, not the other way around. If it seems sensible to represent a data flow by a double-ended arrow, then that's what should be done:

- The DFD de-emphasizes the *control* of flow. The following DFDs are both *wrong*.

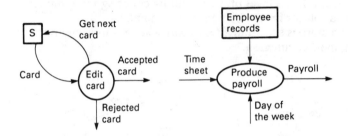

- Each function has a unique and descriptive name.
- Each function name must be defined either in a *structure rule* or by *partitioning*.
- Partitioning of a function results in addition of an extra *level*. The data flows in successive levels must be *balanced*; in other words, they must be mutually consistent. The following diagrams are not balanced:

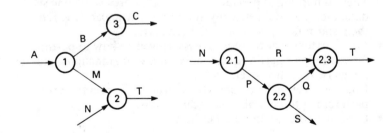

M has disappeared from the lower level and S has appeared.
- A *context diagram* defines the system boundary.

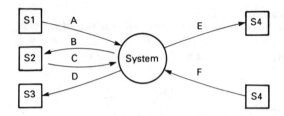

- Below the context diagram level the next level down (showing all the primary partitions) is the level 0 diagram. There will be either a level 1 diagram or a structure rule for each function bubble in the level 0 diagram; a level 2 diagram or a structure rule for each function bubble in the level 1 diagram, and so on. You can tell the level of a diagram by counting the number of decimal places in its function bubble numbers.
- A data store is shown in a DFD only when it forms an interface with another function:

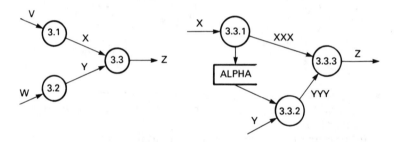

Alpha is entirely local to 3.3. It has no role to play in the higher-level diagram. At the first level at which a data store appears *all references to it must be shown*.
- There is nothing to preclude a set of data stores being one single database. The data actually seen by a particular function are then that function's view of the database.
- To the extent that there is an easy answer to how to partition a function, don't partition into more than seven functions (plus or minus two) at any level.
- Create conceptually meaningful interfaces. Expect the extent of partitioning to be higher at higher levels.
- Continue partitioning until either:

The lowest level function bubble can be described by a reasonably short structure rule; or
Each function bubble conversion is simple.

- A data flow diagram is about *what the system does*.

2.6.2 Data models

- Each table in a database consists of at least one column.
- Each table is simple in construction. For each row of the table there is one (and only one) entry in each column. All rows contain the same number of data items.
- Each row of a table is uniquely identified by the values in one or more columns. These identifying columns constitute the key. The values of all the non-key columns 'depend-on' the key.
- Cross referencing between tables is provided by foreign keys. Every foreign key value must be the same as a primary key value in some other table.
- A *data model* represents both the real world and the tables in the database. The data model maps one to the other.
- Each table in a database is represented in the data model diagram by an entity type box. Both the entity type and the database table represent just one kind of real-world thing. We show an entity type name in the box and, optionally, a set of attributes. Each entity type name corresponds to a database table name. Each attribute name corresponds to a database column name.

```
 _____
/         X          \
|  a,   b,   c,   d   |
_____/
```

- All entity type and table names are unique. Attribute names are unique within an entity type and column names are unique within a table.
- Cross references between entity types are represented by a relationship line, with a *relationship name*. The relationships in this chapter are all *one-to-many* relationships:

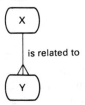

One X <u>is related to</u> many Y's
One Y <u>is related to</u> one X

- Relationship names are unique and ideally constitute an English-language predicate.
- The *owner* (the 'one' end of a relationship) and the *member* (the 'many' end of the same relationship) form an English sentence with the relationship name:

- The set of English sentences in the data model provides a structural description of the system being modelled.
- A data model is about *what the system remembers*.
- This chapter has only outlined data modelling. We shall take up the story again in Chapter 7.

2.6.3 Mini-specs or structural rules

- We have not presented any details about specifying functions and prefer to leave that discussion until Chapter 6.

Discussion points

2.1 We have suggested that a data store should only appear on a data flow diagram when it forms part of the interface between function bubbles on the diagram. We defined a data store as a repository of data for subsequent retrieval. Discuss these restrictions. Do you think they are useful or would some other formulation of data store rules be more helpful?

2.2 One of our suggestions for the proper place to stop functional decomposition is when the conversion is simple; that is, one input data flow into one, two or three input data flows; or one, two or three input data flows into one output data flow. Discuss the relative merits of describing such a simple function by listing the structural rules or by further decomposition into functional bubbles of smaller scope.

Are there merits in stopping functional decomposition *before* a simple conversion is reached?

2.3 We say that there is nothing to preclude a set of data stores being one single database. Are there any potential conflicts resulting from the way we have formulated rules for data stores (a data store is only shown when it forms an interface with another function; at the first level at which a data store appears, all references to it must be shown). If there are any such conflicts, how can they be resolved?

2.4 'A data model represents both the real world and the tables in the database. The data model maps one to the other.' Discuss.

Exercises

2.1 'In a single branch supermarket, members of the public select goods and take them to the checkout. The cash receipts are paid into the bank by Accounts. Point-of-sale data are used for re-ordering new supplies. Re-ordering strategy is influenced by market research analysis of public behaviour.

'The Purchasing department sends purchase orders to suppliers of goods and files two copies of each purchase order in the purchase order file. When goods are received from a supplier they are accompanied by a delivery note. The relevant copy of the purchase order is sent to Accounts. One copy of the purchase order, with the delivery note, is filed in the Purchasing department.

'When Accounts receive the supplier's invoice they pay the supplier, provided that a certified purchase order is held. All cash receipts and payments are recorded in the appropriate ledger.'

Chart the above description by drawing a context diagram, and as many level 0 and level 1 diagrams as you deem appropriate.

Comment on the most sensible place to start charting. Do you draw the context diagram first or should you start at some other place?

2.2 Draw a data model for the Coquotte Company, following the guidelines set out in Section 2.4.

2.3 Suggest an appropriate data model for the system described in Exercise 2.1.

Mark in the desirable relationships and give them appropriate names.

2.4 The British Drivers' and Vehicles' Licence Centre is responsible for issuing drivers' and vehicle licences, maintaining records of registered vehicles and licensed drivers and sending out renewal reminders as necessary. The records they keep for each vehicle show the changes of 'keeper' and any modification for that vehicle. The records for each driver show any licence endorsements and suspensions.

(a) Identify the entity types in the above description. Suggest appropriate attributes and primary keys.
(b) Construct a data model. Appropriately name each relationship in both directions.
(c) Suggest possible entry points to the database.

References

1 Tom de Marco, *Structured Analysis and System Specification*, Prentice-Hall, Englewood Cliffs, NJ (1979)
2 Barry Lee, *Basic Systems Analysis*, Hutchinson, London (1984)
3 Michael Jackson, *System Development*, Prentice-Hall, Englewood Cliffs, NJ (1983)

Chapter 3

Management and control

3.1 Realms of control

As far as system design is concerned we can categorize three different realms of control. First, there is the control of businesses and public enterprises to ensure that they achieve their purposes. Second, there is the control of development projects to ensure that budgeted progress is achieved and that the projected gains from the project are realized. Finally, after the redesigned system is installed and working there is the control designed to ensure that the *integrity* of the database is conserved, that the desired *throughput* of transactions is achieved, that the *response* time required to respond to users of the system is acceptable and that *access* to the database is properly controlled.

In this chapter our concern is with the *control of businesses and public enterprises*. The other three realms of control are ultimately intended to support these business needs. There are chapters describing these realms later in the book.

3.2 Process management and control

We have said nothing about managing Coquotte: only about what is supposed to happen. In fact we clearly excluded 'control' from our data flow diagrams in Chapter 2.

If we speak of managing any organization we must mean that we are clear about *what we are trying to do* (our purpose) and about *how we are going to set about doing it*. Let's sketch what additional data flows this might imply for Coquotte. 'Managing' has been described as *planning, organizing, leading* and *controlling* [1]. Perhaps 'leading' isn't easily fitted into a data flow diagram (unless we represent messages such as 'England expects that every man this day will do his duty' as data flows!).

If 'planning' is the process of deciding what is to be done, while 'organizing' is the process of putting the plan into practice, then the management data flows for any sub-system in Coquotte might be outlined as Figure 3.1. Let's suppose it's the Casting Shop being described.

Figure 3.1 shows both data flows and material flows. There is always a problem about mixing flows in this way. We met the same difficulty with 'events' and 'data flows about events' in Chapter 2. Our belief is that it is legitimate to include a material flow if the flow contains information which is needed for decision making. Clearly, in Figure 3.1 the material flow fits this requirement. We have shown it with bold arrows to differentiate from data flows.

The 'feedback' data flow contains information about what the actual effect of a transformation process is. It may relate to a measurement of the quality of the concrete panels, although this is by no means the only aspect of the Casting Shop activity which is subject to control. The productivity of the workers, prudent and thrifty use of raw material and tools, observance of delivery schedules; all these can and should, to some extent, be monitored, the measurement compared to a standard and consequent action taken. There should be as many control activities as there are purposes of the sub-system, *but the control procedure will differ in each case.*

The *standard* may be some constant statement of required width or viscosity of the wet concrete. We are then discussing *negative feedback.* If the standard is the expectation that more panels will be produced than were manufactured the week before *and this feedback helps to achieve this*, then it is *positive feedback.* If no feedback information is used at all in the planning and organizing activities, then we have *open-loop control.* Much more commonly there is some feedback, and we speak of *closed-loop control.* You must be clear that the feedback information used in closed-loop control can be either positive or negative.

'Controlling' has been represented as the 'Feedback', 'Rework-requirement' and 'Allocation-instructions' data flows, and the 'monitor', 'compare' and 'allocate' processes. 'Planning and organizing' is described by the data flows into and out of the 'plan and organize' bubble.

It would be helpful to summarize these various information flows to show the structure of a management information system designed to service a planning and control process. We did just this for our board-sailing system in Section 1.2. We have categorized the information flows as:

Data about the input
Feedback data
Data from the environment

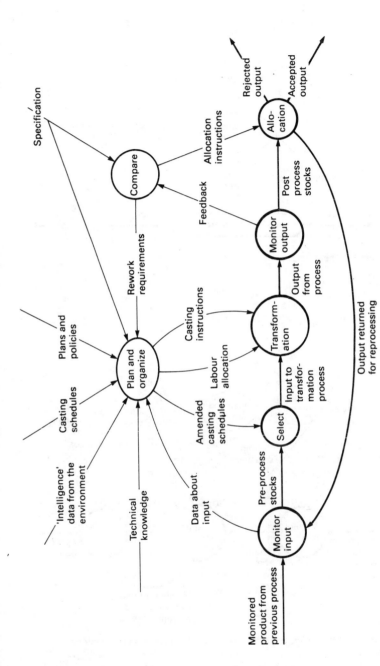

Figure 3.1 'Production' material flows and 'control' data flows for the Casting Shop

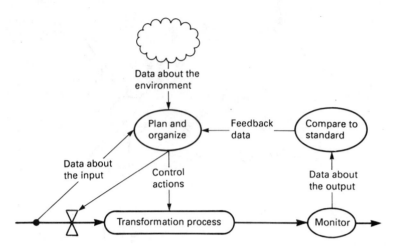

Figure 3.2 The management control cycle

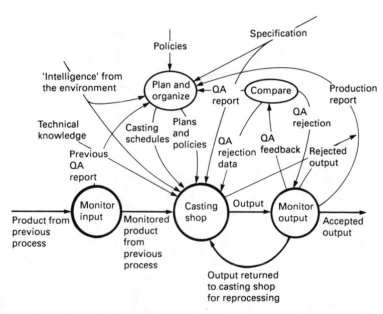

Figure 3.3 'Production' material flows and 'control' flows in the environment of the Casting Shop

Each of these data flows is represented in Figure 3.2. Would you pause now and relate the data flows summarized in Figure 3.2 to those shown in Figure 3.1? If all the function bubbles in Figure 3.1 are thought of as part of the casting shop sub-system, then the management process for the next level up (manufacturing) could be as Figure 3.3. If Quality Assurance is separate from the casting shop and reports directly to the manufacturing manager (what's in a title? It may be Works Manager or Production Manager) then the Quality Assurance feedback can properly be seen as outside the Casting Shop sub-system. This doesn't mean that there is no feedback information inside that sub-system!

We will return to feedback control when we discuss the management of computer system development, and when we look at the control of data flows in a real-life implemented information system. For the moment, let's emphasize a very important message. It is essential to keep system descriptions clear. When we first draw a DFD of a system *we wouldn't normally include the control data flows*. This is not meant in any way to minimize their importance.

3.3 Levels of management

If you look again at Figures 3.1 and 3.3 you may get the impression of a set of Russian dolls with smaller and smaller management systems inside them, which are, in all important respects, similar systems (Figure 3.4). The comparison is not misplaced. There is, however, a different emphasis at different levels of an organization.

Petit[2], in an often-quoted diagram (Figure 3.5), suggested three levels to a management system in an organization – the *technical core activities* (making moulds, casting concrete panels, invoicing customers, estimating prices for new contracts); the *organizational level* (appointing staff, training staff, making rules for requisitioning stock, designing computer-based information systems, negotiating rates of pay for different jobs); and the *strategic level* (company goals and objectives, marketing strategy, relationships with government and local authorities, trade association cooperation and agreements).

To a very large extent, the activities of the three levels really are different in most organizations. Many of the decisions made in the technical core will be *programmable* ('If A and B are true, then do C'; 'If corner panels are required for delivery on 28 May, and they require fourteen days to manufacture and deliver, then schedule

Figure 3.4 Levels in a management control hierarchy

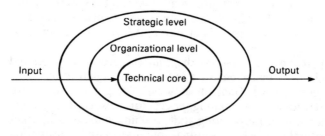

Figure 3.5 Petit's concept of three organizational levels

them for casting before 14 May'). Because so many decisions are programmable, much use will be made of *formal* or previously designed information systems.

In the example above, the decision to do C depended only on a knowledge of A and B. Therefore an information system which provided values for A and B would be quite adequate. Most of the routine technical activities can be characterized in this way –

preparing schedules, replenishing stock, issuing despatch notes and invoices, processing payments received from customers, allocating labour costs to a contract, etc.

It isn't only the operating decisions themselves. Most of the controls applied to these technical activities are programmable. In the second example above, there won't be any ambiguity about whether the panels were or were not delivered on 28 May.

We've said that much use will be made of formal information systems in the technical core. A programmable decision necessarily implies that we know what information we need to make that decision. This doesn't mean that we don't need *informal* information systems at that level. A cement kiln is attended by a Burner: a person responsible for maintaining correct temperature in the kiln. Commonly, a Burner will check the instrumentation by judging the flame colour inside the kiln by eye. No one has designed that information system!

At the organizational level decisions will have more of a *judgemental* element. The decisions which have to be made are less predictable and the relevant information less easily defined. It would be foolish, for example, to appoint John as an assistant to Sarah if the person making the appointment knows that they have a bitter personal dispute. The informal information system is relatively more important than at the technical core. The control mechanisms are also less programmable. It would be foolish to penalize a manager for missing his production targets if his maintenance engineers were observing a national overtime ban declared by their trades union.

Nearly all existing computer-based information systems are related to the technical core activites. As we try to provide support at the organizational level the term *decision support system* has become popular. Rather than provide the information which is known to be required for a programmable decision, the information system seeks to make relevant information available to be used at the decision maker's discretion.

It's very important to realize that the distinctions being made in this description are for purposes of understanding only. A vehicle scheduler working, for example, for a supermarket chain could be provided with computer-produced schedules detailing despatch of lorries to branches. If the scheduler is allowed discretion about whether or not he uses the schedules then he is using a decision-support system. This is true even though he is definitely operating at the technical core. If our supermarket scheduler is allowed to use his judgement in issuing schedules it will undoubtedly do wonders for his feeling of job satisfaction.

We have left the strategic level of decision making and control until last. Decisions here must be virtually entirely judgemental. They will be once-off decisions. The occasions for these may be at random intervals or they may follow, for example, a 'five-year plan'. In either case, if the decisions are based on a formal information system rather than an assessment of the environment as it exists at that time, the organization will come unstuck. Ultimately, the control in an organization is imposed by the environment: failure to attract investment, to attract recruits, to sell products.

3.4 Open systems

The previous section detailed how technical core activities may be strongly dependent on a formal information system to make programmable decisions. The strategic level was presented as making judgemental decisions based on informal information. The organizational level was seen as somewhere in between.

In each case, but especially at the technical core level, the control cycles of 'monitor', 'compare', 'decide' was the framework for discussion. We can see this as a picture of the management activity which shows it as striving for a *steady state*. The information system designed to do this can best be called a *maintenance system*. A 'maintenance system' can still be a 'decision-support system'. If the decisions made are directed towards supporting a steady state then we are speaking of maintenance.

Let's be quite clear. An organization which neglects its maintenance system is headed for disaster. Many companies have collapsed because of inadequate controls, not through any failure of innovation; but steady-state maintenance cannot be enough.

In Chapter 1 we spoke of a board sailor having to adapt his system or even to alter the purpose of the system because of pressure from the environment. In exactly the same way, an organization needs an *adaptive mechanism* as well as a *maintenance mechanism* if it is to survive. There isn't much call today for the products of a firm manufacturing waggon wheels!

Steady-state maintenance doesn't cater for the forces of creativity, play, excitement, love, joy, mission, and all the other irrational drives which go to make us human. Without them we'd still be in our caves. Steady-state maintenance is analogous to the well-adjusted, well-organized but boring individual!

3.5 The design of management information systems

We have described formal and informal systems. We have also attempted to show that at different levels of an organization the mix of formal and informal will differ because of the different kinds of decision being made. Attempts to design information systems have undoubtedly *overemphasized the formal*; have tended to *ignore uncertainty*; and have assumed that *programmable decisions* are a desirable ideal.

Earl and Hopwood[3] have presented a classification of decision situations and the information system appropriate to each situation. They classify in terms of certainty of objectives and certainty of the relationship between cause and effect. Technical core activities will usually have *high certainty* on both dimensions. Strategic level activites will have *low certainty*. The administrative level will occupy an intermediate position (Figure 3.6). An 'answer machine' is one which will carry out programmable decisions. This is a suitable description of nearly all computer-based information systems. 'Learning machine' has a number of very similar labels. If we conceive the decision maker and the information system as both parts of the learning machine, then we have a decision-support system. 'Expert system' and 'Intelligent Knowledge Based System' (IKBS) are both terms which have been used for systems that are able to learn from the correctness or incorrectness of previous results. 'Dialogue machine' involves a 'what if?' approach to decision making. Simulation in all its various forms is an obvious basis for dialogue and for reconciling differing goals.

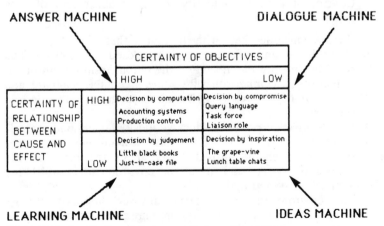

Figure 3.6 A classification of management information systems

It would profit system designers to use such a framework when approaching system design. If the designers think in terms of answer machines then they should confine themselves to technical core activities. If they wish to address the problems of the administrative level then they must think of learning machines or dialogue machines. The strategic level needs dialogue machines and ideas machines.

In any information system there is a balance between the *perceived objectives or goals*, the *decisions* that are taken to achieve those goals and the *information* that is available. Each will influence the other two. If the information available is tightly constrained by a formal system then the decisions made will tend to be based on that information, and the goals pursued will be to make the reported information reflect well on the decision maker. If the Coquotte information system reports the daily tonnage of concrete cast by the Casting Shop then the Casting Shop foreman will try to make that amount high.

If that is the system purpose accepted by the designers, then all is well. If the purpose is different from that, then more thought about the information system is needed.

3.6 Summary

- Realms of control:

  Control of businesses and public enterprises;
  Control of development projects;
  Control of database integrity, of the management of data resources.

  We are concerned here with the first of these.
- Control may entail feedback, giving closed-loop control. The requirements are *monitoring* of the output from a transformation process, *comparison* with some acceptable standard and *allocation* of the resources required to achieve the desired standard.
- If no feedback is provided, then we speak of open-loop control.
- In addition to feedback information, a management information system should provide data about the input to the application system and about the environment in which the application system operates.
- The environment of a particular workshop, or of any department within an organization, may also be monitoring the output of that workshop and comparing it to a standard.

Management can be seen as successive skins of an onion, with the highest level of management as the outer skin. Each level provides the immediate environment for the next subordinate level.

- The concerns of different levels of management differ. Petit classifies into strategic, organizational and technical core levels.
- Technical core decision making tends to involve programmable decisions and *formal* information systems. Strategic-level decision making is largely judgemental.
- 'Monitor', 'compare' and 'allocate', as processes attempting to achieve a steady state, are, in the long run, inadequate. Systems are open, and subject to all kinds of environmental changes. Open-system concepts recognize the place of creativity, joy, sense of achievement and innovation. Not only do we need a maintenance system we also require an adaptive one.
- Decision situations have been classified according to the degree of certainty of objectives and of the relationship between cause and effect. A high level of both of these provides a suitable environment for answer machines. Most computer applications to date have been just this.
- Less certainty of objectives, and of cause and effect, poses a need for ideas machines. Between these we have dialogue machines and learning machines.
- System designers should use such a framework to guide system design.

Discussion points

3.1 'Control is a necessary component of any human activity.' Discuss.

3.2 Give examples of both open-loop control and closed-loop control from the field of cookery.

3.3 A faculty of a college is governed by a faculty board which meets at regular intervals. Give suggestions of open-loop control and closed-loop control in the conduct of their business.

3.4 'A management information system should provide data about the input to the application system and about the environment in which that application operates.' Give examples of such data for:

(a) A family bakery business;
(b) A college.

3.5 Discuss the merits of characterizing the strategic, organizational and technical core levels of management in terms of the lengths of their different planning horizons.

3.6 Do you see divisions of the management process into these three levels as a necessary feature of management?

3.7 Is an informal information system that part of the information system which hasn't yet been formally designed? Should an organization aim to formalize all its information flows?

3.8 Does a system designer prescribe the decisions which will be made by prescribing the information available in a decision-support system?

3.9 Discuss the circumstances in which there might be a low certainty about objectives and of the relationship between cause and effect. What might be the characteristics of a computer-based information system which attempted to address the problems of this area?

References

1 Henri Fayol, *General and Industrial Management*, Pitman, London (1949)
2 Thomas A. Petit, 'A behavioural theory of management', *Academy of Management Journal*, December (1967)
3 Michael J. Earl and Anthony G. Hopwood, 'From management information to information management', *The Information Systems Environment*, edited by M.C. Lucas *et al.*, IFIP (1979)

Part 2

System design

Chapter 4

How to design information systems

4.1 Users, operators, analysts, programmers and others

The title of this chapter is deliberately provocative. It assumes that there is a *method*, which, if followed, will lead to a *design* that is satisfactory to the users of the system. This brings us to the old problem of definitions. What is a user? What is an operator? What is a systems analyst? What is a programmer? We shall assume that a *user* is anyone who, on a routine basis, provides data which are fed into an information system (an information provider) or receives data which are produced by an information system (an information receiver).

A person who handles data within the system but who isn't particularly interested in the meaning of those data (keyboard operator, data controller, computer operator) we shall call an *operator*. Analysis will most probably be carried out by a *systems analyst*, while the person who constructs the final system will usually be called a *programmer*. *Specification* of the system to be constructed will be shared between users, systems analysts and programmers.

We don't have a satisfactory word for anyone concerned with *implementation*. (The business of trying to get the system working in the way intended.) Many people will be involved in this process. We'll need to come back to it after we're clearer about the methods of systems analysis, specification and construction.

Finally, it's increasingly common that *database administrators* (DBAs) take responsibility for the definition and management of the data resources of an organization.

Just to complicate things further, it's possible that in some organizations all or some of these roles (including that of 'user') may be acted by the same person.

At the moment we're just identifying the roles. We will return later to the behaviour of people in these roles.

4.2 An overall view of design

Let's be generous at this stage and assume that our users are some of the few people in the world who actually know what they want. Later we can bend that assumption a little and see where that gets us! Let's also use the tools we've developed for describing systems to represent *the system for designing information systems*.

The formal design system is described in Figure 4.1. The picture in Figure 4.1 is idealized. It assumes that the design starts with a clean statement of 'users' requirement', and follows an orderly path to reach an audited system, together with a list of exceptions. The 'exceptions' contribute to the knowledge of how the system can be still further improved, and so take us back to the beginning again with a new 'user requirement'! This going around and around the same sequence leads us to the popular name the *project life cycle*.

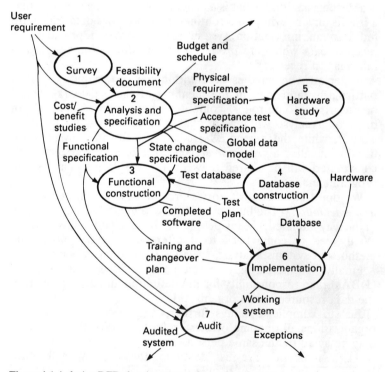

Figure 4.1 A design DFD showing system design functions

There's much more going around and around which the DFD doesn't show. When programmers try to construct programs they will typically find that the 'functional specification' isn't quite right. During implementation the supposedly completed 'software' (the set of programs written by the programmers) won't match the test plan or the functional specification. Even if the software matches the functional specification, and the functional specification is a close fit to the user requirement the story isn't finished. As the user gets more experience he or she *will want to change the user requirements*. 'Oh and whilst you're about it could you just . . .?' 'What I actually meant was . . .!' 'I hadn't realized the effect of . . .!'

In fact, the title 'user requirement' conceals a wide variety of reasons for a design project to be started in the first place. It may be a general feeling of unease by user management or that a newcomer to the scene has brought new insights. The problem-owner may have been on a course or visit which has induced some 'lateral thinking', or it may quite respectably be that someone has been taking around a solution looking for a problem. Whatever the genesis, the user requirement should be argued through until it includes some *terms of reference*; or, more plainly, a statement of *what it is we are trying to do*.

We believe that the documents in our design DFD serve a very useful role and *should* be produced, but it's important *not* to assume that system design necessarily follows the orderly path of Figure 4.1. One very plausible explanation of the design process argues that usually *the solution comes first*! At the least, this means that a system designer will approach the design problem with all his or her accumulated experience of previous solutions for other problems. The design solution to the current problem will be only marginally different from those old solutions.

If indeed there are substantial similarities between the old and the new problems, then this must be a perfectly acceptable design method. Financial systems, production control systems, inventory control systems; all exist in the same national culture, legal framework or set of standards established by the various professional bodies concerned. Part of the secret is to recognize similarities with past work even when they aren't immediately obvious. It's rather like a chess player being able to recognize winning patterns among the pieces.

It goes further than that! It's possible that most of us can only conceptualize a problem *in terms of solutions of which we are already aware*! Unless we know what can be done, we can't define a problem. Put the other way, a problem can only exist if there is a set of known possible solutions. If there are no solutions there isn't a problem. Only the occasional design genius is capable of real innovation!

The innovator extends the set of possible solutions, but innovation carries the risk of failure. The beauty of York Minster or of Santa Sophia was only achieved after many builders' walls and roofs had fallen down (Figure 4.2). If everyone stays within the limits of the tried and tested, then human progress stops[1].

Whatever attitude you may take to the idea that the solution comes first, there is one aspect of this which must be accepted by any well-managed system development organization. *Many jobs will have been done before, somewhere*: if not the whole job, then part of the job; or part of part of the job. The smaller the unit, the more general it is. Every building construction uses nails.

We use language to speak and write to each other. We are able to communicate because of shared understanding of meaning. Specialist workers devise esoteric labels with a wealth of meaning to the initiated ('data models', 'structure-clash', 'fourth-generation language'). Once the label is understood, there is no need to explain its meaning repeatedly. (Just as we may only be able to formulate a problem in terms of a known solution set, so we may be able to define an idea only if we have words to label that idea!)

As with language, so for system design. If there is a widely useful function of whatever size, then code it in as general and efficient a way as possible; label it; carefully define its input and output interfaces; then use the function whenever its use is appropriate.

System design then becomes rather like writing a poem or a symphony. What are you trying to do/say? What functions/words/chords are available for you to do/say it? How do we fit the functions/words/chords together?

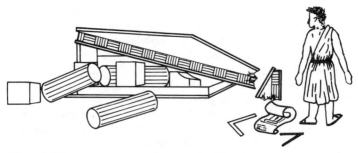

Figure 4.2 If we are to progress, there must be failure!

In any construction there is a need to preserve the wholeness; the coherence of the complete artefact. At the same time, we will be doing detailed work on a small part of the artefact. Michelangelo had to keep in mind a vision of the whole ceiling of the Sistine Chapel while he was painting in the detail of someone's right foot.

We can balance the demands of 'wholeness' and of detail by partitioning. We can divide the whole system into parts, even though *the parts don't, at that stage, exist!* At the beginning of this book we spoke of a system consisting of parts. The partitioning doesn't go on for ever. Eventually we will find that we have defined a function for which we have got the standard building blocks. So far, we can describe the process as *top-down design*; but it doesn't stop there.

We will find that the function we have built is either not quite what we imagined or that we were not absolutely clear what it had to look like before we built it. Either way, we are likely to go back and redefine *what we are trying to do*, and perhaps alter the top-down partitioning that we've previously decided upon. *We can't really be sure what we are trying to do until we've done it.* This is true whether we are engaged in writing a book or designing an all-singing-dancing computer-based simulation system.

In Section 3.5 we said that there is a balance between perceived objectives, decisions and the information that is available. Crime writers tell us that they don't always know what characters are going to be like when they start creating them. Building a function can easily change the mind of the builder about what he or she is trying to do and about the way to do it.

We should now be able to put together a recipe for system design:

1. Agree with your client what you are trying to do. We can see this 'What you are trying to do' as a set of *objectives* or *goals*. Try to strip this of all extraneous noise. Your objectives are different from the underlying *purpose* of the system. Write down a definition of that purpose. Be clear about the boundary that has been set to limit this new application. Understand the application and what its purpose is.
2. Be aware of the constructional pieces and tools already available to you. If you are planning to use a software system for generating the new application, then learn how to get maximum benefit from that application generator.
3. Construct your data model. This describes the structure of that part of the real world for which you are designing an

information system. The data model defines what your information system needs to remember if it's going to do its job. If you get your model right, you can make progress.

4. Get access to a database constructed to your data model. It may be a genuine working database or (better) a test database purpose built for your design activity.
5. Partition your whole application within the chosen boundary so that you can design new functions fitting into a particular structural pattern.
6. Use the tools and constructional pieces you have, to design the new functions. Don't stop at one outline solution. Don't worry too much about system purpose at this stage. (Brainstorming? Or 'I keep six honest serving-men (They taught me all I knew); Their names are What and Why and When and How and Where and Who'[2]). Don't be too reluctant to change your database definition if it seems to be appropriate.
7. Reassess what you are trying to do, and how the task has been partitioned, each time you design a new function.
8. Evaluate your solution and select the one which you now feel is most appropriate to what you now believe you are trying to do.
9. Build the functions and put them all together to construct a new artefact of the new application system.
10. Test the new application exhaustively and initiate any corrective action.
11. Implement, and audit the result.

The structural pattern is the key. You may call it 'Jackson System Design'[3]; or 'Warnier–Orr diagrams'[4]; or 'Structured English; or, if you are writing a poem, 'sonnet form'. Arguments about which pattern is the correct one tend to be about how many dimensions of the problem you can include in one framework. The really important thing is to have a framework! Without that there can be no creative discussion.

There is still a snag. It is the opinion of many systems analysts that users don't know what they want. Why should they? They are being asked to speculate about their desires in an environment that they have never experienced. They are usually busy people with pressing problems which demand their attention now.

Current ideas on prototyping address this problem. If we can produce a crude working system in two days then there isn't too much need to make sure this it's the right system. 'Here's a system. Try it! If you don't like it tell me why not; then throw it away and I'll build you a new one!' The more tried and tested building blocks are available to us, the easier this policy will be.

One obvious advantage comes from the balance between objectives, decisions and the information that is available. It's probably much more reliable to deduce what a decision maker is trying to do from the decisions he or she makes than to ask the decision maker. Whether the objectives have never been formally identified, or whether the decision maker is not willing to admit in public what they are, makes no real difference. Either way, the stated goals are of no value to the system designer except as a statement of what the decision maker says he or she is doing.

Closely related to the ideas about prototyping is the development of Fourth-Generation Languages, or 4GL. These currently take two general forms. One form allows the specfiication of the system requirements in a very high-level language (for example, Structured English, decision tables, 'Higher Order Software'), and the subsequent use of a 'program generator' to produce the object code which drives the system. A second form of 4GL conceives a system as consisting of storage data tables, visual display unit (VDU) screens, printed reports and a data dictionary defining all the parts and their relationships with each other. The 4GL ('Oracle', 'Info', 'Information', etc.) provides support for designing each element of a new system on the VDU screen and for relating the various component parts of the system into a coherent whole. Practice differs between different 4GL.

Whatever the form of the 4GL, its use as a prototyping tool can follow a number of patterns. It may be that a system designer rapidly completes a system and then hands it to a user to try out. This is the suggestion we made above. A different approach is that the prototype emerges as a result of a constantly refining dialogue between designer and user; each step forward is a result of discussion between both groups of people. A third approach is to conceive the system as interfacing with the user in the VDU input and output screens and in the reports generated by the system. Prototyping methods are then used for the design of these screens and reports, and these components are linked into the whole system by more traditional design methods.

Whatever prototyping approach has been adopted, it is a mistake to regard the agreed prototype as the final system. It's a tool for developing the requirement specification (both the functional specification and the data model). The aim has been rapid development, not efficient operation. A final comment, though, on 4GL: if they are useful for developing a prototype, they may be equally helpful in developing the agreed system.

We have spoken at length about the user requirement, and we've outlined an approach to turning this requirement into a design. We still need to say something about the documents in Figure 4.1. Some of these deserve and will get chapters to themselves. We'll deal with others in this chapter.

This section has suggested one approach to design and some possible variations on that approach. The following chapters will put some more flesh on these ideas. Our belief is that the design process itself must be designed! The designers must, if only subconsciously, decide how they are going to set about their task.

4.3 Feasibility document

The essential feature of the feasibility document is that it is produced *early*! It's silly to lay down cast-iron rules, but the management of the organization should be looking for a feasibility document some three weeks after the start of a design project.

The purpose of the document is *to provide the data on which to decide whether to abort the project or to allow it to continue*. Theoretically, this decision can be made at any stage, but in practice, the longer a project continues, the more entrenched the vested interests in that project become. It doesn't become more likely to be successful; just harder to stop! One study conducted by the National Computing Centre [4] concluded that 80% of projects which got past the feasibility study stage went through to implementation, regardless of how well designed they were! However illogical it may be, we all have the feeling that we must get some benefit from money already spent.

If, then, the feasibility document is about continuing or aborting we can specify what should be in the feasibility document. It must clearly state what it is we are trying to do; it must also explore whether this objective is feasible. What do we mean by feasible?

First, there is *economic feasibility*. Can it pay? It isn't necessary to prove that the proposal is going to be profitable. What is necessary is that the possible benefits must match the expected costs. If there is a user requirement for cost reduction, then the scope for savings cannot exceed the existing costs. If the economic case depends on increased turnover, or on a more desirable product, then the scope for increase and improvement must be identified and the assumptions made explicit. *Technical feasibility* is simply a statement that what is proposed is within the scope of existing technology. Finally, *operational feasibility* is whether the proposal is practically possible. If there is a proposal for a computer-based sales record system, and it's known that Fred, the Sales Manager, is bitterly opposed to computers, then there's a dilemma. Either you can have the record system or you can have Fred. You can't have both.

A side product of the economic feasibility examination is that we identify the cost and resources budget for the completion of the next design function, that is, the process of analysis and specification; and that we identify the schedule for the completion of analysis and specification. Each development stage establishes the constraints for the next stage.

4.4 Documents produced from analysis and specification

This is the most fundamental part of system design. We acknowledge a debt to Tom de Marco[6] in formulating the basic document needs as the functional specification, the data model and the state change specification. We've also listed the acceptance test specification, the physical requirements specification, and the budget and schedule:

1. *What the system does – the functional specification*
   We shall be using the data flow diagram with supporting structure rules. The functional specification is a result of functional analysis. The specification will also necessarily tell us the frequency of each data flow and the response time which is appropriate for each function. It will inform us which functions are to be performed by people and which by computer. It will define what processing is done by the system.
   There is a proper sequence about functional specification. The parts of the system which you will attempt to design first are those that are most frequently used or most sensitive in their effect on the business of the organization. If these sub-systems are successfully implemented, then development can reach the less critical areas.
   It should be true that sometimes the organization's response to a functional specification is to postpone further development in favour of some more sensitive functional area.
   Once a functional specification is agreed, there should be a moratorium on further suggestions or demands. This doesn't mean that a functional specification is sacrosanct; only that nothing will ever be constructed if the specification of what you are trying to do is different from day to day.
2. *What the system remembers – the data model*
   The data model strictly models the real-world entity types relevant to the organization's business. It also defines the things

we want information about, and what information we want about them, as well as access paths to that information.

The data model is a product of data analysis. This is as vital a part of the process of system design as functional analysis, and proceeds alongside functional analysis.

3. *How the system behaves – the state change specification*

   The specification describes the relationship between operator and system. For a system using VDUs it can be synonymously called 'dialogue design'. For a large batch-processing system it may be represented by a series of 'run charts'.

4. *The acceptance test specification*

   It's all too common for the acceptance test to be designed after the construction of the new system. The danger must be that the acceptance test is related to what has actually been constructed, rather than what the users require. It is surely vital that a clear and complete statement of what you are trying to achieve is made before construction begins. The acceptance test specification is just that. If you change your mind about what you are trying to do, this is the time to alter the acceptance test specification.

5. *Physical requirements specification*

   The name is self-explanatory. The hardware requirements of a particular system design must be specified as a guide to subsequent hardware selection. The topic is outside the scope of this book, and won't be taken any further. (Don't interpret that as denigrating the importance of this function.)

6. *Budget and schedule*

   Not until the analysis and specifcation stage of system design is it possible to get a reasonable estimate of the potential costs and benefits of redesign. Once this stage has been passed the chances of aborting a project, or making a substantial change of direction, are quite small.

   The budget sets out the resources of every kind which you assume to be required when you carry out the system evaluation. Along with the acceptance test specification and the schedule, the budget is output data from system evaluation. As soon as we say that, we have to qualify it. The budget can never be static. There must be regular review stages (Monthly? Six-monthly? Yearly?) when evaluation is done again. At each of these stages several decisions must be made:

   Do we abort?
   Do we need to change the goals (things we are trying to do)?
   What resources do we need to achieve the goals, given our present knowledge?

How long will the job take (the schedule), given our present knowledge?

The *schedule* is closely related to the budget. It sets out a time scale for completion and all the stages towards completion. Like the budget, it will need to be reviewed from time to time as more and more information about the system is built up. Eventually your forecast of completion date will home in on the true, real-world completion date!

In spite of all we have just written about the budget and schedule not being static, there are two very good reasons why the original budget and schedule should never be thrown away.

The first reason is that any organization must try as hard as it can to get its estimates right. Only if these are somewhere near the mark can you expect to make sensible allocation of resources. It's negative feedback! When a job, or a stage of a job, has been completed you need to compare its use of resources with the original estimated use of resources. It's not an admission of weakness; it's an attempt to do better next time!

The second reason is really an amplification of the first. A consultancy firm, or a profit centre system development group within a large organization, may develop systems for users on fixed-price contracts. Your original estimate is what you are going to be paid on ! It's a good idea to try to get it right.

It will be helpful in Figure 4.3 to partition the 'analysis and specification' function bubble in Figure 4.1. Functional analysis doesn't have a one-to-one relationship with data analysis. Particular functions will almost certainly be redesigned more often than it's necessary to redesign the data model. The data model is a map of the database which gives a solid foundation on which new functional applications can be built. As each application progresses, so *reconciliation* between the functional application and the data model must be necessary. Perhaps new data attributes must be added or old ones modified.

Functional analysis can profitably be partitioned a little further (Figure 4.4). The new logical DFD, supplemented by the user requirement expressed as a set of structural rules, is the 'what you are trying to do' statement that we asked for in Sections 4.2 and 4.4.

Let's have a last word on the analysis and design bubble of Figure 4.1. Don't regard all these data flows as holy writ. We're not saying you must work this way. We're suggesting a framework which we think is useful.

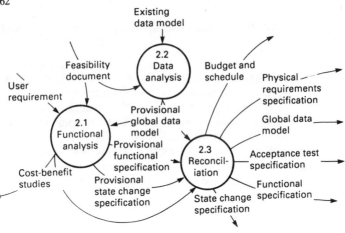

Figure 4.3 The analysis and specification function

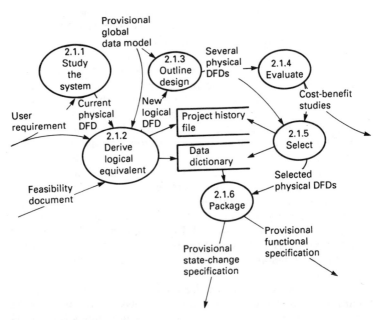

Figure 4.4 Functional analysis

4.5 Documents produced from the functional construction function

The title of this section illustrates the difficulty of describing a system for designing systems! We are describing the function for building functions.

4.5.1 Training and changeover plan

The main statement that needs to be made is what the training and changeover plan isn't! It isn't a teaching programme prepared by the system analysts which is then presented to the users as a first step to implementation. Indeed, implementation starts as far back as the user requirement.

The training and changeover plan includes *user manuals* (unless this has been adequately coped with by 'user-friendly' VDU screen design); computer operator manuals (with a similar rider); a learning programme designed to transmit any necessary skills; and a detailed programme for changeover from the old to the new system. It includes all these things; but it will be quite useless *unless the user's commitment has already been won.*

There are many different ideas about changover plans. These seem to reduce to:

A pilot scheme
Parallel running
Burn your boats, once-for-all changeover

There isn't an obvious choice; horses for courses! The problem with a pilot scheme is whether what can be done on a small scale by a dedicated group of people can be translated to a larger context. It at least gives a chance to iron out the bugs.

Parallel running sounds attractive, but users, like most people, are busy people. The needs of *today* tend to drive out development for tomorrow. The system which is updated will be the one needed to run the business *now*. If the system developers wait for the new system to have the integrity, or truth, of the old one they might wait for ever!

And sudden changeover? You may be forced into that, but the problems are obvious. Whichever plan you adopt, your chances aren't good unless the user has given his or her commitment.

4.5.2 Completed software

The thing which needs to be said is that any software (the code with which we tell the computer what we want it to do) is explained by a detailed set of documents. Without that, if you want to modify the system, it might be cheaper to throw the lot away and start again. In the interest of system maintenance, *documentation is essential*! This is no less true if you are buying your software rather than writing it yourself.

The form of the documentation is suggested throughout this book. You will need carefully annotated 'programs' or some explicit description of the application structure (Structured English, for example). You will require data flow diagrams and data models. You will need the data dictionary entries. With some 'fourth-generation languages' you may be able to expect that the system documentation is an automatic by-product of system development.

4.6 Documents produced from the audit function

Briefly, have the expectations of the system (what you were trying to do) been met[7]? If not, what do we do about this system and about the methods we use to develop future systems?

Perhaps most of our expectations have been met, but there are a few loose ends; or perhaps there are some new ideas about development and enhancement. This should prompt initiation of the whole process again, with new user requirements. And this seems a good place to end the chapter.

4.7 Summary

- The people concerned with a computer-based information system can be labelled as users, operators, analysts and programmers (who could also be termed constructors or builders). We can also identify those people who are concerned with implementation and those who are database administrators.
- We use the term 'project life cycle' as the framework for describing the design activity.
- Many jobs, or parts of jobs, will have been done before. There is no mileage in reinventing the wheel each time you want to move a load!
- Innovation carries the risk of failure; but without innovation there is no progress.
- Any design activity must start with a user requirement or statement of what we are trying to do.

- Unless we can conceive design solutions, it is extremely difficult to define a problem. Our prior knowledge of work which has been done already gives us a context in which to decide what we are trying to do.
- We need to have a structural pattern in which to formulate design solutions. Without that pattern we have no framework to progress the design, and we find communication with fellow practitioners extremely difficult.
- Prototyping is one possible approach to the problem of uncertainty over what we are trying to do.
- There are certain milestone 'documents' which chart the progress of an information systems design project:

  Feasibility document
  Function requirements specification
  Data models, both global and local
  State change specification
  Acceptance test specification
  Physical requirements specification
  Budget and schedule
  Cost/benefit studies
  Training and changeover plan
  Completed software
  Test plan
  Exceptions revealed by audit.

Discussion points

4.1 Are information systems designers attempting to produce information systems which are acceptable to the potential users of those systems?

4.2 A Chief Accountant of a certain company once remarked of the design and implementation of new systems:

> 'We try to persuade the users that there is something for them in the new system; we encourage them to inject their own ideas into the design activity; finally, if they don't cooperate, we fire them.' Discuss this statement.

4.3 'Most of us can only conceptualize a problem in terms of solutions we are already aware of. Unless we know what can be done, we can't define a problem.' Discuss this statement.

4.4 'Arguments about which (structural design) pattern is the correct one tend to be arguments about how many dimensions of the problem you can include in one framework.' What do we mean by dimensions? Why is it difficult to embrace all dimensions in one framework? What dimensions are easily included in a data flow diagram? What are left out? What dimensions are included in a data model? What are left out?

4.5 'It is the opinion of many systems analysts that users don't know what they want.' Discuss this statement.

4.6 Why should a feasibility document be produced early in the life of a project? Would it not be better to continue the project until details about eventual costs and benefits are more certain and then decide whether to complete the work?

4.7 What the system does – the functional requirements specification.

What the system remembers – the data model.

How the system behaves – the state change specification.

We assert that these are the three key documents of a system design activity. This prescription is not universal. Others have argued for different ways of specifying the information requirements. Identify the underlying needs of information requirements specification and the extent to which our three candidates satisfy this need.

4.8 The Production Controller of a steel works once asserted in a conversation: 'Changeover was going very badly. The new production control system was inadequate because all the stock updates were put through on the old card system. In the end I came into work one Sunday morning and burnt all the old cards.' Comment on the wisdom of the Production Controller's attitude.

References

1 H. Petrosky, *To Engineer is Human*, Macmillan, London (1986)
2 Rudyard Kipling, 'I keep six honest serving-men'
3 Michael Jackson, *System Development*, Prentice-Hall, Englewood Cliffs, NJ (1983)
4 K.T. Orr, *Structured Requirements Definition*, Ken Orr & Associates (1981)
5 W.C.W. Morris (ed.), *Economic Evaluation of Computer Based Systems*, Book 1, *Report of the Working Party*, NCC Ltd (1971)
6 Tom de Marco, *Control of Software Projects: Management, Measurement, and Specification*, Yourdon Press, New York (1982)
7 Andrew Chambers, *Computer Auditing*, Pitman, London (1981)

Chapter 5

Functional specification and functional analysis

5.1 The context of functional analysis

In this chapter we are studying the *functional analysis* function of Figure 4.3 and two of the data flows which originate from it:

The provisional functional specification; and
The provisional state change specification.

The only purpose of the word 'provisional' is to establish that after functional analysis is apparently finished it is still necessary to reconcile the results with any separate data analysis and with the current global data model. For the rest of this chapter we shall drop the word 'provisional'.

The state change possibilities are explored in Chapter 8 and at a more fundamental level in Chapter 13 on human–computer interaction (HCI). Here we shall concentrate on the design process, not on the form of the HCI. The state change specification is really a component part of the functional specification. We shall also comment on the *acceptance test specification* and its relationship with the functional specification. The cost-benefit studies originating from the functional analysis function are *not* described here.

Both data analysis and functional analysis are concerned with the *information requirements analysis* of systems. Data analysis attempts to identify the information we need. Functional analysis is the study of the way that information is made available for decision making and routine processing within the system. The end result of functional analysis is the functional specification telling us what we must do and the state change specification gives us the fine detail of the users' interactions with the system. In many ways, the functional specification is *the most important document we produce during a design activity*.

There are very few charting techniques in this chapter that we haven't already described elsewhere. What we are trying to do is present a way of deploying those tools to aid the process of analysis.

Analysis has to start somewhere. We mentioned the 'user's requirement' in Chapter 4. Anyone embarking on analysis must recognize that the problem which has been stated is not necessarily the true problem. For example:

> 'We believe that the stock we receive is not being recorded properly, because we seem to be continually overstocked.'

This statement is of value as the user's belief. However, that belief must be challenged. Only if there is a good robust statement of *what we are trying to do* or *where we want to be at* can there be any hope of delivering the goods. The first stage of analysis must be one of *problem definition*, starting out from a fuzzy problem area. It isn't unknown for users to find after they have been helped to an understanding of what the problem is that they themselves then realize the solution without further mediation by analysts or information system specialists!

The problem definition must recognize that human activity systems are social systems, technical systems and economic systems. We consider systems as economic systems in Chapter 9 and systems as social systems in Chapter 13. Systems as technical systems must depend on the particular industry in which they are based. That is outside the scope of this book. From here on, we shall assume that we know what we are trying to do!

5.2 An overview of analysis and specification

Throughout the activity we are asking questions:

What? Why? When? How? Where? Who?

Answers to these questions will suggest other questions which need answers.

The data flow diagram at the top of Figure 5.1 is taken directly from Figure 4.4. Figure 5.1 is a framework for analysis and outline design specification. We still speak of 'outline', because the preferred design has still to be selected from all the candidate designs and that preferred design must be 'packaged' to produce the functional specification.

The display shows a multi-step activity:

1. Study the system to obtain the facts about the tasks performed.
2. Analyse those facts to determine which tasks are logically required.

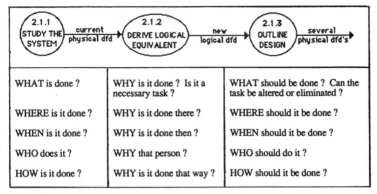

Figure 5.1 The basis of analysis and specification of outline designs

3. Decide on the most appropriate design solutions to complete those tasks.

The potential users of the system must be involved all along the way. *Implementation starts the day the project begins.* If the commitment of the users is not given then the design work will be abortive. Part of the process of winning commitment is proper presentation of tentative solutions. Whether the work is done by analysts or by users, we must have a fourth step in the analysis and specification activity:

4. Present tentative solutions to the user community.

These four steps give the basis for the following sections of this chapter.

5.3 Obtaining the facts

Although we are addressing ourselves to functional analysis, the strategies and techniques described in this section are similar to those required for data analysis. There are certain basic things that an analyst needs to do:

1. Understand the organization and what he or she is supposed to do in the organization. Who reports to whom about what? What roles do different people perform?
2. Somehow, elicit the relevant knowledge that the people in the organization have.

3. Get a copy of any relevant document or message that is used, with operational detail filled in on the fields of the document.

Let's look at each of these in turn.

5.3.1 Organizational structure and the role of the client

Figure 3.5 suggested three broad levels in an organization. They are interconnected; especially the technical core and the administrative level. Even if the 'user requirement' is entirely within the technical core, the administrative level will need management and control data about the system. If the user requirement is for 'management information' or for 'decision support' at the administrative level, then it won't be possible to provide this unless we as designers understand the technical core and the data flows within that core.

At whatever level the system is studied, the study takes place *within a functioning system, with responsibilities and prerogatives which must be observed.* If you want to talk to the weighbridge checker, you will need to talk to the Goods-Inward Foreman first; and before him, you will need to talk to the Chief Storeman. Systems are designed *for* people *by* people. If a so-called designer starts off by stepping on toes, he had better make sure that he has enough power to get away with it! Whether the system he then designs is going to be worth the candle is quite another story. We have written about participation by users in the design activity in Chapter 13.

A person may 'own' a problem and then design for a solution on his or her own behalf. Alternatively, the *problem owner* may commission someone else to do the analysis and undertake the design. In that case the problem owner is the *client*, and the client is all-important. A good design is, by definition, one which satisfies the client. The client may be the owner of a business, the Managing Director, the head of a department, or (in the case of Michelangelo and the Sistine Chapel) the Pope.

We shall write about conducting interviews below. An interview with a client has some very particular requirements of its own. Fundamentally, after interviewing the client the potential designer must know:

1. What is he or she being asked to do?
2. How will the client and the designer measure how well it has been done?
3. What resources are going to be available to do it?

4. How is the designer to be introduced to the people in the organization?
5. What are the constraints? What must be left alone? What shouldn't be said?
6. When must it be done by?

If the designer represents an outside contracting organization or if the client is proposing a contract to buy some proprietary software from a software house, there are some additional things that the client and the contractor must agree:

1. What precisely are the *deliverables*?
2. Are there any *penalties* for non-delivery?
3. What *documentation* is to be supplied about the product by the designer?
4. Is the client to be given the facilities to *amend* the product?
5. Will amendment by the client *invalidate* the contract?
6. What future *maintenance* of the product is the contractor offering?
7. What *costs* is the client incurring, both for present work and for future maintenance?
8. If the contractor should go of business, who will *own* the original product coding and documentation? How will the client get *access* to the coding and documentation?
9. Can the contractor use the client's name as a *reference* for future clients?

5.3.2 Knowledge elicitation

We have listed collection of all the documents used in a system as a separate strategy. Certainly collecting documents will add to our knowledge about how the system works. Apart from that, knowledge elicitation must come from:

1. Highly structured questions distributed as *questionnaires*;
2. *Interviews* with people working within the system; and
3. *Observation*.

A questionnaire supposes that the analyst knows precisely for which questions answers are wanted (see Figure 5.2). The use of a questionnaire only makes sense if responses are wanted from a lot of people, and some consistent framework for analysis is needed. Essentially, an analyst who sends out a questionnaire is trying to measure something. We won't say any more here about measurement, but it is the same topic as the 'utility' which we discuss in Section 9.8.

How many minutes after close of trading does stock-checking take in your branch ?

Would you say that the Customer Complaint Form is

easy to understand	_____
complicated, but clear	_____
incomprehensible	_____

What proportion of goods supplied to customers in your branch are returned as unsatisfactory ?

Not more than 1%	_____
More than 1% to 5%	_____
More than 5% to 10%	_____
More than 10%	_____

Figure 5.2 Some possible questions on a questionnaire

An interview has much in common with a questionnaire. Above all, it is *structured*. The purpose of the interview is for the analyst to elicit relevant facts and opinions from the person being interviewed. If the analyst doesn't know any questions that need answers, then there isn't much point in having the interview!

The difference between an interview and a questionnaire is in a *flexible response*. We said at the beginning that answers to questions will suggest fresh questions. It would be silly to rigidly lay out the structure of the interview in advance and to stick to it. The analyst cannot know all the questions that need answers before the interview starts.

It's possible that the analyst (let's call her Janet) may be superior in the organization to the person being interviewed. It is much more likely that the person being interviewed (let's call him Fred) will feel no particular obligation to Janet. In those circumstances Janet will only get the information which she needs from the interview if she succeeds in creating a climate in which Fred feels comfortable, and well disposed towards her. It's a social encounter, and all the considerations about what makes a social encounter work do apply.

An interview must take place somewhere. Whether it is at Fred's workplace or somewhere else must depend on a combination of the inclinations of Fred and the place where Fred's knowledge and opinions are most likely to be elicited correctly. If they both have to shout to make themselves heard, the quality of communication will be low.

Like any good book, an interview has a beginning, a middle and an end. If Janet and Fred have arranged an interview, she should be there on time, and she should be dressed in the way Fred would expect. There is no benefit in adding a possible point of friction to the interview. She must introduce herself, and explain clearly why she has sought this interview. If she intends to make any notes during the interview she should ask his approval. So much for the beginning.

By the words that are used, and by her general 'body language', Janet needs to make it clear to Fred that he is a person who matters. This means that Janet should seek opinions as well as facts, and prompt Fred for his ideas on improvements; that the encounter should be courteous and appropriately friendly; that on no account should Janet ever be patronizing; and that she should *listen*. If she uses the encounter to propound half-baked solutions then the interview fails in its basic purpose to elicit facts and opinions. If she spends the time while Fred is answering to think about the next question then she could have saved herself the bother of asking the question.

We spoke above about taking notes. It's tempting to try to tape-record the whole encounter. Our opinion is that this inhibits rather than helps the encounter as a social occasion. In spite of this, notes must be taken at the time. Memory is fallible. One writer has suggested that 50% of what is heard is forgotten within ten minutes[1]!

We believe that a prime characteristic of a good analyst is a willingness to ask stupid questions. Janet has failed if she goes away before she understands what she has been told.

Also, the interview has an end. If a certain time period has been agreed by Janet and Fred, then it should be kept to. Before they part, Janet should recount from her notes what she thinks Fred has said. If this is difficult because of the complexity of the subject then she should undertake to send him a copy of the *discussion document* as soon as she has prepared it (which should be by tomorrow!). Feedback is necessary. Janet must make sure that what she *believes she heard* is the same as what Fred *believes he said*. A guideline to the quality of the interview is that at the end of it both Janet and Fred should feel that there is nothing preventing her coming back again to check some doubtful information.

Fortunately for analysts, 'work' is what fills the waking lives of most of us. If something takes up so much of our time, we are usually enthusiastic in talking about it. The job of the analyst will be to guide the discussion in the 'right' direction rather than to go rigidly through a checklist of questions. Just occasionally there might be someone who, either out of suspicion or general cantankerousness, is deliberately obstructive. If this is how Fred insists on treating Janet then she has no choice but to go back to the client and report that Fred's attitude makes it impossible for her to do her job.

What an analyst can never do is to deflect suspicion by making glib promises which he or she has no power to keep. If Fred is worried about losing his job, then he must talk to his boss about it. Janet's job is to collect facts and opinions.

Observation is the last recipe for knowledge elicitation that we describe. The boundary with interviewing is fuzzy. During an interview an analyst may ask the person being interviewed to fill up a form or to make an entry on a VDU screen. While 'observing', an analyst may need to ask questions about what is going on.

An analyst 'observes' to find out about document flows, the details about values put into a form field or how a report is used. It isn't a work study. The analyst must convince the people being observed that they are not in any way being tested. *The analyst should not need to explain his presence.* We said above that a potential system designer must agree with the client about how he or she is to be introduced into the organization. This means that everyone concerned is warned in advance by their management about what is going on and why it is going on.

5.3.3 Recording document and message contents

It should be true, that as a result of an interview, an analyst collects a copy of each document that is received, or filled in, or used by the person interviewed. If any kind of verbal or telephone message is regularly sent or received then the analyst needs a description of that message. If a VDU screen is used, then the analyst will want a definition of that screen.

The collected copy of each document is a *completed* copy. The way the document is actually used may be different from the use envisaged by the person who originally designed the document. The analyst must record what the *content* of each field on the document is, how many *replications* of that field there may be (e.g. twenty separate stock item lines for each customer order document) and any *rules* and peculiarities about the way the field is filled in.

As far as the document as a whole is concerned, the analyst needs to record:

1. The *frequency* of use (e.g. school-attendance records are completed once a day for each class; one order document is completed for every customer order received);

2. The *volume* (e.g. in one school, there are attendance records for each of 30 classes; an average of 150 customers orders a day are received, each for an average of 100 stock item lines); and, if it is appropriate,

Clerical Document Specification NCC	PURCHASE ORDER FORM		SR		PO		S41	I
Stationery ref. ST101		**Size** A4		**Number of parts** 3		**Method of preparation** HANDWRITTEN		
Filing sequence Order Number			**Medium** PADDED SHEETS		**Prepared/maintained by** DEPARTMENT BUYER			
Frequency of preparation/update PER ORDER			**Retention period** 6 MONTHS		**Location** COPY 2 - PURCHASING COPY 3 - DEPT. BUYER			

		Minimum	Maximum	Av/Abs	Growth rate/fluctuations
VOLUME		35 x 1 PER DAY	70 x 33 PER DAY	45 x 9 PER DAY	$+ 7\frac{1}{3}$ % p.a.

Users/recipients	Purpose	Frequency of use
ACCOUNTING OFFICE COPY 1 - SUPPLIER COPY 2 - PURCHASING	To INITIATE STOCK REPLENISHMENT	DAILY

Ref.	Item	Picture	Occurrence	Value range	Source of data
1	Supplier Name	30 A			Stock Card
2	Supplier Address	100 A			Supplier List
3	Order Number	99999		1 to 99999	Pre-printed
4	Order Date	DD-Mon-YY			Today
5	Order Value	9999.99			Sum of 12
6	Originating Dept	NN		1 to 25	
7	Delivery Date	DD-Mon-YY	0 to 1		Suppliers Quotation
8	Merchandise Number	99999	1 to 20	1 to 99999	Stock Card
9	Description	30 A	1 to 20		Stock Card
10	Order Quantity	9999	1 to 20	1 to 9999	Stock Card
11	Purchase Price Per Unit	999.99	1 to 20		Suppliers Quotation
12	Cost Of Purchase	9999.99	1 to 20		10 x 11

Notes
VOLUME : 1ST FIGURE IS NUMBER OF ORDERS, 2ND FIGURE IS ITEMS PER ORDER.

S 41			
Author JW	**Issue** B	**Date** 1-JUL-90	

left margin: © 1989. The National Computing Centre Limited

Figure 5.3 The National Computing Centre's clerical document description form (Courtesy of NCC Blackwell Joint Venture)

3. The *retention time* required for that document or message (e.g. class-attendance records are kept for one year, order documents are retained for six months from the date of the order).

The data dictionary will have entries describing each documented message. We gave some examples of data flow in Figure 2.2. The format of that description is clearly inadequate for a complicated document.

Figure 5.3 shows the layout of a *document description* designed by the British National Computing Centre[2]. The properties described above are all covered. 'Picture' conventions are the same as those we use in Section 10.5 on data dictionary 'domain descriptions'. Computer-based data dictionary descriptions of documents must be more tightly formatted than descriptions drawn on a piece of paper, but the information that a designer needs can and must be included in a data dictionary document description.

Figure 5.3 is a clerical document description. The National Computing Centre has also designed documents appropriate for computer document description, both for input and for output documents. Later in this chapter we shall need to say more about the description of VDU screens. For the moment, we shall close our story about collecting facts.

5.4 Analysing the facts: physical and logical data flow diagrams

The first tool of functional analysis is the *physical data flow diagram* (physical DFD). In Section 2.4 we said that a physical DFD describes what has actually been seen to happen and that a *logical DFD* describes the system which we logically need in order to achieve the system purpose.

In Figure 5.4 we display parts of a number of discussion records prepared by analyst Janet Wright after interviews in the Sellmore retail department store. Janet is investigating the procedures used by the store for stock replenishment. The form of the discussion records is again that used by the National Computing Centre[2].

Figure 5.5 displays a physical DFD derived from these discussion documents. In this diagram we have suggested a device that we didn't use in Chapter 2. We have used soft boxes similar to the entity type boxes in an Entity-Relationship-Attribute diagram. There is no possibility of confusion, because entity type boxes and function boxes can never appear on the same diagram. The

Title	System	Document	Name	Page
Sellmore Retail Store	SR	1	Stock replenishment (buyer)	1

Participants Janet Wright	Date 2-Apr-90
Frederick Jukes, Department Buyer	Location Sellmore

Objective/Agenda	Duration
To establish the relevant data flows	1005 to 1030

Results:

1. Three copies of a purchase order are prepared by the department buyer.
2. Each purchase order is approved by the Store Manager.
3. Copy three is retained by Mr Jukes and filed; other copies go to the Accounting office.
4. When Mr Jukes gets the Receiving Report he compares it to the copy three purchase order, and if correct, files them both together.

Title	System	Document	Name	Page
Sellmore Retail Store	SR	2	Stock replenishment (accounts)	1

Participants Janet Wright	Date 3-Apr-90
Mary Smith, Chief Accountant	Location Sellmore

Objective/Agenda	Duration
To establish the relevant data flows	1130 to 1150

Results:

1. When the Accounting office receives a purchase order from a department buyer, they check whether that deparment is 'open to buy' with respect to that merchandise. If so, the purchase order is recorded, and the 'open to buy' for that deparment is reduced.
2. Copy one of the purchase order is then mailed to the firm supplying the merchandise (the Supplier). Copy two is sent to the receiving department.
3. The supplier's invoice is eventually received from the Purchasing department after they approve it for payment.
4. The amount to be paid is entered into the Purchase ledger.
5. The invoice is filed.

Figure 5.4a Some discussion records from the Sellmore department store (Courtesy of NCC Blackwell Joint Venture)

purpose of using them in a DFD is to allow both the organizational department name and the functions performed by the department to appear together. You may find this helpful.

No data stores appear on the DFD. They are all local to one function, and therefore don't form an interface between functions.

We have not drawn a separate context diagram, and therefore have shown the supplier as an external entity on the DFD. We believe that context diagrams are useful tools for describing system boundaries but will be returning to boundaries in a later section.

The discussion records say nothing about payment to the supplier. If that payment must be entered in the Purchase ledger, and that ledger is a data store local to the Accounting Office, then

Title	System	Document	Name	Page
Sellmore Retail Store	SR	3	Stock replenishment (purchasing)	1

Participants Janet Wright	Date 3-Apr-90
John da Cruz, Purchasing Manager	Location Sellmore

Objective/Agenda	Duration
To establish the relevant data flows	1415 to 1450

Results:
1. The Purchasing department compares the receiving report with the purchase order to ensure that the merchandise received is the same as that ordered.
2. Copy two of the purchase order, and the receiving report, are filed.
3. The invoice from the Supplier is received by Purchasing. If it agrees with the filed purchase order, the invoice is approved and sent to Accounting.

Title	System	Document	Name	Page
Sellmore Retail Store	SR	4	Stock replenishment (cosmetics manager)	1

Participants Janet Wright	Date 4-Apr-90
Charlotte Brown, Cosmetics Department Manager	Location Sellmore

Objective/Agenda	Duration
To establish the relevant data flows	0900 to 0915

Results:
1. The department receives copy two of a purchase order for new merchandise from the Accounting office.
2. A receiving report is prepared when the new merchandise is received.

Figure 5.4b

the supplier payment *must* be shown as a data flow from the Accounting Office function.

The check by the Store Manager can be seen as a *control* function, which shouldn't be shown. It is essential to maintain the simplicity of a DFD. It is a matter of controversy whether this is treated as control, and left off, or as important information which must be included.

There is another feature of Figure 5.5 that we must explain. The Accounting Office, we are told, checks whether the Cosmetics department is 'open-to-buy' with respect to the merchandise being ordered. This could be interpreted as a data flow from the Management system, outside the Stock Replenishment system boundary. That is the way we have charted it.

Alternatively, we could see this information coming from a data store held by the Accounting office function, which records

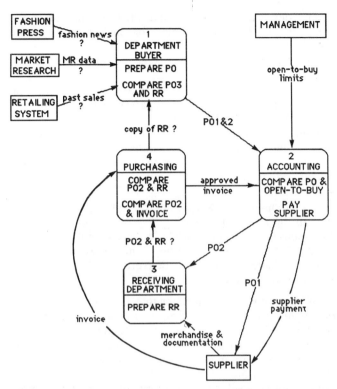

Figure 5.5 A level 0 DFD for stock replenishment by the Sellmore department store

cumulative sales to date of each merchandise category. If this data store also records the 'open-to-buy' limits then these limits would have to be updated from time to time by some other system, probably the management system. The 'open-to-buy' data store seen by the Stock Replenishment system is then a *local* view of the 'open-to-buy' data store.

The facts that were gleaned from Janet's discussions are very limited, and some obvious follow-up questions need to be asked:

1. Why and when does the Department Buyer prepare a purchase order? We have made some assumptions about the information involved in this decision but Janet will need to check this.
2. Is the Department Buyer a member of the Purchasing department? If he is, why are there two comparisons of the received report and the purchase order? How do either the

Purchasing department or the Department Buyer obtain the receiving report? We have assumed that he gets a copy from Purchasing, but this needs checking.

3. What happens if the Store Manager doesn't approve the purchase?
4. Why is the purchase order made out and approved before the 'open-to-buy' is checked? Is the Department Buyer aware of the state of his 'open-to-buy'?
5. What does the Cosmetics department do with copy 2 of the purchase order before new merchandise is received? Is the merchandise received directly from the Supplier? Where is the new merchandise received and how do Cosmetics know it has arrived?
6. Why is the Supplier's invoice compared to the purchase order rather than the receiving report?
7. What happens if only a part of an order placed with a supplier is delivered? Although this question demands an answer, for simplicity we have assumed full deliveries in the rest of the discussion in this chapter.

These are just a few of the questions that Janet must ask herself while drawing her physical DFD. If answers to the questions exist, she will find it much easier to resolve them by taking the diagram to the users and discussing the discrepancies with them. Realization that the diagram is incomplete will prompt users to see the point of her questions.

Some of the answers will be straightforward, some will be more difficult. The Department Buyer may distrust the Purchasing department and wish to make a check of his own. Simply deciding to eliminate the second check won't make any difference; it will still go on! Perhaps the Department Buyer is quite legitimately looking for an assurance that merchandise whose procurement he originated has arrived. There may be conflicts of interest in this particular system, as in any other system, that Janet must be aware of. The DFD is an aid for getting to the facts.

To achieve more richness in our picture we must partition or decompose Figure 5.5 to demonstrate separate *logical* functions. Our picture in Figure 5.6 is oversimplified. In any real exercise we would hope that when we go down a level we partition into from five to seven functions, not two. Look back at Section 2.4 for a discussion of partitioning and levelling.

Function 3, 'Receiving department', in Figure 5.5 contains only one logical function. This means that there isn't any scope for further partitioning. The remaining functions are all partitioned according to the rules we gave in Chapter 2.

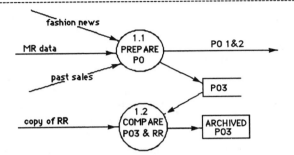

Level 1 diagram 1 for function 1: DEPARTMENT BUYER

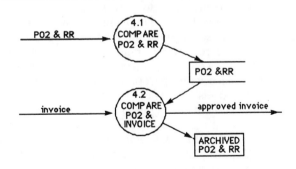

Level 1 diagram for function 2: ACCOUNTING OFFICE

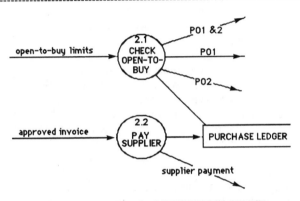

Level 1 diagram for function 4: PURCHASING DEPARTMENT

Figure 5.6 A functional decomposition of the Sellmore department store's stock replenishment system

The 'PO3' (purchase order copy three) data store, the 'PO2 & RR' (purchase order copy 2 plus receiving report) data store and the 'Accounts Receivable' local view all appear in the level 1 diagrams in Figure 5.6. This is because these data stores are all now part of the interface between different functions.

The final storage of copy 2 of the purchase order, of copy 3 and of the receiving report are shown as *sinks*. These are all *archived* data which are not going to flow anywhere anymore. A *data store* consists of data held for subsequent conversion into a data flow. The several level 1 diagrams do display clearly *which departments are currently responsible for which data stores* and *for which archived data*. You may find this useful.

We must always be on guard against storing data which are never read. The data stores in Figure 5.6 are all *local*, so we can make a check by inspecting the diagrams. We shall come back to this point presently.

From the level 1 diagrams we must develop a new *logical DFD*, showing the functions and data flows that *we believe must take place* if the system is to do what it is supposed to do. The Stock Replenishment system is a tool with a use, as we said in Chapter 1. Janet, as the analyst, must make quite sure that she knows what that use is[3,4]. Janet's Figure 5.5 physical DFD already has a logical element since it describes a system which is *for* stock replenishment. Function 3, 'receiving department', is also logically functional since it represents the stock replenishment function of one of Sellmore's retailing departments. The analyst must progressively refine the physical DFD until she is sure that she has a clear logical statement. She'll probably need several attempts at it; and she musn't be afraid to do it over again!

The functions in the logical DFD must be within our chosen boundary. We spend some time on boundary in our next section. The functions in the real system must take place with adequate system controls, and we include a section on system control later. They must take place with appropriate timeliness, and response time, which we also discuss. These points don't all emerge from our discussion documents in Figure 5.4 but that again is because we are trying to keep a simple picture.

The final logical DFD will *not* include any reference to departments. Departments are concerned with particular solutions, not logical statements of requirements.

The checking of copy 3 of the purchase order by the Department buyer remains a difficulty, since we have not identified any data flow which results from that check. What is logically required is that the Department Buyer is informed that the merchandise he requested has arrived. Checking the 'open-to-buy' is, of course, strictly a control action, but the open-to-buy limits are a necessary input to the ordering decision.

We assume that the external entities (whether they are sinks or sources of data) and the data flows across the Stock Replenishment system boundary are unchanged from the level 0 physical DFD of Figure 5.5. They are all included in the logical DFD.

Unique naming of functions is as important as naming any object or person. In Section 2.4 we numbered our functions hierarchically right down from Coquotte Company level. In this chapter we have only worked within the Stock Replenishment system. To uniquely number our logical DFD functions we should perhaps call them SR1, SR2, SR3, and so on. If you prefer more descriptive titles, then SR1.ir, SR2.os, SR3.cd and SR4.ps may be appropriate. For the rest of this chapter we have assumed that 'ir', 'os' and 'cd', or their upper-case equivalents, are unique names. Generally, we cannot assume that the physical DFD function numbers can necessarily be carried across into the logical equivalent.

All names, whether of functions, of data stores or of local views, must be described in the data dictionary.

The ORDER DATA data store needs more discussion. We represent it as the *entire* data storage needs of the Stock Replenishment system. Within that system the local view of this data store required by function 2 (order to supplier) is different from the local view required by function 3 (check delivery). Each function has its own local view. The local view for function 3 could reasonably be named 'CD ORDER DATA' and for function 4, 'PI ORDER DATA'. We'll have more on that in Section 5.6.

If in fact ORDER DATA is a set of local views of a *database* then there must be other systems with access to the same database. For example, the Retailing system will need to update the record of the quantity in stock for each item of merchandise which is held. That makes it more complicated to check that every column of a database table is both written to and read. We shall come back to this point in Section 5.6, but to assist that analysis, we have numbered all the reads and writes in the figure (R1, R2, W1, . . .). This numbering sequence would be taken as a single sequence right through the whole scope of the database.

Beware! It is always a temptation to load more representation onto a diagram. Our R1's and W2's are useful devices, but anything which reduces the simplicity of the display must carry a cost in ease of understanding.

One last word. There is no contradiction in our Department

Buyer being a sink for data, outside the information system, and also carrying out a function within the system.

From the final logical DFD we must progress to a variety of possible *new physical DFDs*, one for each possible design solution; but that is for Section 5.9!

5.5 Analysing the facts: boundary considerations

We have spoken several times of the need to reconcile the fine detail of a design with the overall wholeness and coherence. Michelangelo had the same problem with the ceiling of the Sistine Chapel every time a foot or a hand had to be painted in. Again, the need for flexibility and modularity of system design makes it very necessary that we know precisely what each part of a system

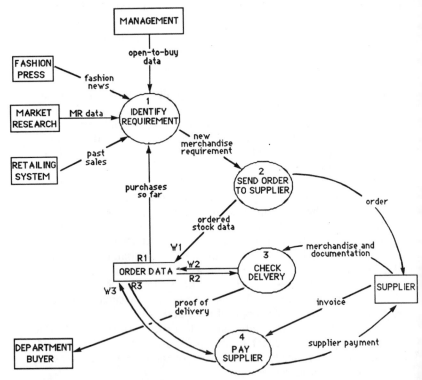

Figure 5.7 A final logical DFD for Sellmore's stock replenishment

does. We meet these needs by the close definition of boundary that we mentioned in Chapter 2.

The size of the system that we include within the boundary is quite important. Every organization has time and cost constraints. Should we simply redesign the Sellmore Stock Replenishment system, taking six person-months to do it, or should we try to get the benefits of an integrated system by redesigning the Stock Replenishment system, the Retailing system and the Management system, at a cost of two person-years? If we just opt for the Stock Replenishment system, then we must be clear about the boundaries of what we are doing, not least so that any future work fits comfortably with what we do now.

The essential feature of the boundary of an information system is that it can be defined in terms of data. It is either expressed in terms of the data which flows across that boundary or of the *local view* of a data store which is seen within a particular boundary. The PURCHASE LEDGER view in Figure 5.6, and the various ORDER DATA views in Figure 5.7, illustrate this. For the Sellmore department store, some of the boundaries are shown in Figure 5.8.

The thick wavy line in Figure 5.8 outlines the system we are interested in. Once this boundary is fixed, we still need to determine the boundaries of individual functions within the

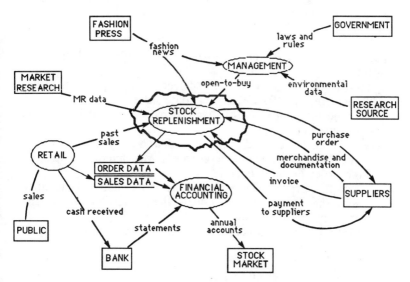

Figure 5.8 System boundaries at the Sellmore department store

system. There is a good chance that when we come to develop new physical solutions the individual *applications* that we design will correspond to the functions on the final logical DFD.

There isn't one final time when boundaries must be fixed. If you start on a study you will necessarily assume a boundary separating the things you are going to look at from those you don't think you are going to look at. Life is too short to expect to look at everything. If you try to, you will see nothing. As the study progresses you will become more committed to particular boundaries, but for a while there will be some flexibility. By the time you have drawn a final logical DFD you will probably be reluctant to change your boundary.

5.6 Analysing the facts: the local data model and users' access requirements

We have devoted Chapter 7 to data analysis. This doesn't remove the need to carry out *local data analysis* related to the particular functions included within a system.

Necessarily, the *local data models* resulting from the analysis must depend on what procedural rules are assumed for a function. If we take function 3, 'check delivery', on the logical DFD of Figure 5.7, the procedural rules expressed in Structured English (Section 6.2.1) might emerge as:

For each supplier's order received at the Sellmore department store:
  If the OrderNumber of the received order equals an Order Number in the ORDER DATA data store
  And the SupplierName of the received order equals the data store SupplierName
  And for each mechandise line included in the received order:
    The MerchandiseNumber equals a MerchandiseNumber in the order in the data store
    And the OrderQuantity equals the actual delivered quantity
    And the OrderQuantity equals the OrderQuantity in the order in the data store
  And there are no unreceived merchandise lines in the order in the data store
  Then
    Accept the received order,
    Inform the Department Buyer,

Mark the order in the data store as 'received',
For each merchandise line included in the received order:
Increase the StockQuantity recorded in the ORDER
DATA data store by the OrderQuantity;
If the DueDate of the received order is later than today's date
Then
Enter a 'late delivery report' against the relevant supplier in
the database;
Otherwise
Reject the received order,

Which might be summarized as:

1. If everything is correct about the received order then accept it;
2. If it is late but everything else is correct then accept it, but make
a 'late delivery report';
3. If a received order is accepted then update all the relevant
StockQuantities in the data store;
4. In all other circumstances reject the order;

The 'late delivery report' is another example of control data,
which we don't normally include on a data flow diagram.

The various 'reads' and 'writes' to the ORDER DATA data
store can be tabulated as in Figure 5.9. If the analysis table is
presented in sequence of base table name, then it can very quickly
be seen whether each column of any table is both being written to
and read. Remarkably, we have experience of several systems in
which data are written to a column but never read!

The local data model must reflect every attribute demand placed
on it by the procedural rules. We display an appropriate model in
Figure 5.10.

We've used the two terms 'local view' and 'local data model'
apparently interchangeably. In fact a view is strictly a single table,
based on one or more database *base* tables. If it is based on more
than one base table it is unlikely to be normalized (Chapter 7) and

Data store or database name	Read or Write	Data object		Function name
		Base table name	Column name	
ORDER DATA	R1	MERCHANDISE LINE	MerchandiseNumber	Identify requirement
ORDER DATA	R1	MERCHANDISE LINE	OrderQuantity	Identify requirement
ORDER DATA	W1	SUPPLIER ORDER	SupplierName	Send order to supplier
ORDER DATA	W1	SUPPLIER ORDER	OrderNumber	Send order to supplier
ORDER DATA	W1	SUPPLIER ORDER	DueDate	Send order to supplier
ORDER DATA	W1	MERCHANDISE LINE	MerchandiseNumber	Send order to supplier

Figure 5.9 Part of a Read/Write analysis for the ORDER DATA data store

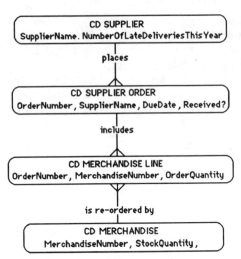

Figure 5.10 Local data model for the 'check delivery' function in the Sellmore stock replenishment system

it is likely to have some restrictions on the data manipulation of the database than can be performed through it. The simplest approach is to see the view as derived from a single base table.

'Local data model' is a wider description. As we have used it, it is *precisely* the data model which is relevant to one particular function. The entity types included in the local data model may themselves be represented in the database by *views* of particular base tables. Each function could, if the designer and client so will it, have its own local data model. The *aggregation* of all the local data models should be equivalent to the *global data model*, however that global model is derived (Section 7.9). The ability to define different local data models does give the system designer the facility to limit the data that users carrying out a particular function have access to. It thus allows control of access to data, if this is a requirement of the system.

We haven't exhausted the possibilities of local data models. In Chapter 7 we present the idea that a view (and therefore a local data model) may contain statistical data. The Store Manager may have different information needs from anything we have looked at so far. The following are some suggestions:

1. Average supplier order value for the past month;
2. Standard deviation of supplier order value for the same period;

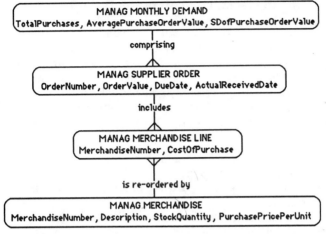

Figure 5.11 A local data model appropriate to the Store Manager's function

3. Frequency distribution of supplier orders by value;
4. Listing of all purchase orders received late, in order of lateness;
5. Listing of all currently overdue orders;
6. Listing of total purchase cost of the merchandise comprising the top 20% of purchases;
7. Listing of all the merchandise not ordered this year;
8. Stock value and stock quantity of Eau d'Amour Shampoo.

The Management system (MANAG) local data model which satisfied these information needs would be as shown in Figure 5.11. Every time the MANAG MONTHLY DEMAND view is invoked, the table contains the average demand for each product over the relevant reporting period and also the standard deviation of demand (SDofDemand). If a relational database management system (RDBMS) is in use, then the definition of these statistics is included within the view definition. If a program-based data management system is in use, then the definition must be within the program.

In this book we are not principally concerned with the way that views are implemented but with the proper specification of logical requirements. Normally, a local data model relates to the system described in the final logical DFD. If we are linking one local data model to one function, then that function is a function on the lowest level to which we partition a logical DFD.

5.7 Analysing the facts: control considerations

In her investigations Janet has identified several control points for the Sellmore Stock Replenishment system, apart from the separate Management system dealing with the Store Manager's information needs. It would be a very poor system designer who assumed that 'normal' procedures are necessarily going to take place.

For the sake of clarity, we de-emphasize control in a data flow diagram. Nevertheless, the control points and identification of exceptions are vital. Let's list some:

1. The Department Buyer's decision to raise a purchase order is checked by the Store Manager.
2. The quantities and cost of a purchase order are checked against the 'open-to-buy'.
3. The merchandise delivered from the supplier is checked against the purchase order.
4. The invoice received from the supplier is checked against what was ordered and what is known to have been delivered.
5. We identified a 'late delivery report' in Section 5.6.

For each of these checks, an analyst must be sure what is being checked and why it is being checked, and what happens if the check should fail. In some instances ('open-to-buy') there is a predetermined limit which must not be exceeded. In others (merchandise delivered from the supplier), the check looks for any shortfall. Is the purchase order marked in some way to indicate this shortfall? Is the shortfall recorded in some other way? If there is a shortfall, how does Sellmore make sure that the follow-up delivery is actually received, and related to the original order?

Control has other implications. If data are to be manipulated, or stored in a database, any integrity constraints on those data must be enforced. In general, if it is possible to make rules defining the structure of the data, *then those rules should be formally defined*.

Noble and Abbod[3] quote the 1965 offical Scottish health statistics as recording that 'during that year there had been 520 married patients under the age of fourteen, there had been 8 male patients with malignant neoplasms of the cervix or body uterus, 19 female patients with enlarged prostates, 20 male patients had aborted, 20 male patients had experienced discomfort and complications of childbirth or pregnancy, 181 male patients had been discharged from gynaecological wards, and 335 patients over the age of one had suffered infections of the newborn; of these 60 were aged seventy five or over'. Noble and Abbod were working in Aberdeen. There is no reason to suppose that Scottish health statistics are any less reliable than those from any other source.

We have much to say about structural rules in Chapters 6 and 7. Chapter 10 discusses how these rules are recorded in the data dictionary. The rules define both the operating constraints on the system ('merchandise is only accepted if all details of the goods received agree with the purchase order') and the required integrity of the database ('only numeric characters, a decimal point or a null value, are allowed in this field').

The last control feature that we are going to mention is the need to *control access* of people to parts of the system which may be sensitive. We have not the space to discuss access control here, but note that the recipe for fraud is that people who might otherwise behave honestly may give way to temptation if they realize that some asset is insuffiently controlled and can be misused or can be appropriated for their own use.

5.8 Analysing the facts: data volumes, timeliness and response time

In Section 5.3 we mentioned recording frequencies and volumes of all data flows. An analyst making a study of a system will record these in appropriate data dictionary entries. The importance of these data about data is that they describe the amount of processing that a system will have to do. In turn, the amount of processing will have a direct effect on the *response time* or the amount of time that a system takes to respond to a request.

For batch-processing systems (Section 8.3) the designers are able to assume that a response can be delayed for several hours. A VDU terminal operator, as will a person waiting in a car at a red traffic light, will tend to get irritated if nothing happens after about fifteen seconds. The system can gain a little more time by sending out encouraging messages, just to show the user that he hasn't been forgotten; but users' patience is always limited.

It is very important that a designer does know what the response time requirements are within a system so that hardware may be adequately specified. Function 2 in the Sellmore logical DFD, 'order to supplier', or 'os', doesn't contain a response element apart from a check on the domain integrity (Section 7.6). There seems to be nothing preventing an 'immediate' response relating to domain integrity and a much later response tabulating just which orders have been processed, if this is a part of the information requirement. Function 3, or 'cd', in the same logical DFD seems to demand a much faster response. A decision turns on the function. Either the received order is going to be accepted or it will be rejected.

Timeliness is a related but different concept. The Sellmore Store Manager wanting data about the value of merchandise held may want the answer within five minutes, but may be satisfied with yesterday's data. Most of us, if we ask our bank how much money we have, will be told that figure for close of business on the previous day. On the other hand, if an airline or a hotel booking agency has to rely on yesterday's data then some customers are going to be left two to a seat or to a bed.

Both timeliness of data and appropriate response time are vital pieces of information requirements analysis. If we are going to succeed in providing them in the right quality, we need data about *data flow frequencies* and *data flow volumes*.

5.9 Deciding the most appropriate design solutions

Within the scope of this chapter we can identify six aspects of this:

1. What must be produced?
2. What procedural or structual rules must be enforced?
3. What are the local data needs (local data model), function by function?
4. What are the system boundary and the function boundaries, and how are these mapped to applications?
5. What is the most appropriate division into functions which are best performed by people and those which are best performed by computers?
6. How do we define the acceptance test which will eventually determine whether the completed software does what it's supposed to do?

We cannot really say any more about timeliness and response time here, because their final values will depend on the particular choice of hardware which is made.

We expect that, first, several competing outline designs will be produced as candidates for evaluation. After selection of the preferred design, it will be packaged and presented as the functional requirement specification. It is this document which is the basis of subsequent design, and is the defining document telling us what we are trying to do.

5.9.1 Acceptance test specification

We don't believe that this document deserves a long separate treatment. This is not in any way because it is unimportant. The role of the acceptance test is very like that of an examination sat by an examination candidate. If the application which has been developed passes its acceptance test then it is given formal status as an authorized application within the organization. The difference between an authorized application and a successful examination candidate is that no change to an authorized application can be permitted unless the changed application is once again authorized by passing a proper acceptance test.

Every feature of the acceptance test must be derived from the functional requirement specification. Whatever all singing and dancing features the completed software may have are irrelevant unless they have been specified as a functional requirement. Any lack of facilities in the software when compared to the functional requirement is a failure[4].

If you believe that features in the functional requirement specification are irrelevant by the time you get to the acceptance test, then *change the functional requirements specification* and *change the acceptance test specification*. Don't ignore them. Naturally, any change to either specification must be properly approved, as we outline in Chapter 11.

5.9.2 Functional requirements specification

It must be clear by this stage that functions can be decomposed into smaller functions. The partitioning is arbitrary, but for convenience we shall refer to the largest function we have identified (Stock Replenishment system) as a *system* and to the component functions (check delivery) as *applications*.

We present below the skeleton of the functional requirements specification which we believe is needed. We number the various paragraphs as 'S . . .' for 'specification . . . .'. You must expect that you will not understand all the paragraphs on first reading. We describe the conventions in Chapters 6 and 7. Come back to this specification skeleton after you have read those chapters.

S1: The statement of system purpose ('to facilitate the replenishment of merchandise stock-holdings') and the statement of costs and benefits which are expected.

S2: The data model. This may have a wider scope than the system we are specifying or it may be tailored precisely for that system. The procedural rules governing domain integrity and table integrity (Chapter 7) are an integral part of the data model and must be included. The bulk of these rules can be specified by an ERA diagram.

S3: Mapping of the data model to the database. We expect that, like the data model, this can usually be expressed diagrammatically. The particular form of the diagrams depends on the database management system being used (Network, IMS, Relational). If the data model is mapped to a simple file management system, then we show the various files and their contents.

S4: The final physical data flow diagram. In the case of the Sellmore Stock Replenishment system, this would closely follow the form of the final logical DFD of Figure 5.7. In addition to the detail in that figure, the diagram should indicate the human functions and the computer functions. We suggest that function 1 (identify requirement) should be a 'human' function; the remaining functions (order to supplier, check delivery, and pay supplier) we see as 'computer' functions.

The physical DFD identifies both system boundary and the application boundaries.

S5: System level procedural rules. These system level rules are those that are not easily displayed as part of the data model. Typical examples would be access to privileges.

There are three user classes:

Class 1: Users with 'read only' privilege;
Class 2: Users with 'read and update' privilege;
Class 3: Users with application supervision privilege.

A further system level rule might specify the table locking sequence:

'Locks on tables, or on any updatable views defined on those tables, shall be sought only in the sequence:

SUPPLIER
SUPPLIER ORDER
MERCHANDISE
MERCHANDISE LINE'

S6: Functional decomposition. This must be based on the final physical DFD for the system. For the Sellmore Stock Replenishment system it is quite limited:

'SR   Stock Replenishment system
    SR1.ir   identify requirement

SR2.os	order to supplier
SR3cd	check delivery
SR4.ps	pay supplier'

S6.* Application name and description. This must specify 'Human' or 'Computer':

S6.*.1 Local data model (if one is defined)

S6.*.2 Application level procedural rules
'Rule cd1: Deletion not allowed;
Rule cd2: Insertion allowed only if user has class 3 access privileges;'

S6.*.3 Application decomposition. List all the 'blocks' included in the application. We are basing this on the 'ORACLE' database management system requirement that database tables are queried and updated through a 'block' on a VDU screen. Other 'DBMS' will have different mechanisms for updating tables.

S6.*.3.* Block name and description

S6.*.3.*.1 Block level procedural rules:
'Rule cd3: Pre-Update MERCHANDISE LINE
Update owner MERCHANDISE within
'is re-ordered by' set NewStockQuantity
= StockQuantity + :orderquantity;'

S6.*.3.*.2 Block decomposition. List all the 'fields' included in a block. We are making the assumption that one database table column is queried and updated through a 'field' in a 'block'.

S6.*.3.*.2.* Field name, description, and procedural rules.
Typical examples of these procedural rules are the 'default on insertion' rules described in Section 7.7.

S7: VDU screen descriptions. This is *not* the same as the block descriptions in paragraph S6.*.3.* above. We intend that under this heading a designer displays the screen layouts, such as that in Figure 5.12.

S7.* Screen name and layout, including names of all blocks and fields on the screen.

S8: Document or Report layout. Again, we intend that an example of each document or report is produced.

S8.* Document or Report name and description.

S8.*.1 Document or Report example.

S8.*.2 Document or Report decomposition. We assume that there are separate sections or 'blocks' to each document or report.

S8.*.2.* Block name, description and decomposition into fields.

S8.*.2.*.* Field name and description.

S9: *State change specification.* We present this as the last paragraph of the functional requirements specification because it is strictly about the way that a user relates with the system rather than the functional requirements placed on the system.

If some of the screens in the system design are menu screens then we expect a diagram of the state change possibilities to be included (Figures 8.17 and 8.19). Menu screens are still screens, and we expect them to be defined under paragraph S7 above. If it is necessary that menu screens contain 'control blocks' or 'control fields' in order to allow navigation to occur, then we expect those blocks and fields to be defined under paragraph S6 above.

Navigation of a system by a user demands some 'Help!' provision. This may be included in the 'prompts' on a screen; it may be in 'Help!' messages which can be obtained by a user pressing the 'Help!' key on the keyboard; or it may be on 'Help!' screens which can be reached via a menu. We expect that all these messages are defined within the appropriate block descriptions or as a screen description.

We cannot be more precise about the provisions of the state change specification because it depends so heavily on the particular system development software being used.

Throughout this section on the functional requirements specification we have used Section 6.3 as the basis for our presentation of procedural rules. If it is necessary to present these rules as a series of Structural English statements, or as an Entity Life Cycle diagram, then the functional requirements specification will have a rather different appearance. We have discussed both those forms in Section 6.2. We hope that our presentation here is adequate to demonstrate what should be included in the specification, regardless of the form of rule presentation preferred.

In paragraph S7 above we suggested that screen layouts should be included in the functional requirement specification. Figure 5.12 presents part of such a layout. For most VDU screens currently in use the screen size allows 80 columns and about 21

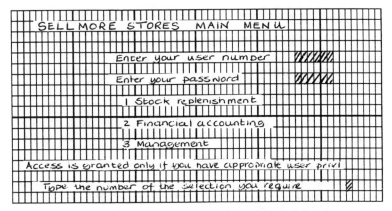

Figure 5.12 A screen design for Sellmore's stock replenishment system

rows. One row on the screen may be dedicated to error or exception messages from the computer system to the user.

5.10 Presentation of solutions to the user community

The purpose of such a presentation may be twofold:

1. To offer the *client* (who may or may not be a potential user) an opportunity to approve the proposals, to reject them, or to ask for modifications.
2. To solicit the further help of potential users in producing a redesigned system with as wide acceptance as possible.

It would be wrong to visualize the system designers as working away in isolation, and then, after a suitable period of gestation, publicly meeting the users to reveal the holy writ. Chapter 13 explores the need for a close participative relationship between designers and potential users all the way along the path from the first conception right up to the audit of the completed and implemented system. However close the degree of cooperation (and indeed of integration) between designers and users, there is no way that the design team can avoid eventually declaring 'this is what we propose to do'.

The structure for such a presentation follows the same skeleton as the functional requirement specification. There is no point in exploring every single procedural rule if the community have the functional requirement specification available to them, but any aspect which directly touches the working lives of the users must be examined.

All that we said at the beginning of this chapter about the interview being a social occasion applies to the presentation. The flow of data is now *both* ways, between designers and users, but the onus is clearly on the designers to contruct the occasion to facilitate that flow:

1. Use presentation aids: overhead projectors, flip charts, models.
2. If you present anything, make sure that it is clear enough or large enough to be seen.
3. Don't stand in front of what your are displaying.
4. Make sure that you can be heard.
5. Try to avoid annoying mannerisms. What are you going to do with your hands?
6. Get some variety into the presentation; don't rely on only one person's voice.
7. Look at the people you are presenting to.
8. Listen to what is said to you.

5.11 The Sellemkwik case study: a medium-sized garage

The aim of this case study is to provide an overview of the tools and techniques used in the design of a computer-based information system. We will not give a full system specification since this could itself fill a whole book! We hope that you will take this opportunity to practise the use of the tools and techniques. The statement of objectives, problem definition and background information are derived from a *feasibility study* already completed.

5.11.1 System purpose

The General Manager of the parent company has been asked what the purpose of the system is and has identified two objectives:

To make a profit; and
To satisfy the customers.

As with any set of objectives, they seem to conflict, but a moment's thought shows them to be interdependent. Satisfying the customer should lead to increased profit (by increasing trade). A higher profit should lead to increased customer satisfaction (by allowing more investment in equipment and facilities). It is also probable that the managers of the company wish to make a profit so that they can continue to do the work they enjoy doing. Most companies make a profit in order to exist, rather than exist in order to make a profit[5].

5.11.2 Problem definition

The General Manager identifies the problems of the garage as:

1. A fall in profit of 7% in the last financial year;
2. An increase in customer complaints;
3. A reduction in the number of regular customers.

The garage staff are aware of the problems, and have various views as to their cause:

1. Two other garages have opened in direct competition in the immediate vicinity.
2. The manager believes that the mechanics are lazy, and don't do their jobs properly.
3. The mechanics blame the Stores for not supplying the parts they need.
4. The Stores staff complain of lack of forward planning.
5. The storekeepers often complain, loudly, that their stores are full of obsolete parts.

5.11.3 Background information

The garage has three business sectors:

1. The shop and forecourt petrol sales;
2. Used-car sales;
3. Car repairs for breakdown and accident, servicing and MOT Certificates.

The shop and petrol sales make a satisfactory profit, and have not been studied any further.

Used cars are purchased at auctions or by part exchanges with customers buying cars. Cars are subject to repair and renovation before resale. The maximum number of cars purchased in one day is ten, but it is more usual to purchase this number over a week. The number of private cars going through the workshop daily depends on the types of servicing or repairs required.

The members of staff in the garage are:

Manager (1)
Secretary (1)
Sales Staff (3)

Forecourt attendants working shifts (3)
Chief Mechanics (2)
Mechanics (8)
Storekeepers (2)

The General Manager of the parent company sees this garage as a pilot system which, if successful, could be implemented in other locations. She is willing to provide funds for an investigation initially confined to *purchasing and selling cars* and to *repair and servicing*, covering:

1. Preparation of transaction documents;
2. Updating of records and schedules; and
3. Information that will be useful to management in meeting the business problems.

Exercise 5.1
List the points that you want to clarify with the General Manager before you start your investigation. Set out a schedule for the conduct of the investigation for presentation to the General Manager.

5.11.4 Description of procedures

The following information has been obtained by you from a mixture of interviews and observation carried out after the original feasibility study. The information should be related to the physical

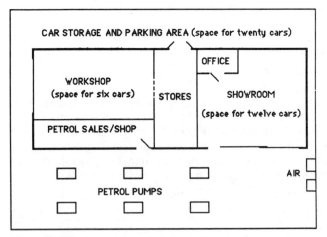

Figure 5.13 Physical layout of the Sellemkwik Garage

layout of the garage, displayed in Figure 5.13. Repairs, servicing and requests for MOT Certificates are booked in at the shop by customers either by telephone or in person. The approximate time allocation for these tasks is:

Thirty minutes for a MOT Certificate;
Between two and three hours for a service;
Variable periods for repairs, estimated by a Chief Mechanic.

A *daily schedule* is prepared for the mechanics by a Chief Mechanic. An individual *job card* for each car is given to the mechanic allocated to the job. Emergencies are only dealt with if time allows.

The data entered on a job card are:

1. The current date;
2. The period of time spent on the job by the mechanics, with signatures;
3. The part number, description, price, quantity and value of parts and material;
4. The car registration number;
5. Whether the car is a private vehicle or has been purchased by the garage for resale;
6. The Chief Mechanic's initial time estimate for completing the job;
7. Data about the customer if the car is a private one.

The mechanics use an *internal order form* to withdraw parts from the Stores. The data on the internal order form are the current date, the time, the part number and description of the parts withdrawn, and the storekeeper's and the mechanic's signatures. When parts are given to a mechanic the job card is updated with the value of the parts. If the parts are not available the storekeeper will telephone the suppliers to check when the parts can be obtained and to request urgent delivery.

When a car is booked for service or repairs a Chief Mechanic gives a *post-dated internal order form* to the Stores for those parts he believes will be needed. He keeps one copy for issue to the mechanic. Parts are set aside by the Stores under allocation. When the allocated parts are issued to the mechanic, the job card is updated.

A manual *stock record file* is kept in the Stores in part number sequence. A microfiche file of supplier's details is also kept in the Stores in supplier name sequence.

When cars are purchased for resale a *purchase invoice* is prepared by the sales person giving details of the sale by the previous owner and the *purchases account file* is updated. After repair and renovation a car is offered for sale. When a sale is completed a *sales invoice* is prepared and the *sales account file* updated. Copies of both the purchase invoice and the sales invoice are kept in the office, together with Road Fund Licence, MOT Certificate and vehicle insurance documents. Mechanics' *timesheets* are filled in from the job cards and their wages calculated. This function is carried out by the secretary, in the office (see Figure 5.14).

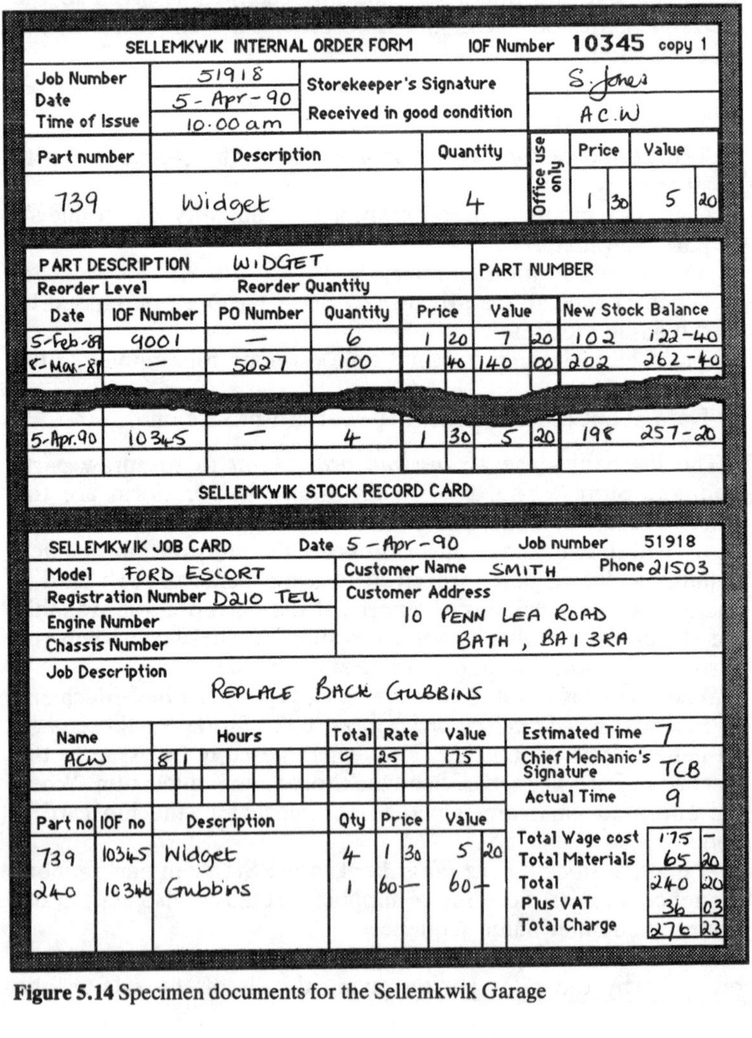

SELLEMKWIK INTERNAL ORDER FORM IOF Number 10345 copy 1

Job Number	51918	Storekeeper's Signature	S. Jones
Date	5 - Apr - 90	Received in good condition	A C.W
Time of Issue	10·00 am		

Part number	Description	Quantity	Office use only	Price		Value	
739	Widget	4		1	30	5	20

PART DESCRIPTION WIDGET PART NUMBER

Reorder Level Reorder Quantity

Date	IOF Number	PO Number	Quantity	Price		Value		New Stock Balance	
5-Feb-89	9001	—	6	1	20	7	20	102	122-40
8-Mar-89	—	5027	100	1	40	140	00	202	262-40
5-Apr.90	10345	—	4	1	30	5	20	198	257-20

SELLEMKWIK STOCK RECORD CARD

SELLEMKWIK JOB CARD Date 5 – Apr – 90 Job number 51918

Model FORD ESCORT	Customer Name SMITH Phone 21503
Registration Number D210 TEU	Customer Address
Engine Number	10 PENN LEA ROAD
Chassis Number	BATH, BA1 3RA

Job Description REPLACE BACK GUBBINS

Name	Hours		Total	Rate	Value	
ACW	8	1	9	25	175	

Estimated Time 7

Chief Mechanic's Signature TCB

Actual Time 9

Part no	IOF no	Description	Qty	Price		Value	
739	10345	Widget	4	1	30	5	20
240	10346	Gubbins	1	60	—	60	—

Total Wage cost	175	—
Total Materials	65	20
Total	240	20
Plus VAT	36	03
Total Charge	276	23

Figure 5.14 Specimen documents for the Sellemkwik Garage

5.11.5 Data flow diagrams

Exercise 5.2
Draw a context diagram and a level 0 physical DFD, reflecting the above data (use Figures 5.15 and 5.16 as checks).

The most controversial point is whether the Stores is a part of the system or a part of the environment. We haven't any information about how the Stores normally replenishes its stock of parts, but we are told about an emergency telephoning function by the Stores. This illustrates excellently the problems of boundary definition!

We shall show a 'provide parts' function within the system. The Stock Replenishment system we represent as a part of the environment, but we have no details of any data flows to that system. The interface is probably realized by a separate view of the stock records file.

We also have no details about payments by customers or about the role of the bank. We know that there must be a banker somewhere out there in the environment, but we haven't found out about the data flows between the Sellemkwik Garage and the bank. Finally, we have abbreviated 'internal order form' to 'IOF'.

It is worth noting that the data flow between 'execute jobs' and 'provide parts' is *towards* 'provide parts'. The reverse data flow is 'signature on job card'. It is a *data flow* diagram not a material flow diagram!

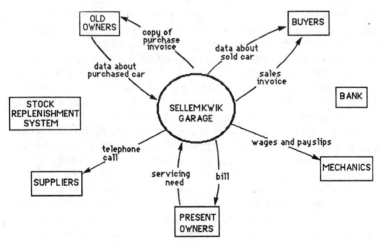

Figure 5.15 A context diagram for the Sellemkwik Garage

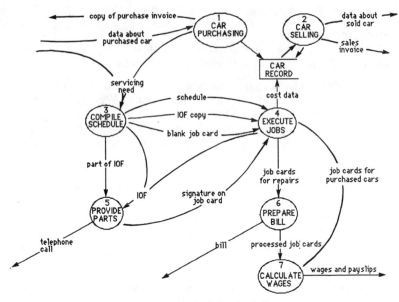

Figure 5.16 A level 0 physical DFD for the Sellemkwik Garage

There is no contradiction between showing mechanics as external entities outside the system and the fact that it is the mechanics who 'execute jobs'. The data flow diagram describes data flows in an *information system*. The mechanics perform a task within that information system *but they are not themselves components of the information system*. They aren't data flows, or data stores, or functions. *They are people.* If we label a function within a DFD as 'mechanics' or 'Chief Mechanic', we intend it to mean 'what a mechanic does' or 'what the Chief Mechanic does'. It is because of this problem that we prefer predicates ('execute jobs') or gerunds ('servicing') as function labels.

This physical DFD should prompt some discussion and ideas. For example, there is no evidence of any collection of historical data or preparation of summary statistics to help management. Again, would it help the Stores to forward plan if they had access to the schedule? Can one secretary adequately cope with 'car selling', 'car purchasing', 'bill calculation' and 'wage calculation'?

We don't have to provide any answers yet. We should first extract from what we have a statement of what *must* be done to complete the tasks being examined.

Exercise 5.3
Draw a logical DFD for this system within the same boundary as
the physical DFD and check against Figure 5.17.

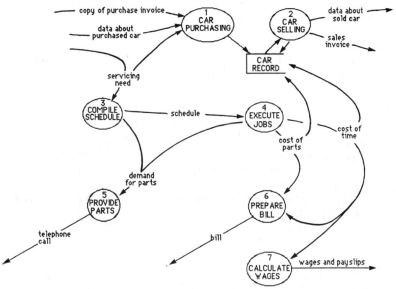

Figure 5.17 A logical DFD for the Sellemkwik Garage

We haven't changed the functions between the physical DFD
and the logical DFD. The same tasks must still be performed. We
have isolated out the actual data which must flow between
functions and have removed the arbitrary flow of job cards first to
'bill preparation' and then to 'wage calculation'. Function 4,
'execute jobs', and function 5, 'provide parts' seem the most
amenable to further analysis.

Exercise 5.4
Set out the structural rules for data manipulation within the
'execute jobs' function. Draw a local data model derived from
these rules.

5.11.6 Physical data flow diagram for the Sellemkwik garage

Whatever the final outcome of logical design, the physical
constraints are still in existence. The garage is still a collection of

buildings and offices and people working in them. Cars are bought at auctions, and somehow the data describing those cars must be entered into the record system. If there is any consolidation of records into a database, how will all the interested people get access to those data? Which functions are best performed by people and which by computer?

Exercise 5.5
Draw physical DFD of a proposed system for the Sellemkwik Garage. Indicate the human functions and the computer functions.

5.11.7 The data model for the Sellemkwik garage

Data analysis is a parallel activity to functional analysis. Before we attempt data analysis we must have some 'back-of-the-mind' idea of what the system is all about. As data analysis progresses so reconciliation with the demands of functional analysis will cause revision of the list of attributes of the various entity types. If this is your first reading, and you haven't yet read Chapter 7, then omit this section!

Exercise 5.6
List the entity types which are involved in the Sellemkwik garage system. The basic list must include:

CAR	Something which is purchased and sold and is renovated by jobs;
MECHANIC	Who executes jobs;
CUSTOMER	Who commissions jobs;
PART	Which is held in stock and is issued for jobs.

Each of these can be named and identified by a simple key with one attribute.

The purchasing and selling of cars does not involve any other entity types on our list. It must therefore be seen as to do with attributes of CAR. A likely list could include the name and address of the seller, the name and address of the purchaser, the date when Sellemkwik bought the car, and the date when Sellemkwik sold the car. The attribute list must mean that if a car is bought and sold twice then it will be recorded twice in the database. Could this cause any problems?

A PART is held in stock, but it is difficult to think of any attributes of something called STOCK. 'Total stock value' could be a candidate, but this is a secondary value. It is simply the sum of the values of all the parts.

All our entity types seem to relate to something called JOB. This must then be a *relationship entity type*. One JOB is related either to CAR or to CUSTOMER, depending on whether it is commissioned by a customer or is to do with the renovation of a car. This suggests that we might find a use for *sub-types* of the entity type JOB. One JOB may require many parts and be executed by many mechanics. The relationships with these two entity types are therefore many-to-many.

The TIMESHEET has a reality, because it necessarily records one mechanic's work for one wages period. The TIMESHEET should appear on the data model. By a similar argument there must be a place for SCHEDULE.

Since our system boundary does include emergency telephone calls to suppliers we must provide for a SUPPLIER entity type. A SUPPLIER supplies PARTS. Are all part identities supplied by Sellemkwik? What happens if two suppliers have different identifying part numbers for the same part?

Exercise 5.7
Draw a data model for the Sellemkwik Garage. Mark the model to represent any structural rules which you deem appropriate. Display the attributes of each entity type.

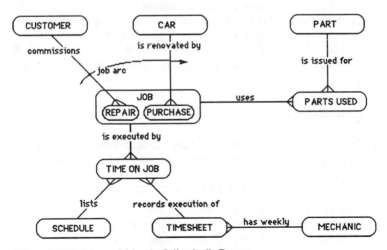

Figure 5.18 A data model for the Sellemkwik Garage

5.11.8 Management and marketing information

So far, we have suggested nothing which would meet the General Manager's desire for information useful to management in meeting business problems. The basis for that information must be the data model such as that displayed in Figure 5.18. Possible examples are:

1. Weekly reports on the allocation of stock to jobs;
2. Comparison of estimated and actual repair times;
3. Comparison of CAR.PurchaseDate and CAR.SellingDate;
4. Weekly report on the sales value of 'dead' stock;
5. Historical summaries of performance to assist both job scheduling, and marketing.

Would it be a good marketing strategy to remind car owners that their MOT Certificates are about to expire? Which market sectors should we concentrate effort on?

Exercise 5.8
Describe the management and marketing information which you would wish to see if you were the Sellemkwik Garage manager. How can this information be derived?

5.11.9. Functional requirements specification

Exercise 5.9
Write a functional requirement specification for the 'execute job' function of the logical DFD in Figure 5.17. Assume that this is the first stage of a development programme which will eventually cover the whole Sellemkwik Garage system. *State clearly what benefits and costs you expect if this specification were implemented.*

5.12 Summary

- The starting point of analysis must be definition – what are we trying to do? In Chapter 4 we represented that as the users' requirement.
- The overview of the functional design activity is:

    Study the system to obtain the facts;
    Determine which tasks are logically required;
    Decide the most appropriate design solutions;
    Present tentative solutions to the user community.

Throughout this activity, we are asking questions:

What? Why? Where? Who? When? How?

- Obtain the facts by:

    Understanding the structure of the organization;
    Eliciting the knowledge of people in the organization;
    Collecting relevant documents.

    In particular, an analyst needs to understand from the client what he or she is being asked to do.

- Knowledge elicitation may be by questionnaire if a highly structured response is required from a large group of people, or by interview. The interview allows a flexible response. The interviewer cannot know all the questions that need to be asked at the time when the interview begins.

- An interview is a social occasion, which takes place in order to allow the interviewer to elicit information from the interviewee.

- Knowledge elicited by questionnaires and interviews is supplemented by observation of the activities of the organization.

- Recording information requires the use of two main documents:

    Discussion records
    Physical data flow diagrams

- Analysis of information requirements requires preparation of logical data flow diagrams.

- Deciding the most appropriate design solution requires that the designer knows:

    What must be produced;
    What rules must be enforced;
    The local data needs;
    The system boundary;
    The most appropriate human and computer functions;
    Definition of the acceptance test.

- The acceptance test specification must be derived from the functional requirements specification.

- The functional requirements specification is perhaps the most important document produced. This should be quite formally constructed.

Discussion points

5.1 'A physical data flow diagram describes what has actually been seen to happen, a logical data flow diagram describes the

system which we logically need in order to achieve the system purpose.'
Might there be circumstances in which the two diagrams are identical? What is implied if the name of a function is that of an organizational department ('Accounting' on the Sellmore physical DFD)? Does the label 'Accounting' on that DFD suggest any potential mapping problems when the whole Sellmore information system design is developed?

5.2 Why have we included the Departmental Buyer as an external entity on the Sellmore logical DFD and a function 'identify requirement' which we know is executed by the Departmental Buyer? Is this the best way of representing the situation?

5.3 In Section 5.9.1, paragraph S5, we specify a sequence in which locks can be granted on tables. Why is this done?

References

1 Charles Handy, *Understanding Organizations*, Penguin, Harmondsworth (1987)
2 The National Computing Centre Ltd, *Data Processing Standards, Systems Documentation Manual* (1970)
3 C. Gane and T. Sarson, *Structured Systems Analysis*, Prentice-Hall, Englewood Cliffs, NJ (1979)
4 Tom de Marco, *Structured Analysis and System Specification*, Yourdon Press, New York (1979)
5 Ralph Cornes, *The Guardian*, 1 September 1988
6 Peter Checkland, *Systems Thinking, Systems Practice*, John Wiley, Chichester (1981)

Chapter 6

Procedures and rules

6.1 The Careful Manufacturing Company

The presentation in this chapter is based on a very simple system for supplying products to customers. We believe that this will be better for the learning points we want to make than the Coquotte case study presented in Chapters 2 and 3 and the Sellmore case study in Chapter 5.

The Careful Company supplies its wares to a set of *customers*. A separate account is kept for each customer. A customer can place *orders*, each of which consists of several *lines*. Each line relates to exactly one *product*, held by Careful as a stock item. For example, Careful manufactures widgets, and customer J. Smith and Sons may order twenty widgets as one line of an order for perhaps a hundred different products. If insufficient stock is available to meet an order for a particular product, then the quantity actually available is delivered. We have not included any procedures for eventually delivering the shortfall.

The Data Flow Diagram is shown in Figure 6.1. CUSTOMER and SUPPLIER are each both *sources* and *sinks* of data. We can also call them *external entities*, outside our *information* system. We have omitted the context diagram, and start in with a level 0 diagram.

Although the customers themselves are outside our information system we shall certainly 'create customers', and we shall record orders received from our customers. The data model we use will represent all the 'things' of interest to us, including customers.

The level 0 DFD in Figure 6.1 is simplified, and includes only two functions: 'sales', and 'inventory'. The PRODUCT DATA STORE is required by both these functions; this means that it must appear on the DFD.

Figure 6.2 is a level 1 DFD, partitioning the level 0 DFD. The principle of *balance* applies, and all the level 0 dataflows appear on this chart too. A new data store appears, the CUSTOMER DATA STORE, which is of interest only to the 'sales' function. The level

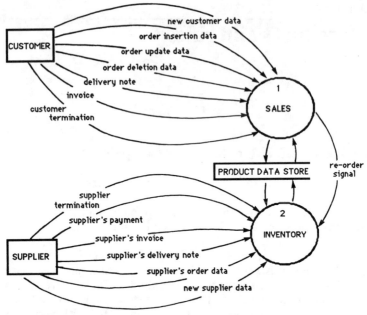

Figure 6.1 A DFD for the Careful Manufacturing Company

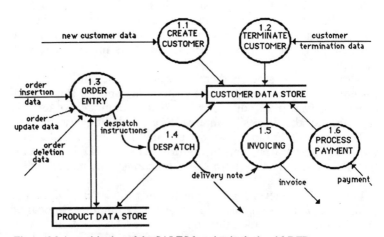

Figure 6.2 A partitioning of the SALES function in the level 0 DFD

1 DFD is a *functional decomposition* of the level 0 DFD in Figure 6.1.

The data model which is appropriate is shown in Figure 6.3. The formulation of a data model is the crucial part of system design. The data model defines what the system remembers. Unless the designer gets that right, there won't be any progress with design.

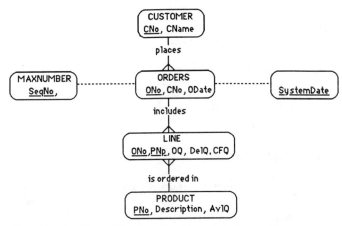

Figure 6.3 The Careful Manufacturing Company's data model

We have ignored the need for stock replenishment to try to keep the system down to a reasonable size. We have also shown the quantity available for orders, rather than the quantity which is in stock. The attributes included allow the system to remember *what stock is available for allocation* and *what has been ordered for immediate delivery.*

We'll give a brief explanation of the meanings of the attributes which we have included:

CUSTOMER entity type
CNo   Customer identification number
CName   Customer's name
Orders entity type
ONo   Unique order number
CNo   Customer identification number
ODate   The date the order was placed
LINE entity type
ONo   Unique order number
PNo   Product identification number
OQ   Ordered Quantity

DelQ   Quantity actually delivered
CFQ   Carried Forward Quantity to be re-ordered at a
              later date
PRODUCT entity type
PNo   Product identification number
Description   Description of the product
AvlQ   Quantity available for allocation to a customer
              order
MAXNUMBER entity type
SeqNo   The maximum number so far given to a customer
              order
SystemDate   'Today's' date

In the discussion below we have also used expanded attribute
names synonymously; thus 'Available Quantity' for AvlQ.

6.2 Transition processing

We need a means of specifying how a new customer or new
customer order is inserted into the database, how an existing order
is updated or deleted, and how an existing customer order is
terminated. This must be done without corrupting the *integrity* or
truthfulness of the database.

We cannot assume that this specification is going to be
implemented as a set of *programs*. The processing prescription
may be dispersed throughout the system. It may be part of data
definitions, or of screen and report definitions, or still as part of
more traditional programs.

Wherever the prescription may lie, there are two broad methods
of specification. We can write a *procedural* specification, such as
the Structured English steps in Figure 2.5. Alternatively, we can
write a set of *non-procedural rules* governing the ways changes to
the database are made and input and output data are handled. A
procedure requires that we define a series of steps which are
carried out sequentially, one after another. If we are working
non-procedurally, any requirement that something is done after
something else must be specified in a rule; we can't assume that
there is any implicit sequence of rules.

We start by taking the procedural route. We shall present the
Structured English approach outlined in Chapter 2, supplemented
by *structure diagrams*. A structure diagram outlines the *life cycle* of
particular entities. If we draw a structure diagram for 'sales' it will
portray the creation of a CUSTOMER; the life history of that

customer, including any amendments to customer data and all the customer ORDERS that that customer places; and finally it will portray the termination of the customer. We show this life cycle in Figure 6.4.

The life cycle story told by Figure 6.4 is that a customer is *created*; the customer may be quiescent during the body of his life or there may be *customer movement*; one movement may *update* the basic customer data or it may be a set of customer *ordering actions*. Finally, the customer is *terminated*. The structure diagram showing this is a *tree*. The topmost box is the *root* and boxes which have no lower connections are *leaves*. The diagram contains several constructs.

First of all is a *sequence*. Each step in a sequence occurs exactly once. 'Sales' is a sequence, and the steps are 'create customer', 'customer body' and 'terminate customer'.

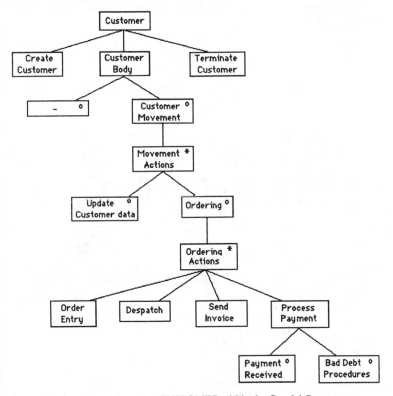

Figure 6.4 Structure diagram for CUSTOMER within the Careful Company

The 'customer body' step is a *decision* (in the sense that more than one option exists). The customer body may be of two kinds. Either there is no movement during the life of the customer or there is some movement. The decision is charted by putting a small circle in the top right-hand corner of the *child* boxes of the decision.

The last construct is an *iteration*. 'Customer movement' is an iteration because there must be many such movements during the body of a customer life cycle. This is shown by marking an asterisk in the top right-hand corner of the *child* box. Constructs in a structure diagram are always indicated by marking the child box.

We have cut off the steps in our customer life cycle very abruptly without showing any details about *order entry*. This is purely a convenience because these steps are shown in Figure 6.5. There are useful insights to be gained from drawing the customer's structure diagram. It gives the time sequence and processing completeness which is quite lacking in either a data flow diagram or a data model.

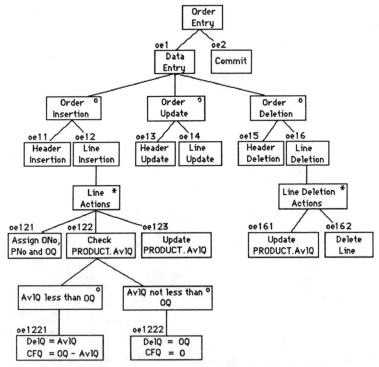

Figure 6.5 Expansion of the 'order entry' component of the CUSTOMER life cycle

Figure 6.4 provides the *structural rules* which define the 'sales' function in the level 0 DFD of Figure 6.1. These rules define the environment in which the company's customers operate. They are also designed to ensure the integrity of any database set up to support this environment.

If we set out the structural rules for the 'inventory' function from the same DFD then we should display the life cycle of each PRODUCT. There could be overlap between the 'sales' and the 'inventory' structure diagrams. 'Customer ordering' is just as much a part of a product's life cycle as it is a part of a customer's life cycle.

In Figure 6.1 we have recognized this link between the two functions by showing a 're-order signal' which would trigger stock replenishment as orders placed by customers reduce stock levels below the re-order level. This data flow is *not* included in any other presentation in this chapter.

Figure 6.5 expands the 'order entry' box of Figure 6.4. The diagram defines the 'order entry' function of the level 1 DFD in Figure 6.2 by setting out the *structural rules* of the system as far as order entry is concerned. It is this diagram which gives a background for the discussion of the next few pages of this chapter.

There really isn't an absolute rule telling us how far functional decomposition should go. The guidelines we gave in Section 2.7.1 would suggest that the 'sales' function in the level 0 DFD *should* be partitioned into the several functional bubbles of Figure 6.2, including 'order entry'.

Figure 6.5 isn't complete. For reasons of space we have left out the 'line update' detail. We have also omitted the detail of the values which are inserted into the order header. What it does show is the time sequence of order entry for any specific order.

We have introduced a step-numbering system. It's essentially the same as the numbering system we used for Figure 2.5. Note that it's only the procedural steps that we have numbered. 'Data entry' is numbered 'oe1' (for 'order entry step 1), but the conditions 'order insertion', 'order update' and 'order deletion' aren't numbered, because they are an integral part of the 'data entry' step. Similarly, 'line deletion actions' is an integral part of 'line deletion'.

6.2.1 Structured English specification

We shall translate this structure diagram into a set of Structured English statements. In exactly the same way as for a structure diagram, Structured English consists of *sequence, decision* and *iteration* constructs. Initially, we shall use the form of the SQL language (Structured Query Language) to make our statements, with a few simple and obvious additions. We shall then translate again into a freer-form natural language.

We shall need to make clear which is the *current row* of any table. Usually this is the row we are currently inserting or deleting. We shall do this by using lower-case letters preceded by a colon. Thus ':pno' is the current product number; ':orders.ono' is the current order number which we are inserting into the ORDERS table and ':line' is the current row of the LINE table.

For simplicity, we omit the case where the orders entry is an *update*. Only *insertion* and *deletion* are included.

```
For each order entry:
  Select the case which applies:
  Case 1: order entry is an insertion.
    Update MAXNUMBER set SeqNo=SeqNo+1 and lock MAXNUMBER
                                                          table;
    Select MAXNUMBER.SeqNo into :orders.ono;
    Assign the value for :cno at the keyboard;
    Select SystemDate into :orders.odate;
    For each LINE entry within includes:
      Select :orders.ono into :line.ono;
      Assign the value for :pno at the keyboard;
      Lock the PRODUCT row where PRODUCT.PNo = :pno;
      Assign the value for :oq at the keyboard;
      Select :oq,0 into :delp, :cfq from PRODUCT
        where :oq <= AvlQ
        and PNo = :line.pno)
      Select AvlQ, (:oq-AvlQ) into :delq, :cfq from Product
        where :oq>AvlQ
        and PNo = :line.pno;
      Update PRODUCT set AvlQ=AvlQ - :delq where PNo = :line.pno;
  Case 2: order entry is a deletion.
    Identify the order number of the order to be deleted as :ono;
    Delete ORDERS where ONo = :ono;
    Update PRODUCT set AvlQ = AvlQ + (select DelQ from LINE,PRODUCT
                                      where LINE.PNo =
                                                       PRODUCT.PNo
                                      and LINE.ONo = :ono)
        where PNo in (Select PNo from LINE
                      where ONo = :ono);
    Delete LINE where ONo = :ono;
    Commit all changes and release all locks;
```

Let's repeat our Structured English in something closer to natural language!

Carry out the following sequence for each order entry
(the entry will be either an insertion, or a deletion):
In the case of an insertion
Increase the value of the Sequence Number in the MAXIMUM NUMBER
table by one, and lock the table;
Use the new Sequence Number as the New Order Number in the ORDERS
table;
Set the Order Date in the ORDERS table to today's date;
Carry out the following sequence for each LINE to be ordered within the
'includes' relationship:
Copy the Order Number in the LINE table from the Order Number just
inserted into the ORDERS table;
Type in the Product Number at the keyboard for entry into the LINE table;
Lock the corresponding row in the PRODUCT table;
Type in the Ordered Quantity at the keyboard for entry into the LINE table;

If the Ordered Quantity is not more than the Available Quantity shown in
the PRODUCT table, for the same Product Number
then
The Delivered Quantity is the same as the Ordered Quantity
and the Carried Forward Quantity is set to zero
Otherwise
The Delivered Quantity is the same as the Available Quantity
and the Carried Forward Quantity is the difference between Ordered
Quantity and Available Quantity;
Update the Available Quantity in the PRODUCT table for the same
Product Number, by subtracting the Delivered Quantity just
calculated, from the Available Quantity;
In the case of a deletion
Delete the entry in the ORDERS table;
Update the Available Quantity in the PRODUCT table by adding the
Delivered Quantity for all the products which appear in an order LINE to the
appropriate Available Quantity;
Delete the entries in the LINE table with the appropriate Order Number;
Commit the changes, and release all locks;

Before we go any further we need to give more details about
Structured English. Both the above examples qualify as Structured
English. What is required is a systematic way of setting out the
steps. There is no need for a list of reserved words or to stick to a
particular form of words to implement an intention. If you prefer
'erase the row in the ORDERS table' to 'delete the entry in the
ORDERS table', then that is the sort of choice you are free to
make.

We have tried to be consistent in the way we refer to data
objects. Thus 'ORDERS table', 'Delivered Quantity' and 'DelQ'
all observe similar conventions. What we must be able to do is to
represent the three basic constructs; *sequence, iteration* and
decision.

Every set of structured English steps is a sequence:

Set the Order Number in the LINE table to that just inserted into the ORDERS
                                                                      table;
Type in the Product Number at the Keyboard for entry into the LINE table;
Lock the corresponding row in the PRODUCT table;
Type in the Ordered Quantity at the keyboard for entry into the LINE table;

---

is a sequence. A complete decision construct is also a step in a sequence. Thus:

If the Ordered Quantity is not more than the Available Quantity shown in the
PRODUCT table, for the same Product Number
then
    The Delivered Quantity is the same as the Ordered Quantity
    and the Carried Forward Quantity is set to zero
Otherwise
    The Delivered Quantity is the same as the Available Quantity
    and the Carried Forward Quantity is the difference between Ordered Quantity
                                                       and Available Quantity;
Update the Available Quantity in the PRODUCT table for the same Product
                                                                      Number
by subtracting the Delivered Quantity just calculated, from the Available Quantity;

---

constitutes two steps in a sequence. The eight lines before the first ';' are one step. Together they form a single decision construct. The remaining two lines form a sequence construct. Thus the whole extract is a two-step sequence construct and it consists of one decision construct and one-single step sequence construct.

The whole Structured English example we have given constitutes a single-step sequence construct. The single step is also an iteration construct. The two phrases we used to signal an iteration are:

'For each order entry:-' and
'Carry out the following sequence for each order entry'

What is required is some form of words which signals that the following sequence construct is to be executed many times.

Several different forms of decision construct have been used. In Figure 2.5 our example was:

If the start is not good
Then
  The starter fires the pistol to recall contestants;
  The starter lines up the contestants on the start line;
  The starter tells the contestant to get ready;
  The starter fires the start pistol;

This is one-decision construct, which contains a four-step sequence construct.
  In this section we wrote:

Select :op,0 into :delq, :cfq from PRODUCT
  where :oq <= AvlQ
  and PNo = :line.pno;

It's rather uncertain whether this decision construct contains a single step or a two-step sequence construct. Two values are being selected into two variables. It does illustrate that there is not always a one-to-one correspondence between different forms of the same type of construct. What *is* clear is that there is just one decision construct.
  Again from this section we have the decision construct we have already cited:

If the Ordered Quantity is not more than the Available Quantity shown in the PRODUCT table, for the same Product Number
then
  The Delivered Quantity is the same as the Ordered Quantity
  and the Carried Forward Quantity is set to zero
Otherwise
  The Delivered Quantity is the same as the Available Quantity
  and the Carried Forward Quantity is the difference between Ordered Quantity
                                            and Available Quantity;

The point to note here is that there is a sequence of steps relating to both an evaluation of 'true' and an evaluation of 'false' for the decision condition.
  This brings us to the last form of a decision construct that we shall display:

Select the case which applies:
   Case 1: order entry is an insertion.
     Update MAXNUMBER set SeqNo = SeqNo + 1;
      -----;
      -----;
   Case 2: order entry is a deletion.
     Identify the order number of the order to be deleted as :ono;
      -----;
      -----;

Clearly, there isn't any difficulty about adding:

   Case 3: order entry is an update.

The decision condition doesn't evaluate to just 'true' or 'false'. There can be as many different outcomes as are dictated by the logic of the situation.

One feature that our example does demonstrate is that decision constructs can be nested within other decision constructs. We have an 'If. . .Then. . .Otherwise' construct within the 'Case order entry is an insertion' clause. This nesting can occur to any depth.

We have tried to show Structured English as having a fairly free form of expression, but with a strict requirement for the three constructs of sequence, iteration and decision. That is what it is basically about. There remain only the measures we can adopt to improve the impact of a set of statements on a reader to assist the understanding of meaning.

Figure 6.6, gives a skeleton for the Structured English example we've been using. Each separate box encloses *one sequence*. Some of the sequence steps are decision constructs and two of them are iteration constructs. Drawing a set of boxes like this is one way of making clear the structure of the set of statements. All the examples we have given have used indentation as a device to display structure. Figure 6.6 is indented and the indentation pattern matches the boxes in the skeleton.

The last device that we can suggest is a structured numbering system. We used this in Figures 2.5 and 6.5. Figure 6.7 repeats Figure 6.6 with numbering added using a sequence similar to Figure 6.5. Since we have omitted 'update' from Figure 6.7, the numbering differs where 'order entry is a deletion'. The steps in a sequence are all sequentially numbered. A nested sequence is numbered as its containing step, with an extra classification point.

A decision construct is given only one number which includes all its sections. The numbering within a decision construct is taken

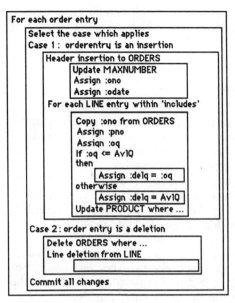

Figure 6.6 The structure skeleton for the Careful Company's order entry

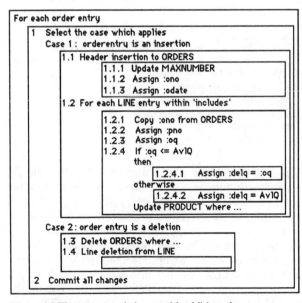

Figure 6.7 The structure skeleton, with addition of sequence

right through. There isn't a separately numbered sequence depending on whether the decision condition evaluates to 'true' or 'false'.

6.2.2 Transition rule specification

Some processing is inherently procedural. For example, Figure 8.11 displays a procedure for sorting rows of a table into sequential order. In the previous section we have outlined a procedural approach to the problem of ensuring the integrity of a database. In this section we outline a rule-based approach.

Where a particular row of a table is referred to, it is specified by the word 'Required'. Thus: RequiredPNo. If a value is updated, the new value is identified by the word 'New'. Thus: NewSeqNo. Finally, a value which has been locked is identified by LockedAvlQ.

Since there is no sequential processing assumption a particular rule may contain a variable which needs to be *instantiated* or given a value before the rule can be evaluated. Let's set out the rules for an order insertion in the order entry function:

Roe1:   Commit all insertion changes to ORDERS and MAXNUMBER and then
release locks

Where commitment is preceded by
Lock the MAXNUMBER table,
Update MAXNUMBER adding 1 to the SeqNo to establish the
NewSeqNo,
Insert one order header into ORDERS;

Roe2:   Insert an order header into ORDERS
Where this requires the following actions
Assign the Required CNo at the keyboard,
Assign NewSeqNo to the ONo,
Assign SystemDate to the ODate;

Roe1 and Roe2 (Order entry rule 1 and Order entry rule 2) attempt to specify exactly the same order header insertion into the ORDERS table, together with necessary updating of the MAXNUMBER table, as we described in Section 6.2.1. The only difference is that we have tried to specify sequence only where it is strictly required. Before we can commit the header insertion to the ORDERS table we must lock and update the MAXNUMBER table, and insert the new order header into the ORDERS table. Part of making the insertion into ORDERS is to assign the newly updated value of MAXNUMBER.SeqNo to ORDERS.ONo.

When all that is done we can *commit* the changes to both the ORDERS and the MAXNUMBER tables!

Roe3: Commit all insertion changes to LINE and PRODUCT and then release
locks

 Where commitment is preceded by
  Commit all insertion changes to ORDERS,
  For each RequiredPNo included in the order
   Insert an order line into LINE,
   Update PRODUCT, subtract DelQ from LockedAvlQ;

Roe4: Insert an order line into LINE
 Where this requires the following actions
  Copy the ONo last inserted into the ORDERS table into ONo,
  Assign the RequiredPNo and the OQ at the keyboard,
  Lock the RequiredPNo row of the PRODUCT table, giving
LockedAvlQ,
  Compute DelQ, and CFQ using OQ, and LockedAvlQ;

Roe5: Select OQ into DelQ, and zero into CFQ
 Where
  OQ is not more than Locked AvlQ;

Roe6: Select LockedAvlQ into DelQ, and OQ minus LockedAvlQ into CFQ
 Where
  OQ is more than LockedAvlQ;

Rules 3 to 6 specify that before we can commit order line insertion to the LINE table we must have done three things; we must have inserted and committed an order header; we must have inserted an order line; and we must have appropriately updated the PRODUCT table to subtract any stock delivered to a customer from the available quantity of stock. Insertion of an order line requires that we check whether we have sufficient stock of that particular part to make a delivery.

We have assumed that the ORDER and LINE insertions are separately committed. Whether that is true or whether the complete order including header and line detail should be committed as a single data object is, of course, dependent on the system requirements.

If we want to specify the rules for an order deletion:

Roe7: Commit all deletion changes to ORDERS, LINE, and PRODUCT
 Where commitment is preceded by
  Assign the order number for deletion to DeleteONo at the keyboard,
  Delete ORDERS using DeleteONo,
  For each LINE
   Compute DeletePNO, and DeleteDelQ, using DeleteONo,
   Update PRODUCT,
   Delete LINE;

Roe8: Update PRODUCT add DeleteDelQ to AvlQ
 Where PNo for the updated row = DeletePNo;

Roe9: Delete LINE
    Where
      Deletion is preceded by Update PRODUCT,
      ONo for the deleted row = DeleteONo;

Roe10: Select PNo into DeletePNo, and DelQ into DeleteDelQ
    From LINE
    Where ONo in the row = DeleteONo;

None of our various formulations is complete. A system designer must expect to specify a more exhaustive set of rules than we have. We have not related our discussion to any particular software system design product. We hope that we have demonstrated two possible approaches to the real problem of defining the rules governing the *transition* of a database from one state to another as new data are added or deleted.

We have not taken any account of integrity rules which are *static*; that is, rules which could be checked by an audit of the database at any time. Those rules will be covered in Chapter 7. Here we are concerned only about rules which can be enforced at the time when a database transition occurs, *and at no other time.*

It is, of course, quite possible that for a particular application the specification of the static rules will be enough; this may be true of a simple cataloguing system for a record collection. Once the administrator of the collection starts lending records out to people and making rules about how the loans are made, then some transition rules will have to be formulated.

6.3 Rule specification using relationships in the data model

Any study of the previous section must suggest that our rules could be simplified by using implicit knowledge. For example, it must be true that any row of a table which is eventually going to be altered in any way must be locked, to prevent other users having access to that row. If this must always be true, then it isn't necessary to spell it out.

Necessarily, if an insertion or a deletion is successful the changes will be committed. Unless the designer wants to make specific rules requiring that (for example) all an order header information and all the order line information is committed as a single 'commitment unit', then we don't need to spell the commitment out. Similarly, if our data model includes designated relationships, there is an implied linkage between the *owner* and the *members* of any *A-Set*, or atomic set (also known as a *fan-set*).

Since one customer order consists of one order header and many order lines, we can say that one row in the ORDERS table relates to many rows in the LINE table. Using our relationship name, one ORDERS row *'includes'* many LINE rows. A particular ORDERS row, and its related LINE rows, constitutes one A-set. Just to make sure that the analogy is clear, we've illustrated it in Figure 6.8 for the cub-scout sports day example of Chapter 2.

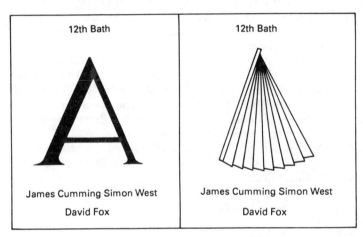

Figure 6.8 An A-set or fan-set, showing owner and member rows

Specifically, we should be able to make a statement within a rule which affects owner and member values:

Update owner PRODUCT within 'is ordered in' set NewAvlQ = AvlQ − DelQ;

If you look back at the data model in Figure 6.3 you will see that the 'is ordered in' relationship links the PRODUCT and the LINE tables.

Including the word PRODUCT within our statement is actually redundant, but we don't consider this harmful. We have continued the convention which we used above, that the prefix 'New' implies an updated value.

If the membership condition of LINE within 'includes' is *mustbe* (look forward into Chapter 7 for the strict meaning of this!), then even when we add a new LINE there will already be an owner within 'includes', and within 'is ordered in'. *Referential integrity* (which we shall explain in Chapter 7) will insist that any Product Number that we refer to in our LINE entry is, in truth, in existence in the PRODUCT table, and that Order Number is, in truth, in existence in the ORDERS table. It follows that there can be no question of adding a LINE *before* the corresponding ORDERS entry.

We can get some further implications from the data model. If any attribute is a key attribute, then since it is helping to uniquely identify one row of a table, there is no need to assert that it is typed, or assigned, at the keyboard. There is no other way that it could get its value! Attributes such as Ordered Quantity are also only constrained by the legal set of values that they can take, and it is unnecessary to make the obvious statement that their values are assigned at the keyboard.

Whenever we assign some value that is already stored in our database to an attribute we shall describe it as the *default value* (SystemDate to ODate; MAXNUMBER.SeqNo to ONo; and current ORDERS.ONo to LINE.ONo). The most convenient place to define these default values is in the rule describing which attributes belong to a table. This we shall do in Chapter 7.

Default values can get complex. The SQL statements that we have already used assign a value to Delivered Quantity and to Carried Forward Quantity:

```
Select: oq, into :delq, :cfq from PRODUCT
   where :oq <= AvlQ
   and PNo = :line.pno;
Select AvlQ, (:oq − AvlQ)into :delq, :cfq from PRODUCT
   where :oq > AvlQ
   and PNo = :line.pno;
```

For consistency, we shall define these default values also within the rule describing the attributes in a table. Again, it's something for Chapter 7!

Finally, if it is clearly necessary that the PRODUCT table be updated before LINE rows are deleted, then there must be an efficient way of signalling this:

```
Pre-Delete LINE Update owner PRODUCT within 'is ordered in' set NewAvlQ
= AvlQ + LINE.DelQ;
```

In less formal language, we are saying that before a row in the LINE table can be deleted the row in the PRODUCT table corresponding *to the same product number* must be updated so that the quantity available is increased by the amount not now being delivered to a customer.

Since the rules are inevitably different from those we set out in Section 6.2.2 we have chosen bold type to label them:

Roe1: Pre-Insert ORDERS Update MAXNUMBER set NewSeqNo = SeqNo + 1;

Roe2: Insert ORDERS into 'places with default values;

Roe3: Pre-Insert LINE Update owner PRODUCT within 'is ordered in'
     set New AvlQ = − :line.delq;

Roe4: Insert LINE into 'includes' and into 'is ordered in' with default values;

We can comment that there is no contradiction in rule 3. ':line.delq' is a value that is about to be committed to the database. Before it is committed, PRODUCT must be updated! Since the default value of LINE.ONo is the current value of ORDERS.ONo, rules 1 and 2 must be executed before rules 3 and 4. For deletion we shall identify the order number of the target order as DeleteONo:

Roe5: Delete ORDERS from places where ONo = DeleteONo;

Roe6: Pre-Delete ORDERS Delete member LINE within 'includes';

Roe7: Pre-Delete LINE Update owner PRODUCT within 'is ordered in' set
     NewAvlQ = AvlQ + LINE.DelQ;

In rule 6 the reference to member LINE means that we are referring to *all* LINES within includes. Clearly, in rule 7 we are referring to the LINE.DelQ which is about to be deleted. The updating of PRODUCT must precede this deletion, otherwise it would be impossible!

We can formulate an alternative rule 6*:

Roe6*: Pre-Delete ORDERS ¬ Exists LINE within 'includes';

This says that an order can only be deleted if no related line entries exist! We can also formulate an alternative rule 5* which pre-empts rules 6 and 7:

Roe5*: Deletion of ORDERS not allowed;

It has seemed logical in this set of rules to use a *pre-delete* and a *pre-insert* construction. There is no reason to avoid *post-delete* and *post-insert* if these seem to be required by the circumstances.

Obviously, more development work is needed before we can be confident of expressing any required integrity rule within the descriptive framework of a data model. Some obvious comments are that we have not used the 'If. . .then. . .else. . .' construct and we have not nested decision constructs. Again, rules 6 and 6* above could, with a little work, be incorporated into the relationship descriptions in Chapter 7. In spite of these reservations, we believe that we have a powerful framework.

6.4 Rules about processing

Realistically, an application is going to require much more complex processing than we can implement with a set of default rules. We adopt an approach which is rather similar to defining default rules. The device of *views* allows us to make complex definitions of values that are to be assigned to a variable. We could define the Average Value of Purchases for each customer for any year or we could define the frequency distribution of demand for all products. If a particular application has need of this kind of processing a view can be designed to support it. View definition is treated in this book as an aspect of data modelling. We deal with this in Chapter 7.

6.5 Summary

- We are concerned with the specification of the structural rules governing the transitions made by particular functions. Integrity or truthfulness of data depends on the proper enforcement of these rules. We have called these structural rules transition integrity rules. Structural rules can be specified procedurally or non-procedurally.
- The procedural specification can be by structure diagrams and by Structured English statements.
- Either method of specification requires three methods of construct:

  Sequence step
  Decision step
  Iteration step

  Any step, of any type, can contain all three construct types as sub-steps.
- A sequence is shown on a structure diagram as a vertical progression of steps:

- A decision is marked by 'o' on the child box:

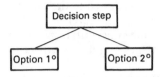

- An iteration is marked by '*' on the child box:

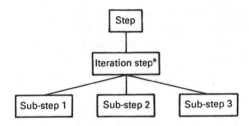

- There are various forms of expressing a Structured English decision construct. For example:
    If (condition)
    Then
      Sequence
    Otherwise
      Continuation of sequence;
- A Structured English iteration construct requires a form of words which signals that the following sequence is to be executed many times:
    For each order entry:–
      Sequence
- Both structure diagrams and Structured English statements can be illuminated by a hierarchical numbering system.
- A non-procedural specification requires that we do not rely on the sequence in which steps are written down. We use the construction:
    Rule name: Step
              [Where (condition)];
    The [] indicate an optional clause.
- It is sensible to specify non-procedural rules using relationships in the data model. The rule prescribes the order in which updating, insertion of data into and deletion of data from tables included in a relationship must occur.

Discussion points

6.1 What dimensions of a problem can be included in the models described in this chapter? Are there any differences in the expressiveness of procedural and non-procedural specification? What advantages or disadvantages might you expect to accrue from taking either route?

6.2 We have specified sequence, decision and iteration steps. Are these three adequate to describe any task?

6.3 We have studied an appropriate example of a pre-insert transition rule. Give suitable examples illustrating the field of application of post-insert, post-update, and pre-query transition rules. Assume that any of these rules can operate over the whole database and over all the current values entered or retrieved into a VDU screen.

Exercises

6.1 Specify the transition rules for the 'check delivery' function of the Sellmore logical DFD, using a non-procedural format.

6.2 Using both a procedural and a non-procedural format, specify the transition rules for:

The 'order to supplier' function of the Sellmore logical DFD;
The 'prepare program' function of the cub-scout sports day DFD in Figure 2.1.

References

1. C. J. Date, *An Introduction to Database Systems*, Vol. 2, Addison-Wesley, Reading, Mass. (1985)
2. Michael Jackson, *System Development*, Prentice-Hall, Englewood Cliffs, NJ. (1983)

Chapter 7

Data modelling and data analysis

7.1 Introduction

We don't intend to repeat the description of the entity
type/relationship/attribute constructs that we gave in Chapter 2. It
would be useful for you to reread the chapter summary in Section
2.7.2 at this point.

Chapter 2 presented only one-to-many relationships between
entity types, and did not explore any of the subtlety of those
relationships. In this chapter we shall try to remedy any omissions.
We shall also present an approach to data analysis.

7.2 The context of data modelling

So far as the process of data modelling is concerned, the context is
provided by the data flow diagram descriptions of *what the system
does*, refined by consideration of what the purpose of the system
is. 'What are we trying to do?' 'Where do we want to be?' and
'What's it for?' are questions which lead us to the formulation of
logical data flow diagrams, and then eventually to functional
requirements specifications, by a process of functional analysis.

If the purpose of the system alters, then the perception of what
we ought to do will change. Changes in purpose may be expressed
as explicit *policy decisions* or they may be subconscious reactions
to events that the decision maker isn't even aware of! *What the
system remembers* is more robust. Even if the purpose changes, *the
things we want information about* often stay substantially the same.

In Chapter 1 we discussed the things you may want to know
about a board-sailing system. Our list included changes in the
design of boards, the weather and sea conditions, and the amount
of congestion caused by other users of possible sailing areas.

One of the authors of this book once asked a group of business
executives to identify the classes of things which were important to
their businesses. A member of a family carpet manufacturing

business said without hesitation 'Patterns, products, yarns, dyes, suppliers, employees, and customers'. Anyone working in a college or university would probably agree on a list of items of interest as including courses or teaching programmes, students, lecturers, researchers, research programmes and rooms or laboratories.

The *relationships* between these classes of things, or entity types, are also robust. We can make structural statements about systems which summarize those relationships:

Yarns *are coloured by* dyes.
Patterns *require* yarns.
Suppliers *supply* yarns.
Customers *purchase* products.
Courses *enrol* students.
Lecturers *counsel* students.

We aren't at the moment bothering about whether you should use a singular or a plural noun to label the entity types, only with the stable relationships.

The things we want to know about entities (that is, the attributes of the entity types) alter with changing policies. *Information, system purpose* and *decisions* are linked in an intimate way. Clearly, if policies explicitly change, different decisions will be made, and different information will be appropriate to the making of those decisions.

If the Careful Manufacturing Company decides that disappointed customers will be supplied with out-of-stock products as soon as the stock has been replenished, then the company will have to remember details of all the outstanding customer orders. If one of the company's competitors supplies its customers as a Cash-and-Carry operation, then that competitor will need to remember very little about its customers.

It's less obvious that changes in the information we collect and record and display also affect decision making. If a local education authority widely publicizes school examination results in the local press, the schools concerned are likely to try to make those results reflect to their credit. If the Careful Manufacturing Company's information system highlights late delivery of customer orders, then the Production Manager and Marketing Manager will give more attention to this aspect in their decision making.

Perhaps the change in recorded information reflects someone's policy decision. Perhaps it has come about for reasons unrelated to policy, or because of a design decision by some unsung systems analyst!

We said above that we can make robust structural statements about the relationships of entity types to one another. The integrity rules which govern those relationships also depend on policy decisions. A rule which allows a student to be a member of a college without being enrolled on a particular course is different in its effects on the database from a rule which insists on enrolment.

7.3 Charting conventions and data modelling concepts

It is an aid to understanding if we can describe our data models diagrammatically. It must help communication of ideas between people if they have a common medium for dialogue. An unambiguous statement of requirements will help to achieve rapid and error-free implementation of the design of an information system. For all these reasons we are justified in developing the concepts of data modelling, and the charting of those concepts, in tandem.

We shall try to represent the entity types, the relationships, the attributes and the integrity rules on our diagrams, so far as it is feasible to do so. In a later section we shall follow this up by formulating the rules more explicitly.

We take as a starting point the entity/attribute description in the chapter summary of Section 2.7.2. We called the description a data model. We often rather loosely refer to the diagram displaying the model by the same name. We shall also use the term *ERA diagram*. The charts we draw *are intended to represent things in the real world*. If they also correspond to tables in the database, that is incidental; we are attempting to model reality.

7.3.1 Keys and key integrity

When we speak of keys, we normally mean *candidate keys*. We'll define primary and secondary keys shortly. A candidate key can take values which uniquely identify one entity, or one row of a data table, with no redundancy. All the tables we presented in earlier chapters had keys with this property. The non-key attributes of an entity type, or the non-key columns of a table, *depend* on the key. This means that if we give a value to the key, we can read off from the table *single values* of all the non-key attributes. It is only because we insist on simple tables, with one single value written into each row and column intersection, that this is possible. If we allowed multiple values, then we couldn't say that the column value depended on the key.

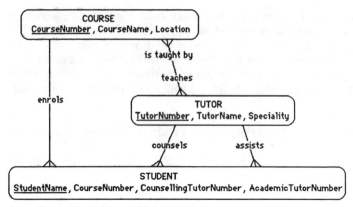

Figure 7.1 A college data model

In Figure 7.1 we have shown all the attribute names unabbreviated, so that the examples are more obvious.

In the COURSE entity type both Course Number and Course Name could reasonably be seen as candidate keys. It is unlikely that TutorNumber and TutorName could both be candidate keys of TUTOR, because people rarely have unique names. This, of course, means that StudentName is not a good choice as a key of STUDENT!

We choose one from among the candidate keys as the *primary key*. Numeric values are often preferred because computers will always see 1, 1.0, 01.0, and indeed +1.0, as the same value. 'John Smith' with one space between the two names might be perceived as different from 'John Smith' with two spaces. Even people, with far more discerning ability than a computer, might be hard pressed to say whether

Teresa Browne
Mrs T. E. Brown
Dr T. Brown
Theresa E. Browne

identifies one person or more than one person.

Our convention for primary key attributes is to underline them:

CourseNumber in COURSE
StudentName in STUDENT
TutorNumber in TUTOR

All the examples so far have one key attribute. The number of key attributes depends on how much needs to be specified to ensure uniqueness. To uniquely identify a person we may have to specify both that person's name and the postal address.

Candidates keys have no redundancy. It would be wrong to specify both CourseNumber and CourseName as primary key attributes in COURSE if CourseNumber uniquely identifies one course entity or one row in the COURSE table. Each of CourseNumber and CourseName is a candidate key, and we choose one of them as the primary key.

Extremely importantly, we must emphasize that *a thing is different from the name of that thing.* 'STUDENT' is the collective name that we can give to a group of real-world entities. 'StudentName' is an attribute which we use to label the members of that group. The name 'John Smith' is not the same thing as the person having that name. It would be very bad practice to name an entity type 'STUDENT' and then to use the same name, 'Student', as the identifying attribute or candidate key of that entity type.

Names tell us both about *oneness* and about *sameness*[1]. If CourseName takes a value in a COURSE table as 'BA(Seismology)' then we have uniquely identified *one* course. If ProductName in a PRODUCT table takes a value 'Widget' then we have identified a group of entities which have in common that they are all called widgets. Perhaps we don't want to know anything about individual widgets, only how many we have in total.

A *secondary key* is a group of one or more attributes, *not constituting a primary key*, on which we wish to make a search. The essential difference between primary and secondary keys is that there is no restriction on duplication of secondary keys. There can be more than one row of a table with the same name, or value, for a secondary key. A secondary key does not give unique identification. If we wish to search through all the tutors to find those whose speciality is 'systems analysis' then that name represents *sameness* among a particular group of tutors.

We can now make a definition of the *key integrity rule*. This states that no null values are permitted in any attribute of a candidate key. The rule has no relevance to secondary keys. A null value is one which either isn't known or isn't appropriate. A record of whether or not he has had a hysterectomy would be inappropriate for a man. If the value of a key attribute isn't known, then clearly it might take any value. It is therefore useless as an identifier of a specific entity.

7.3.2 Relationships and ownership and membership rules

In this sub-section we are talking about simple *binary* relationships (only two entity types involved) which are *one-to-many* relationships. 'Enrols', 'counsels' and 'assists' in Figure 7.1 are all binary, one-to-many relationships.

Taking 'enrols' as an example, *one* course relates to *many* students, while *one* student relates to *exactly one* course. We illustrate this by putting a crow's foot at the *many* end of the relationship line in Figure 7.1.

Let's look for a moment at the question of relationship names. In Chapter 2 we suggested that a relationship be named so that it could be read as an English sentence connecting the *one* end and the *many* end of a relationship:

One course *enrols* many students.

The reality is, of course, that binary relationships are invariably two-way. They wouldn't be relationships if they weren't! The names we give are directional; but there is always a complimentary reverse sense, as shown in Figure 7.2. It is, of course, the same relationship, whichever way we read it!

The direction in which we look at a relationship is important for another reason. The only reason that we have included CourseNumber, CounsellingTutorNumber and AcademicTutor-Number in the STUDENT entity type is because they are *foreign keys* which make the relationships explicit in the database tables. STUDENT.CourseNumber (the CourseNumber attribute in the STUDENT table) points away to a primary key in a 'foreign' table. It is the foreign keys in database tables which allow us to make cross references between tables. The foreign key always points to the primary key of a table. A match is only possible if the two keys have the same value.

We always look for the foreign key at the *many* end, pointing to a primary key at the *one* end. If we try to put the foreign key at the *one* end we end up listing all the students on any particular course:

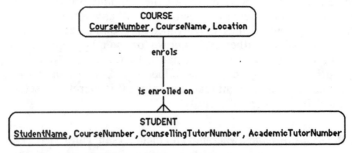

Figure 7.2 A relationship named in both directions

C21, MA(Theology), John, Jane, Elizabeth, Edward,
William. . ., Birmingham

If we enter that into a database table it conflicts with our
requirement for simple tables, with a fixed number of columns and
one entry for each row and column intersection.

The role of the foreign key should be clearer if you look at the
'counsels' and 'assists' relationships. 'Counsels' links one counselling tutor with a group of students by means of the 'CounsellingTutorNumber' foreign key. 'Assists' links an academic tutor (who
may well be the same person!) with a different group of students
by means of the 'AcademicTutorNumber' foreign key. There are
two distinct relationships between tutors and students and the two
foreign keys map these relationships to the database table.

Foreign keys are simply a way of representing a relationship. If
the relationship names are sufficiently clear, we can leave the
foreign keys out of the data model. *There is no way that we could
leave them out of the database tables!*

Wherever it is feasible to do so, we shall, from now on, omit the
foreign keys from our data models. If we are drawing ERA
diagrams to aid clarity and communication we must avoid
overloading with redundant data. Look at Figure 7.3 to see what
we mean.

The relationships we have shown would, in a database, define
sets of data. Each set has exactly one *owner* (a particular course)
and many *members* (a group of students). Together they form an
A-Set, or *fan-set.* If you look back to Figure 6.8, we have
illustrated what we mean by an A-Set.

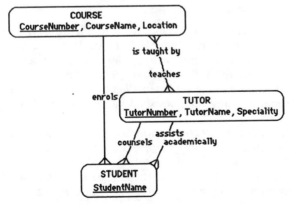

Figure 7.3 A college data model with no redundant attributes as foreign keys

It isn't enough to assert that this, that or another entity type belongs to a relationship. To capture more meaning about reality we need to say something about the strength of that relationship. We do this by declaring the *ownership* and *membership* rules. It's easier to illustrate what this means if we introduce the complementary relationship description:

One student is enrolled on one and only one course.

We can expand this statement in two ways:

One student *may be* enrolled on one and only one course.
One student *must be* enrolled on one and only one course.

The statements say something about membership. If a student *may be* enrolled on a course it implies that we will permit students to exist who aren't enrolled on a specific course!

Let's look at the relationship from the other direction:

One course enrols many students.

The quantification 'many; can be refined:

One course enrols no students or more than no students (*some* students!).
One course enrols one student or more than one student.

These two statements say something about ownership. If a course is permitted to exist with no students we are declaring that COURSE is not required to participate in the 'enrols' relationship.

With this understanding of the meaning of ownership it can be expressed succinctly:

One course may enrol many students.
One course must enrol many students.

We have displayed variations on these rules in Figure 7.4. In Figure 7.4(a) a course must enrol students, but a student need not be enrolled on a course. In Figure 7.4(b) a course need not enrol students, but a student must be enrolled on a course. A bar represents *mustbe* while a circle represents *maybe* or *optional*. If we refrain from marking any line, we shall be implying that the condition is *maybe*.

There is a variety of different conventions used by other authors to represent these 'ownership' and 'membership' rules. We don't intend to explore them here!

At the end of Section 7.3.1 we set out the key integrity rule. We are now in a position to set out the other fundamental rule of entity type/relationship/attribute data modelling. The *referential*

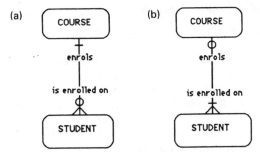

Figure 7.4 Marking data model diagrams to show ownership and membership rules

integrity rule tells us that any value that is referred to *must exist!* If a student is enrolled on a seismology course, then there must be a seismology course in that institution. If relationships are mapped to a database by means of foreign keys, then referential integrity requires that the foreign key value in a member table matches a primary key value in the owner table.

Referential integrity does not rule out null values for a foreign key. A null value simply means that the key doesn't refer to anything. In our college database a null value in STUDENT-.CourseNumber shows that the student concerned is not enrolled on any course. This only breaks the integrity rule if STUDENT membership of 'enrols' is *mustbe*.

7.3.3 Many-to-many binary relationships

In Section 7.3.2 we showed that only if a foreign key contains a *list* of key values can it point to a candidate key at the 'one' end of a one-to-many relationship between database tables. Exactly the same problem exists for any many-to-many relationship.

The 'teaches'/'is taught by' relationship in our college data model is represented by a line with a crow's foot at each end, showing a many-to-many relationship:

One tutor teaches many courses.
One course is taught by many tutors.

If we are to represent this relationship in the College database then either we need a COURSE.TutorName attribute which lists all the tutors on the course:

Luther, Aquinas, Marx,. . .

or we need a TUTOR.CourseName attribute which lists all the courses taught by a particular tutor:

BA(Seismology), BPhilosophy, MMusic,. . .

Either solution would conflict with our requirement for simple tables, with a single value at each column and row intersection. The tables we are looking for are essentially two-dimensional. This gives us a convenient name for them, as *flat tables*.

The data model can be redrawn in such a way that it can be mapped directly to a series of flat tables in the database. To do this we introduce a *relationship entity type* which tells us something more about the 'teaches'/'is taught by' relationship. Like any data object name, the entity type name should be unique and it should be descriptive. We'll call it 'COURSE_TUTOR'. We see no need for particular markings of a relationship entity type box on an ERA diagram.

One COURSE_TUTOR entity, or one row in a COURSE_TUTOR database table, tells us something about the relationship of *one tutor* to *one course*. In the case of the database table, TutorNumber, and CourseNumber would be present in the table as foreign keys. Together they constitute a candidate key for the table, giving unique identity to each row.

Both the data model entity type and the database table would include any attribute which tells us something about the relationship of a tutor to a course. One obvious attribute of COURSE_TUTOR is ContactHours. This tells us for how many hours in any one week (or term, or year; the choice is arbitrary) one tutor is in contact with one course. Another appropriate attribute of the relationship could be the name of the room in which the encounter takes place.

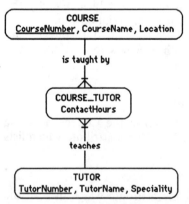

Figure 7.5 Resolution of a many-to-many relationship

These changes are included in Figure 7.5, just for the 'is taught by'/'teaches' relationship. *Note that the crow's feet are at the COURSE_TUTOR end of both lines.* This must follow from the many-to-many relationship.

The many-to-many relationship between COURSE and TUTOR hasn't vanished! We've chosen to represent it in a different way. It would be redundant to include, in addition, any line directly linking TUTOR and COURSE. Note that we have declared that one COURSE_TUTOR *mustbe* related to both a tutor and a course!

If there is no attribute of a many-to-many relationship between two entity types which is of interest then we are happy to represent that relationship on our data model diagram as a single line with a crow's foot at each end. We always name a many-to-many relationship *in both directions,* regardless of how we intend to represent it.

Although the method of handling a binary relationship between two entity types, in which one entity of either type relates to many entities of the other type, is quite general, we need some words of caution. It is possible to be misled into believing that a relationship is many-to-many when this is in fact not true.

We are indebted to Aberdeen University[2] for the background for Figure 7.6. On the face of it, one sheep can be supposed to be related to many matings, where each mating results in a litter of lambs. This is *not* a many-to-many relationship in the sense of Figure 7.5.

Figure 7.6(b) suggests that there *is* a two-to-many relationship in that exactly two sheep 'parent' many matings and that one mating has a progeny of many sheep. If we know that an exact number exists at either end of a relationship then it is sensible to state this. In practice, of course, it's unlikely that a particular pair of sheep would parent more than one mating.

Figure 7.6(c) discloses that the apparent many-to-many relationship can properly be presented as three quite distinct

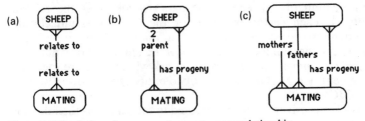

Figure 7.6 Resolution of an apparent many-to-many relationship

one-to-many relationships! One sheep 'fathers' many matings; one sheep 'mothers' many matings; and one mating 'has progeny' of many sheep. Naturally, the same sheep who is a mother or a father is a part of the progeny of some other mating.

Question
Can you suggest appropriate attributes for the two entity types in Figure 7.6?

Figure 7.7(a) again suggests a many-to-many relationship between many tutors, and many students. (We are indebted to the Open University for this example [3].)

In fact, the relationship between TUTOR and STUDENT is that they are equivalent to each other. Both of them can be represented as members of the same relationship, with owner TOWN. The one-to-many relationship is between TUTOR and TOWN and between STUDENT and TOWN.

Figure 7.7 does establish one important point. Although many relationships are binary, there is no case for regarding this as a rule. The entities which are members of a relationship can be of one or several types.

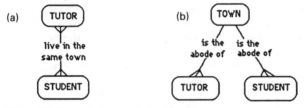

Figure 7.7 An equivalence relationship with an appearance of many-to-many

7.3.4 One-to-one relationships

We can't deny that these relationships exist. All that we want to emphasize is that if the relationship is one-to-one, then identification of one entity automatically identifies the related entity. If each customer order for the Careful Manufacturing Company is separately invoiced, then once we know the unique customer order number, we also know the unique invoice number. In these circumstances it is proper to ask whether we are speaking of one entity type (ORDERS) or two entity types (ORDERS and INVOICE).

If one bus driver is always allocated to the same bus then there is a one-to-one relationship between DRIVER and BUS. It wouldn't

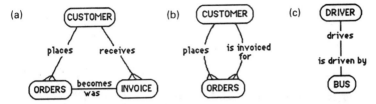

Figure 7.8 The one-to-one relationship and alternatives

be very sensible to suggest that these two are a single entity type. We have shown these options in Figure 7.8.

The 'becomes'/'was' relationship of Figure 7.8(a) is absorbed into ORDERS in Figure 7.8(b). If we want to preserve the notion that not all orders have been invoiced we can identify two different relationships between CUSTOMER and ORDERS.

Figure 7.8 prompts us to make a second extremely important point. Data models are not God given. They represent reality, but it is not true that every person perceives reality in the same way. We the designers impose models on reality. We have equally correctly interpreted a customer order as either one entity type or as two. In Figure 7.8(b) the discrimination moves from the entity type definition to the relationship definition.

7.3.5 Non-binary many-to-many relationships

Returning to Figure 7.5, the relationship included there could be seen as an encounter between a COURSE, a TUTOR and a ROOM. We can take it a little further and make it an encounter between a COURSE, a TUTOR, a ROOM and a TIME. 'The Meditation course will meet Mr Jones in room 352 at 2.00 p.m. on Friday June 12th.'

Figure 7.9(a) shows just this relationship. In Figure 7.9(b) we introduce a LINK entity type which fulfils just the relationship entity type role of COURSE_TUTOR, which we met earlier. ContactHours could well be an attribute of LINK. Figure 7.9(c) displays the situation where we want to know the identity of the room in which the encounter takes place and the time when it occurs; *but we don't want to know anything else about either the room or the time.* We don't want to know what colour the room is painted or how many chairs it has; we don't want to know that this is the time when the pubs open!

There is one new convention that we have used in Figure 7.9. StartTime and RoomName are underlined with dotted lines. They are key attributes, but they don't constitute a whole key. There

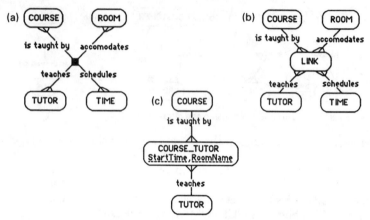

Figure 7.9 A non-binary many-to-many relationship

may be more than one course scheduled to be in that room, to be taught by that tutor, at that time. To uniquely identify one encounter we need the CourseNumber as well. As a foreign key, we are leaving CourseNumber out of the ERA diagram.

This is our third extremely important point. We can sometimes represent a piece of information either as an entity type or as an attribute. In fact we could see a sort of shadow entity type hovering behind most attributes. Figure 7.10 represents STUDENT as a relationship entity type, describing a relationship of degree five. Small wonder we don't want to introduce a special symbol for relationship entity types. Almost any entity type can be made to look like one!

Figure 7.10 can be seen as a sub-classification of STUDENT. It suggests that summaries of student data could be produced

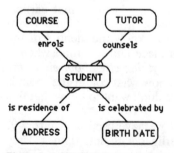

Figure 7.10 STUDENT represented as a relationship entity type

classified by their home addresses, their ages, their courses or their counselling tutor name. We don't regard this as a proper use of a data model! Entity types are included if and only if there is something we want to know about the entities. If we can't identify at least one non-key attribute of a proposed entity type, then we shall not recognize it as an entity type.

7.3.6 Arcs and arc transition rules

This sub-section enlarges an idea that we introduced in Figure 7.8(b). The order that a customer places can pass through several phases. First, it is simply an order. Next, it is an order for which goods have been despatched and an invoice requesting payment is sent to the customer. Finally, it is an order for which payment has been received from the customer.

Introducing the concept of an *arc*, we can say that all these relationships belong to the arc, which we have named 'order arc'. One order can belong to one and only one of these relationships at any one time.

Figure 7.11(b) takes this a little further, but brings us right into the business of transition integrity rules which we described in Chapter 6. The arrow tells us that an order must be related to a customer in the sequence 'places', 'is invoiced for', 'makes payment for', as well as belonging to exactly one of them.

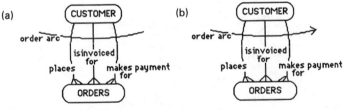

Figure 7.11 An arc, comprising several relationships

We have not yet suggested any convention for saying that an order *must* belong to one of the relationships comprising 'order arc', although clearly it would be a sensible rule to prescribe. Perhaps if we mark each relationship in the arc as *mustbe* it would allow this interpretation. We also haven't an explicit means of permitting an order to belong to more than one relationship, except by failing to declare an arc.

There is also the possibility of more than one entry point into an arc. The sequence could begin with the relationship:

A CUSTOMER makes a reservation for an ORDER,

and a particular order sequence could start optionally with 'makes a reservation for' or with 'places'. Specifying all the possible transition possibilities *is beyond the scope of an ERA diagram*. Complex requirements demand explicit statement as integrity rules.

A customer order is an *event*. It occurs at a specified time, and that time is an attribute of the order. The order itself also describes a relationship between a customer and a group of products that the customer wishes to obtain. ORDER then has to be seen as a relationship entity type. Relationship entity types, particularly if they belong to an arc, correspond very closely to the entity life cycle structure diagram of Chapter 6.

7.3.7 Types and sub-types

The last data modelling concept that we shall attempt to chart is the *sub-type*. Figure 7.12(a) re-labels the COURSE_TUTOR relationship entity type of the college data model as 'SUBJECT'.

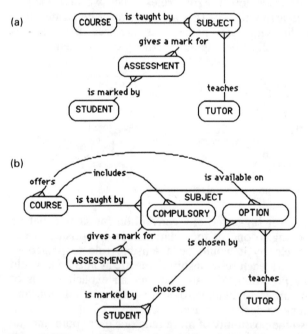

Figure 7.12 Types and sub-types in the college data model

A STUDENT 'studies' many SUBJECTs and a SUBJECT 'is studied by' many students. The relationship entity type which represents that many-to-many relationship could be called ASSESSMENT, describing the progress of one student in one subject.

So far, there are no new concepts. If we change the model so that some subjects are compulsory and others are options chosen by the students then there are different kinds, or sub-types, of subject. These sub-types can have differing relationships with other entity types. We have shown these two sub-types in Figure 7.12(b).

The 'offers'/'is available on' relationship shows that each option is potentially available for more than one course (both BA in Accounting and Bachelor of Law, for example). A course 'is taught by' subjects and each subject 'gives a mark for' assessment of each student. Each student 'chooses' a set of options and one option 'is chosen by' many students. We cannot deduce from the data model how many options each student must choose. That must be defined by the values of an attribute of COURSE, for each course which is available for enrolment.

We have left the 'enrols', 'counsels' and 'assists' relationships out of Figure 7.12. This is purely for the sake of clarity. We have also omitted the ownership and membership rules. Sub-typing could easily be extended. Perhaps tutors come in two sub-types: senior tutors and others. We can postulate that:

A SENIOR TUTOR may act as director of one or more COURSEs.

The relationship between type and sub-type is always an 'is a' relationship:

An OPTION *is a* SUBJECT.
A COMPULSORY SUBJECT *is a* SUBJECT.
A SENIOR TUTOR *is a* TUTOR.

The fact that an optional subject is a subject means that the two must have some attributes in common. We can usually, for example, expect that we can specify the key at type level, and, like any attribute defined for a type, that key will apply to all sub-types. In addition, each sub-type will have its own exclusive attributes which are different from those of any other sub-type and from those of the type itself. We have shown only one level of sub-type, but there is nothing preventing sub-sub-types. At each level, an instance of a type is itself a type, with its own instances.

This completes our discussion of the charting conventions. We have only mapped a small part of the richness of the real world.

Now we need to consider some of the ways these conventions may be used and also some of the aspects which are more difficult to portray.

7.4 Data structures

We need to use the charting conventions introduced in the previous section to describe the variety of structures that we meet in practical applications. The *list* structure within a particular table doesn't merit much further explanation. Each row of a table describes a particular entity, and the attributes that we record about each entity are the same as those we record for all other entities of the same type.

Writers also identify a *lattice* structure. The requirement is that any one entity in a data model (or any one row of a table in a database) can be 'owned' by more than one entity (or row of a table). Thus in Figure 7.12 ASSESSMENT is owned by both SUBJECT and STUDENT. You will agree we feel sure that *any* modelling involving relationship entity types implies that we are working with a lattice.

A *cycle* is an extremely useful device. The requirement is that an entity can 'own' (either directly or indirectly) member entities of the same type. (From now on we shall refrain from pointing out every time that the same statement applies to rows in a table in a database.) Figure 7.6(c) is a cycle; an indirect one this time. A sheep 'mothers' a mating; a mating 'has progeny' sheep; and so back to a sheep 'mothers' a mating.

Figure 7.13 shows two direct cycles. Figure 7.13(a) is the basic organization chart. A person 'supervises' many people/a person 'is responsible to' one person. Figure 7.13(b) is the ultimate data model!

The last data structure we shall introduce is the *tree*. For this, any one entity in a data model is either a *root* or it must be owned by exactly one entity. Branches never rejoin; there are no cycles.

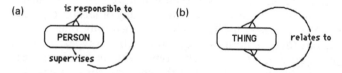

Figure 7.13 Two cycles: an organization chart and the ultimate data model

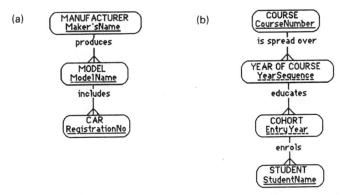

Figure 7.14 Trees, with inherited key values for the college data model in (b)

Figure 7.14(a) shows a tree in which each level of the tree has its own primary key as unique identifier. In Figure 14(b) identification of an entity requires the higher-level keys. A course 'is spread over' several years and each year of the course 'educates' successive cohorts of students. Finally, a cohort 'enrols' individual students. We have shown relevant key attributes in each case, but not the keys inherited from higher echelons.

7.5 Normalization

We do *not* see normalization as an essential step in the design process. An experienced designer should arrive at a normalized data model directly, without going through the steps described below. We have included this section purely because we think it will help you to understand what a normalized entity type really is!

The step-by-step sequence of normalization is something that applies to data tables rather than data models, and so we shall make our presentation in that form. As a starting point, Figure 7.15 is a version of part of the cub-scout data that you saw in Figure 2.3. For simplicity, we have assumed only one race for each event. We have put all the data into one table.

Clearly, this table breaks our basic requirement for flat tables. There *is not* a single entry for each row and column intersection. Also, if these are seen as two records, one for race number one and one for race number two, then the records are of indefinite length.

	SPORTS						
Race Number	EventName	StartTime	Cub-Scout Name	DOB	PackName	PackLeader's Name	Position
1	under 9,80m	2.10 pm	John Bates	3-Apr-82	9th Bath	Linda Evans	second
			David Fox	13-Aug-81	15th Bath	Edna Collins	first
			Rohit Patel	19-Apr-82	2nd Bath	John Miles	third
			Simon Birch	12-Sep-81	2nd Bath	John Miles	–
2	under10,80m	2.30pm	Simon West	31-May-82	15th Bath	Edna Collins	first
			Jason Hewitt	12-Jan-82	25th Bath	Jean Rooke	second

Figure 7.15 The cub-scout sports data in a single table

The first step in normalization is to eliminate any *repeating group*. All the attributes to the *right* of the vertical dotted line form a repeating group. They are repeated four times for the first record and twice for the second. The repeating group is eliminated by splitting the table. The two tables we derive from this are in *first normal form* (Figure 7.16).

SCHEDULED RACE emerges as a table with few rows because it deals only with race data. We have eliminated some of the *redundancy*. All the non-key attributes depend on RaceNumber as the primary key, and in fact this table is now completely normalized. We have called the other table CONTESTANT 1, to show that it is, at the moment, in first normal form. We need RaceNumber as a foreign key in CONTESTANT 1. Without it we should lose information about the races the cub-scouts are competing in.

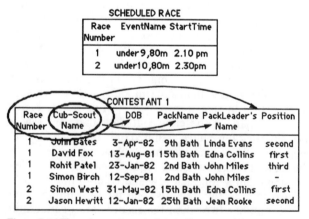

SCHEDULED RACE

Race Number	EventName	StartTime
1	under 9,80m	2.10 pm
2	under10,80m	2.30pm

CONTESTANT 1

Race Number	Cub-Scout Name	DOB	PackName	PackLeader's Name	Position
1	John Bates	3-Apr-82	9th Bath	Linda Evans	second
1	David Fox	13-Aug-81	15th Bath	Edna Collins	first
1	Rohit Patel	23-Jan-82	2nd Bath	John Miles	third
1	Simon Birch	12-Sep-81	2nd Bath	John Miles	–
2	Simon West	31-May-82	15th Bath	Edna Collins	first
2	Jason Hewitt	12-Jan-82	25th Bath	Jean Rooke	second

Figure 7.16 The cub-scout sports data in first normal form

Second normal form requires that all non-key attributes *depend* on the whole key. If you know the value of the key you can read off the non-key attributes from the table. but you cannot do this at all if you know only a part of the key. In Figure 7.16 the cub-scout's race position must depend on both his name and the race number. He could well have run in three different races! All the other attributes depend on Cub-ScoutName only.

Figure 7.17 meets this by splitting CONTESTANT 1 into two parts. We have used '2' in the table names to show that they are in second normal form. Since SCHEDULED RACE is unchanged, we haven't carried it forward.

The advantage in splitting CONTESTANT 2 from CUB-SCOUT 2 isn't obvious in the figure. You will accept, though, that each cub-scout will have exactly one entry in CUB-SCOUT 2. He will have an entry in CONTESTANT 2 for every race he runs in. CONTESTANT 2 is now fully normalized.

Our next step in normalization is the *Boyce–Codd normal form.* Any attribute on which some other attribute depends *must be a key.* In Figure 7.17 PackLeader'sName depends on PackName. PackName must therefore be the key of a table. In fact unless two

CONTESTANT 2

Race Number	Cub-Scout Name	Position
1	John Bates	second
1	David Fox	first
1	Rohit Patel	third
1	Simon Birch	–
2	Simon West	first
2	Jason Hewitt	second

CUB-SCOUT 2

Cub-Scout Name	DOB	PackName	PackLeader's Name
John Bates	3-Apr-82	9th Bath	Linda Evans
David Fox	13-Aug-81	15th Bath	Edna Collins
Rohit Patel	23-Jan-82	2nd Bath	John Miles
Simon Birch	12-Sep-81	2nd Bath	John Miles
Simon West	31-May-82	15th Bath	Edna Collins
Jason Hewitt	12-Jan-82	25th Bath	Jean Rooke

Figure 7.17 The cub-scout sports data in second normal form

CUB-SCOUT 3

Cub-Scout Name	DOB	PackName
John Bates	3-Apr-82	9th Bath
David Fox	13-Aug-81	15th Bath
Rohit Patel	23-Jan-82	2nd Bath
Simon Birch	12-Sep-81	2nd Bath
Simon West	31-May-82	15th Bath
Jason Hewitt	12-Jan-82	25th Bath

PACK

PackName	PackLeader's Name
9th Bath	Linda Evans
15th Bath	Edna Collins
2nd Bath	John Miles
25th Bath	Jean Rooke

Figure 7.18 The cub-scout sports data in Boyce–Codd normal form

pack leaders have the same name, PackName and PackLeader's-Name depend on each other. They are each *candidate keys*. CUB-SCOUT 3 and PACK in Figure 7.18 are in Boyce–Codd normal form. They are fully normalized.

Figure 7.19 displays the normalized data model. We have presented this model before, in Figure 2.4. Normalization thus far can be summed up succinctly[4]:

Non-key attributes depend on the key, the whole key and nothing but the key!

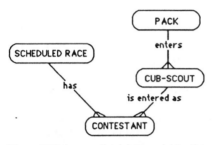

Figure 7.19 A normalized data model for the cub-scout sports data

7.6 Domains and domain integrity

Put simply, *a domain is a set of values*. If we say that an attribute belongs to a domain we are saying that the values that constitute that domain are the only legitimate values for that attribute. Put in formal mathematical terms, we say that an attribute is defined on a particular domain.

There is an obvious practical importance of this so far as database tables are concerned. *Any foreign key must be of the same domain as the primary key to which it points*. If it isn't, then it is not possible to find a match. A more general usefulness of the domain concept is that if several attributes belong to the same domain, it's only necessary to define that domain once!

Our illustration of this is based on the Careful Manufacturing Company data model in Figure 6.3. We have adopted a naming convention that the last word in every attribute name is the name of the domain. The named domains are therefore:

no   as a convenient abbreviation of 'number'.
name   which is fairly explicit.

date   which presupposes a particular form of expressing
                the date.

q   as an abbreviation of 'quantity'.

description   which again is fairly explicit.

'description' does make a useful point. If no ambiguity can result
from it, there is no harm in using the same name for a domain and
for an attribute. In all cases we have used lower-case letters to
distinguish the domain names from attribute names. Attributes are
variables; they can be instantiated with a variety of values.
Domains are *data objects*; they consist of a constant, unchanging
set of values.

It is time to discuss integrity rules again. In Chapter 6 we
described transition integrity rules. In this chapter we introduce
domain integrity rules and *table integrity rules*. The basis for this
classification comes from Date[5]. We are also indebted to Smith
and Smith[6] and Hammer and McLeod[7]. Let's start with the
domain integrity rules. What these do is to define the content of a
domain, and therefore the permissable values for any attribute
belonging to that domain. The structure of each rule is a
declaration of the domain name, followed by the conditions for
membership of the domain:

Domain (no)
Where no is integer,
  no between 1 and 1000;

Domain (name)
Where name is character,
  name includes {alpha caharacters, "-", "'", ".", "space"},
  Width is 20;

Domain (date)
Where date format is 'DD-Mon-YY',
  date between '1-Jan-1901' and '31-Dec-2000';

Domain (date)
Where date format is 'DD-Mon-YY',
  date between '1-Jan-1901' and '31-Dec-2000';

Domain (q)
Where q is integer,
  q between 0 and 1000;

Domain (description)
Where description is character,
  description includes {alpha characters, "space"}
  Width is 30;

'name', and 'date' deserve some comment. We could all recognize which strings of characters might be customer names. We should find it quite difficult to write a full definition of those names. There is therefore a difference between the real-world domain of names and the domain that we are capable of defining to a computer driving a database. It's one of those times when we just have to do the best we can!

The domain 'date' gives problems of usage. American and European practices differ in the way dates are set out. A format which expresses a date as '5-Jun-90' reduces the risk of being misunderstood. The curly brackets {} are the normal mathematical markers for a *set* of values.

There is one small anomaly in the date domain definition. Although the format is given as 'DD-Mon-YY', the limits are, for obvious reasons, expressed as 'DD-Mon-YYYY'.

By implication, every domain includes a null value. We've explained before that a null value takes two forms. Either the value *isn't known* for an attribute of an entity or it is *inappropriate* for a particular attribute of a particular entity.

7.7 Table integrity rules

The transition integrity rules specify what *changes* in database values are allowed. the domain integrity rules specify what values *are allowed to exist* in a database. The table integrity rules specify additional constraints which are imposed on values of an attribute, either because of that attribute's *role in a table* or because of *a relationship with other data objects* outside the table. We are assuming that key integrity and domain integrity are implicit in any database.

The table integrity rules, like the domain integrity rules, are *static*. Most of them can be included in an ERA diagram. Some rules (for example, whether or not null values are allowed for an attribute) are very difficult to put on a diagram. We are going to try to display all the rules, regardless of whether they can be easily charted.

Our schema requires a way of defining two different kinds of data object: *tables* and *relationships*. We shall include *attributes* in the table definitions. We are writing integrity rules for databases, and therefore do specify foreign keys. We have not included any sub-types, but don't see any difficulty in specifying 'TABLE NAME is a sub-type of. . .'. Again, our example is the Careful Manufacturing Company:

ORDERS (ONo, CNo, ODate)
Description: Orders for products are placed by customers
Where ONo belongs to no,
    ONo is key,
    ONo default on insertion is MAXNUMBER.NewSeqNo,
    CNo belongs to no,
    CNo is not null,
    ODate belongs to date,
    ODate default on insertion is SystemDate;

LINE (ONo, PNo, OQ, DelQ, CFQ)
    Description: Each line specifies one product included in a customer order
    Where ONo belongs to no,
        ONo is key attribute,
        ONo is not null,
        ONo default on insertion is :orders.ono,
        PNo belongs to no,
        PNo is key attribute,
        PNo is not null,
        OQ belongs to q,
        DelQ belongs to q,
        DelQ default on insertion is minimum {:oq, owner PRODUCT.AvlQ within 'is ordered in'},
        CFQ belongs to q,
        CFQ default on insertion is (:oq - :delq);

We have stayed with the convention that we introduced in Chapter 6 by using :line.ono and :oq to indicate the *current* value of ONo in the ORDERS table and the *current* value of OQ.

It remains to give examples for relationship definition:

Relationship (places)
Where owner is CUSTOMER,
    Member degree is none or more,
    CUSTOMER deletion is not allowed where member ORDERS exist
    Member is ORDERS via CNo,
    ORDERS membership is mustbe;

Relationship (includes)
Where owner is ORDERS,
    Member degree is one or more,
    ORDERS deletion deletes member LINE,
    Member is LINE via ONo,
    LINE membership is mustbe;

Relationship (is ordered in)
Where owner is PRODUCT,
   Member degree is none or more,
   PRODUCT deletion is not allowed where member LINE exist,
   Member is LINE via PNo,
   LINE membership is mustbe;

We must comment first on the clause 'Member degree is none or more'. This is exactly the same in its effect as 'Ownership is maybe'. The reason that we prefer our version is that it does additionally allow us to declare that a relationship is one-to-one, or even in the case of 'has parents' that it is one-to-two.

Both 'ODate default on insertion is SystemDate' and 'CUSTOMER deletion is not allowed where member ORDERS exist' are *transition integrity rules*. This does conflict with the schema we declared for integrity rules, but frankly we should like to show all transition rules as table rules if we can devise a way of expressing them. Perhaps we should provide for 'Additional transition integrity rules' that we can't fit into the table rules! We shall return to rule definition in Chapter 10.

7.8 'Views' and local data models

If a data model describes the basic information which is available within a particular system boundary, then it follows that we don't need all that information for every application which the system supports, and that we may prefer to have the information presented in a different way. In particular, we may wish to:

Prevent a user from seeing or even knowing about information that he or she doesn't need.
Preserve the names and definitions of data objects seen by a user, even though the database has been changed.
Combine data from different tables to produce a report.
Calculate summary statistics based on the available information.

The mechanism which we use in the SQL language is the *view*. We shall describe views in terms of data tables, rather than entity types. The simplest form of the view is a table which includes only *some of* the rows and columns in a database *base table*. In that sense every table we have referred to in this chapter is a view, since we have never suggested that we were presenting all the attributes that might be contained in a database.

A view may be restricted to only some of the rows in a base table. Thus it might be an abstract from the STUDENT table for those students whose Course Number is C32. The names of columns included in a view may be changed.

We use the style for view creation adopted by the SQL language:

```
Create view STUD (SName, CNumber)
as Select StudentName, CourseNumber
   from STUDENT
   where CourseNumber = 'C32';
```

The table STUD, with the two columns 'SName' and 'CNumber', doesn't actually exist in the database but it can be referred to or invoked by a user in exactly the same way as a base table such as STUDENT.

'STUD' as we have defined it can only participate in the 'enrols' relationship of our college data model, because that is the only foreign key in the view. A data model involving views will therefore probably be different from one which just relates to base tables. From this we get the concept of the *local data model* as the data model seen by one application.

A view can be defined across more than one base table, and thus include a group of attributes which are not in any one base table:

STUD (SName, CourseName, CounsellingTutorName)

A view may include statistics derived from data in several base tables:

STUD (SName, CourseName, AverageAssessmentMark, StandardDeviationOfMark)

This is particularly useful if we are concerned with a local data model describing the management information required for controlling a real-world system.

Whether a table is a base table or a view, the *owner* of that table can grant privileges to any other user to *select* the table in order to read the data; to *update* the table; to *delete* data in the table; and, if the owner so wishes, to grant those same privileges to other users. What the Lord has given, the Lord can take away; and the owner has the ability to revoke any of the privileges that have been granted.

7.9 Data analysis

Writers have suggested that there are at least three different ways of setting about data analysis. The first of these is the *bottom-up* approach. This requires that the analyst goes around the organization collecting every single piece of information; every field on a form; every column in a report; every attribute of stored data; every individual aspect of a message. Next, the analyst must look for dependencies. We discussed what is meant by one attribute *depending on* another attribute when we described normalization. As a result, the analyst can identify entity type sets of attributes, each set depending on a single primary key. Finally, the analyst must look for relationships between the entity types. We've said in several places that the relationships express the structural framework of the system. If you read the English sentences in any of the data models in this chapter you will follow our meaning.

'Bottom-up' sounds elegant, but there is surely a danger of postponing any benefits to be gained from system design indefinitely. By the time the analyst feels able to construct a sensible global data model the world about him will probably have changed.

The second approach to data analysis is *synthesis*. The analyst concentrates on functional analysis and develops a local data model describing the data required by each separate application. These local data models are then synthesized into a single *global data model*.

'Synthesis' is the method of sub-optimization. It supposes that applications developed independently of each other as isolated islands of mechanization are then merged into a coherent whole. It doesn't take account of the truth that the data resource of any organization is the most effective integrating framework for that organization.

The third approach is *top-down*. This is the most realistic approach, and it has consistently been our approach in this book. We have suggested that an analyst should use a data flow diagram as a record of *what a system does*. This is sharpened by the preparation of logical DFDs. That part of the analysis process is *functional analysis*. Parallel to this is the process of *data analysis*. This requires that the analyst identifies the basic types of things about which we want information. The end result is a data model telling us *what the system remembers*.

Identifying a list of basic types of things first of all requires *abstraction*. There is no possibility that the full richness of the real world can be captured by the data model. The analyst must try to distil the essential parts out of the whole scene. Essential to what? Really it has to be essential to 'what the system is for'; which, of course, fudges the distinction between data analysis and functional analysis! You may list a different set of basic types of things if you view an organization as a social system rather than as a technical or economic one.

A list of basic types also requires *generalization*. Three people are three different entities. One may listen to Beethoven and belong to the Boy Scouts of America; another prefers board sailing and heavy metal; the third spends her time canvassing for the Prodigal political party. Once you call them all PERSON, or STUDENT, then you prescribe the profile for each one of them. We could generalize some individual people as MALE STUDENT and others as FEMALE STUDENT. This is justified if *the things we want to know about them* are different for male and female students. If they are not, then defining two different entity types is pointless.

There is an acid test of whether or not you have correctly identified an entity type. Can you list a set of attributes for that entity type; and can you pick out one or more attributes as a key, with all the understanding of what the key of a normalized entity type is? You should be able to see the chosen entity type name as a heading for a table and the attribute names as headings for the columns of the table. If two different entity types both have the same key, or if the two keys are dependent on each other, then you need to ask whether you are really dealing with two entity types or whether it is perhaps one.

You will often perceive that reality is better expressed as a hierarchy, or tree, of entity types. We believe that you should do this only if there is something different that you want to know about each level in the tree. If you are going to define a hierarchy, you must be able to define a hierarchical key.

Once you have a list of basic entity types, it is time to make the structural statements which define the framework of the system. In each case, this will involve an entity type name as a sentence subject, a relationship name which predicates something about the subject, and an entity type name as a sentence object.

Making the structural statements may require *aggregation*, or grouping of entity types together to make entity super-types (which, conversely, could be decomposition into entity sub-types). The requirement would arise from the desire to predicate something about only *some* of the entities of an entity type.

For some of the relationships which you define you will see a need to define attributes of that relationship. This will involve defining relationship entity types.

Let's suppose there is a need for a system enabling a firm of software suppliers to manage and control their development projects. The *external entities* on the DFD are likely to include clients, analysts (doing the actual job of development) and the managers of the design process needing information about how everything is progressing.

The list of basic entity types about which we want information overlaps this list more than a little. It must include clients, contracts with clients, analysts, and the computers or other devices on which development work takes place. Some of these require fairly constant stores of information (clients and contracts). Some are resources (analysts and computers). For any resource the managers want to know how much of the resource has been committed to any specific task and when it is committed.

The process of data analysis and functional analysis cannot operate independently for ever. Periodically, there must be reconciliation between them. This may make it necessary to go back and do something again. Both processes are iterative.

Both functional analysis and data analysis should progress as top-down. Once the inputs and outputs to and from a function have been identified, once a significant part of the data needs have been modelled, development of that function and that part of the global database can continue. Benefits can be gained progressively instead of being postponed until the arrival of a new Jerusalem, when all the analysis is finished.

Construction of any function, or of any part of the database, increases our knowledge of the total system. As work progresses our perception of what we are trying to do will change. We will be totally sure what we are building after we have built it!

Data analysis is not an activity with a short planning horizon. The data resource is as significant as any other corporate resource. The ability of the organization to thrive in the future may depend on the quality of the data planning that is done now.

7.10 Summary

- We are not repeating the data-modelling conventions described in Section 2.7.2.
- The key integrity rule states that no null values are permitted in any attribute of a candidate key.
- A binary relationship can be identified by two names, one for each direction of the relationship. We give preference to a name which predicates something in the one-to-many direction.
- The ownership and membership rules specify whether rows in both owner and member tables may be linked to those in other tables by the relationship, or must be linked to rows in other

tables by the relationship. We accept suitable marking conventions for the ERA diagrams to show these rules.

- The relationship integrity rule requires that any entity which is referred to must exist.
- We will not normally show foreign keys on data models.
- Many-to-many relationships, whether binary or non-binary, commonly possess attributes. Display of these attributes requires identification of a relationship entity type interposed between the entity types involved in the relationship.
- We identify by a dotted underline key attributes in a relationship entity type, or in a tree, which do not relate to primary keys in other entity types.
- A thing is different from the name of that thing.
- Some features of reality may be represented as either
    Different entity types, or
    Different relationships between entity types.
- Some features of reality may be represented as either
    Different entity types, or
    Attributes of entity types.
- An arc represents a situation where two entity types are related by more than one relationship, and a particular entity is only allowed to belong to one of those relationships.
- An entity type may include entities with differing relationships with other entity types. This requires identification of type hierarchies, with sub- and super-entity types.
- We can represent reality as lists, cycles or trees.
- Normalization requires us to represent first, second, third or fourth normal form. Up to third normal form the normalization can be summarized as:
    Non-key attributes depend on the key, the whole key, and nothing but the key.
- Attributes and table columns may be defined as belonging to domains. A domain is a defined list of values which can legitimately be inserted into any column which belongs to that domain. Domain integrity rules define these sets of values.
- Table integrity rules specify constraints imposed on values of an attribute either because of that attribute's role as part of a table or because of a relationship with other data objects outside the table of immediate interest.
- Many of the constraints can conveniently be displayed on a data model diagram.
- An abstract of a database table which is appropriate for one particular task, or to which access can be granted to a particular group of users, is a view.

- A local data model is the part of the database which is appropriate to one particular function. Such a model could well consist of one or several views.
- The activity of data analysis can be tackled in a variety of ways. Our preference is for a top-down approach. We believe that most people who are familiar with a problem area can identify the classes of things about which information is needed.

Discussion points

7.1 We attempt to capture more meaning in our data models by marking diagrams to show ownership and membership rules, sub-types, relationship entity types and arcs. By doing this we risk losing the simplicity of expression which so helps understanding. Discuss the merits of this attempt to capture meaning.

7.2 A data model, complete with domain integrity rules and table integrity rules, presents a static model of reality. How serious a handicap is this in attempting to model reality?

7.3 Would you say that two different analysts, attempting to model the same situation, would be expected to arrive at similar data models?

7.4 'A data model represents reality; it also represents the database stored in a computer's data store. The model maps one realm to the other. Additionally, the data model records the retrieval access paths which are available within a database.' Discuss this statement.

Exercises

7.1 Produce a set of tables formatting the data in the following description:

John Smith is a farmer. He farms 350 acres with a mixed product. The farm is called 'Prospect', a name given by John's grandfather when he bought the land in 1920.

The farm has recently given a steadily expanding profit. It was £10 500 in 1984; $10 700, £11 000, £11 700, in 1985, 1986 and 1987. In 1988 and 1989 profit was almost steady at £11 750 and £11 730.

The stockman, Jim Purvis, is the only full-time employee. He lives with his wife in a tied cottage on the farm. Unsurprisingly, it's called 'Rose Cottage'. Jane Purvis is a full-time worker too. All her time is spent on the cottage, on Jim and on their 6-month-old baby Sarah.

John Smith is married to Sue Smith. She's a potter, and also owns her own business, based at the farm. She set it up ten years ago under the name 'Quality Pots'. Presently, she has reached an output of some 500 ovenware pots a year. Things haven't been easy, with losses of £1500, £500 and £250 over the three years to last year. In 1989 it was better, with a profit of £1300.

Sue employs two people part time. They are a childless married couple named Chris and Mavis Jones. They live in the neighbouring village of Ercwell.

Sue doesn't have much chance to get bored, because she raises and markets the turkeys on Prospect Farm.

Mark Smith is fifteen, and Emma Smith is twelve. They are John and Sue's only children. Emma is interested only in school and horses, but Mark does a daily newspaper round for Vic Toogood, the newsagent in Ercwell. Mark delivers all the newspapers to people who live in the village itself. The job seems fairly safe because Toogood gets a steady income of about £5000 from the business to meet his bachelor costs. He's been trading ever since he finished his National Service in 1957, and he's not looking for a move. Apart from Mark, his widowed mother Ellen helps with the business.

Draw a data model diagram representing the situation.

7.2 A travel agency keeps a record of all tours which it organizes, including the state of payment account for each potential traveller. Additionally, a mailing list is kept of people who have in the past, or may in the future, make bookings for a tour.

A tour involves a particular airline, one or more than one hotel, one or more than one resort, a particular country in which the resorts are situated, and perhaps a particular bus operator. Each of these entities possesses its own characteristic attributes.

The travel agency has a policy of periodically reviewing performance by airline, hotel, resort, country and bus operator. They also review by time of year. A satisfactory tour will normally be repeated the following year. If there are unsatisfactory features, then the records kept should help to correct the problems.

The data recorded for each entity also make it possible to prepare accurate publicity brochures very quickly.

Draw a data model representing this situation.

References

1. William Kent, *Data and Reality,* North-Holland, Amsterdam (1971)
2. S. M. Deen, A database case stuoy on a sheep-breeding project, based on a database implemented by Stephen Knowles and others of Aberdeen University Computing group for a research group of J. B. Owen in the School of Agriculture at Aberdeen University
3. The M352 course – Computer based information systems, Block 2 – conceptual modelling, Open University (1980)
4. S. M. Deen, Comments at the First British National Conference on Database (1982)
5. C. J. Date, *Introduction to Database Systems,* Vol. 2, Addison-Wesley, Reading, Mass. (1985)
6. J. M. Smith and D. C. P. Smith, 'Database abstractions: aggregation and generalisation', *ACM TODS,* **2,** No. 2, June (1977)
7. M. Hammer and D. McLeod, 'The semantic data model: a conceptual data modelling mechanism', in *Advances in Database Management,* edited by T. A. Rullo, Heyden, London (1980)
8. D. S. Bowers, *From Data to Database,* Van Nostrand Reinhold, Wokingham (1988)
9. C. W. Bachman, 'Data structure diagrams', *ACM SIGBDP Journal,* **1,** No. 2, March (1969)
10. ANSI/X3/SPARC Study group on database management systems: Interim report', *ACM SIGMOND Bulletin,* **7,** No. 2 (1975)
11. P. P. Chen, 'The entity-relationship model: towards a unified view of data', *ACM TODS,* **1,** No. 1 (1976)
12. ANSI/X3/SPARC Study group on database management systems: Framework report on database management systems, AFIPS (1978)
13. C. W. Bachman and Daya, 'The role concept in data models', *Proceedings of the Third International Conference on VLDB* (1977)

Chapter 8

How the system behaves

8.1 An overview

In this chapter we will discuss the technology of collecting data, getting it into a computer, spelling out to the computer what should happen to the data, and storing and retrieving data as necessary. In general, the requirements are that we should be able to give a label to a data object (whether the data object be a set of records, one particular data item, or a program which we wish to use); that we should be able either to retrieve the data object or to put it somewhere where we will be able to find it later; that we should be able to do what we have to do with that data object (use it, update it, delete it, or display it for people to see); that we should be able to do this sufficiently quickly to be useful (*the response time*); that while we're doing all this we preserve the *integrity* and accuracy of the database; and that we should organize our management of the database in such a way that we get through all the business we have to (*the throughput*).

We shall need to look briefly at the collection of data. It's a field which changes very rapidly, and we'll stick to general principles rather than specific techniques. We shall also need to look at *system state*. If we want to conduct a transaction with a computer system, it must be *in a state in which it can listen to our request*. It's no use dialling a telephone number on a pay-telephone if it's actually asking us to put money in. It's no use telling the cash dispenser in the bank how much money we want, when it's asking for our account number. In neither case will the system understand the language we're using. It will either go on asking for what it wants or it will give up and start ignoring us!

We shall need to look at the organization of the data store. We list below the aspects that we are going to cover:

1. General principles of data collection;
2. The different system states of a batch-processing application. This can be displayed as a *run-chart*;

3. The way that data are organized in a data store for a batch-processing application;
4. The different system states of a demand-processing application (often called *dialogue design*);
5. The ways that data can be organized in a data store for a demand-processing application.

8.2 Data collection

Our starting point is the assertion that data relate to some *event*. Someone has completed a repair job; one person has purchased something from another; a production schedule has been produced; a student's exam script has been marked; a coil of steel has been moved from one location to another; a solicitor has held an interview with a client; radioactive gas has escaped.

We expect that the data relating to this event should be transferred into the computer data store as quickly as convenient, with the minimum amount of transcription from one medium to another. The more often data are copied, the higher will be the cost of data collection, and the higher the chance of corruption of the data.

'Once upon a time' data relating to any event were written on a piece of paper. The piece of paper was gathered together with other pieces of paper into an *input batch*. The whole batch of documents was taken to a *data preparation* room where the data were transferred to punched cards using key-punching machines. Finally, the cards were put into a card-reading machine to input the data to the computer.

Usually, before the punched cards were input to the computer they were put through another keyboard machine for *verification*. The verification operator typed the same key strokes from the same source document, to ensure that the data on the piece of paper had been correctly transposed onto punched card. Quite often, the key punch machine was effectively a small computer, with a capacity to be programmed. This meant that the key punch was capable of performing some validity tests on the data and rejecting blatantly wrong input.

Today, the same task is still widely performed. It is more likely that the key strokes made by the operator will record data directly onto magnetic disc or tape. Often many workstations will be linked to one processor, which is capable of storing the input data onto magnetic disc or tape. The processing power is many times greater than was the case with card-punching machines and more complex checks on the validity of the data are possible. Batches of data can still be verified, but the verifier's key strokes will be compared against data *already in a computer data store*. When a batch of data is complete and verified, it can be output onto a disc

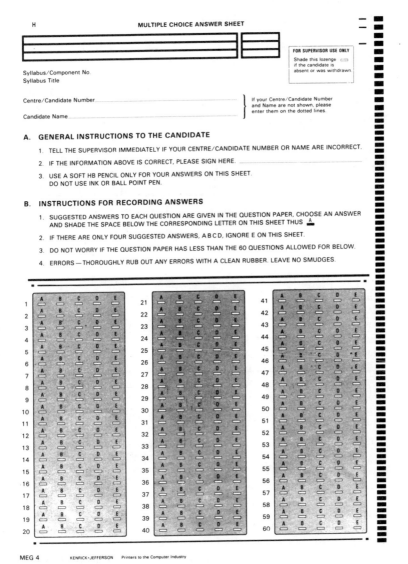

Figure 8.1 Optical Mark Reading (Courtesy of Southern Universities' Joint Board)

or tape and the data batch can then be input to the 'mainframe computer'.

One refinement to the system just described is that documents are not necessarily sent to the data-preparation room. The data-preparation desk may be in the user's office, remotely connected to the data-preparation computer. This gives us *Remote Batch Entry*.

For a very long time people have attempted to by-pass the data-preparation keyboard. *Optical Mark Reading* (OMR – Figure 8.1), *Optical Character Recognition* (OCR – Figure 8.2) and *Magnetic Ink Character Recognition* (MICR – Figure 8.3) attempt to eliminate all or part of the need for using a keyboard to transfer data from a piece of paper to a medium which can be read directly by a computer.

Figure 8.2 Optical Character Recognition

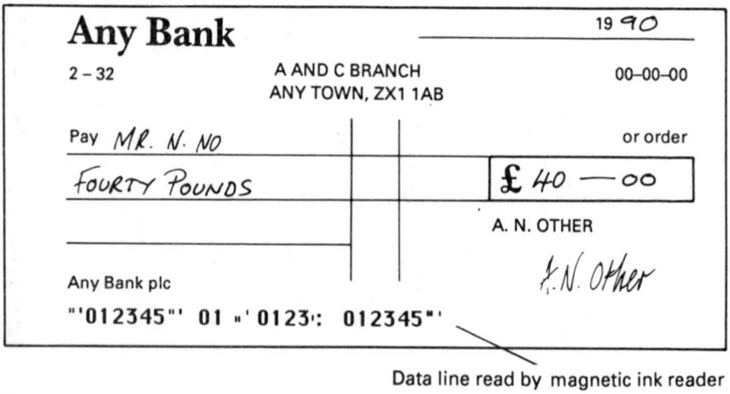

Figure 8.3 Magnetic Ink Character Recognition

All this time there has been enthusiasm for a device which can read handwriting. There has been some success, but perhaps the problem has become rather *passé*. Today, many people are happy to key data with a portable keyboard rather than write it on a piece of paper. There has been much success in going right back to the data-producing event itself to record the data. Finally, work is being done to allow a person to *talk* directly to a computer.

Let's look at progress in getting back to the data-producing event. The most straightforward is perhaps using sensors to record temperature changes, machine movements or weights (Figure 8.4). *Bar codes* (Figure 8.5) have allowed movements of lorries,

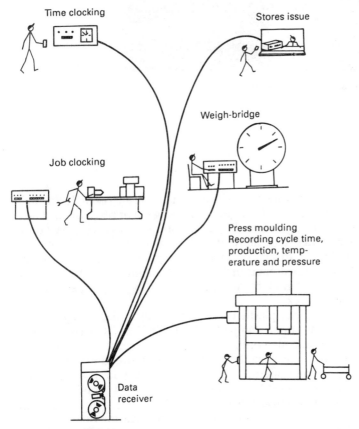

FACTORY DATA COLLECTION

Time clocking

Stores issue

Weigh-bridge

Job clocking

Press moulding
Recording cycle time,
production, temp-
erature and pressure

Data
receiver

Figure 8.4 Recording changes in the state of the system

Figure 8.5 The use of bar codes to record movement past a scanner

railway waggons and pieces of machinery on an assembly line to be identified and recorded as the lorry, waggon or piece of machinery passes a sensing device. Bar codes printed on grocery packets or retailers' price tags allow data for sales analysis and for stock replenishment to be collected at the *point of sale* as goods are purchased by customers at the cash till (Figure 8.6). The reading of the bar code can be by a fixed sensor or by a 'light pen' brushed over the display.

The ubiquitous plastic card can carry data identifying a person or an object, either stamped onto the card in OCR characters or bar code or encoded onto a magnetic strip on the card. By putting a card into a card reader, data can be recorded about a *person* (with a personal identifying card) borrowing a *book* (again with an identifying card) from a library (Figure 8.7); obtaining money from a cash dispenser; or using a credit card to make a purchase. Again, a hand-held reading pen can be used for reading instead of a fixed sensor.

Figure 8.6 Point-of-sale data collection by bar codes

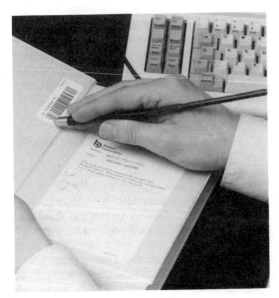

Figure 8.7 Bar codes used in borrowing a book from a library

Whether the point of data capture is a person using a keyboard, an automatic temperature sensor or a plastic card being pushed into a card reader, there is a range of possibilities about the response that the system gives. At one extreme the data may simply be passively collected into a batch for subsequent input to a computer. At the other extreme the terminal reading the data may be connected directly to the database being updated. If this is the case then any inconsistency or exception reports which arise can be reported back to the terminal immediately, and the data corrected while the situation still exists.

The intermediate situation is that a certain amount of consistency checking is performed immediately (ensuring that a valid user number and password has been offered, for example) and the data then added to a batch to be processed at some later time. Possibly an immediate *data retrieval* response may be given (valid Personal Identity Number and card number and a report on the cash balance in the bank account, for example), but *updating* of the bank account may be postponed until after the close of business for the day.

We've said quite a lot about collection of data with subsequent batch processing. *Demand processing* assumes that a user requires a response from the system within a short period (seconds or milliseconds). If you want to find out your bank account balance from a cash dispenser machine you will initiate the *transaction* by pushing your cashpoint card into the card reader. A large area of data collection for demand processing involves a user conducting a *dialogue* with a computer system via a keyboard and a screen. The dialogue may be conducted in words or it may be in graphic symbols such as those used by architects and engineers when they design a structure (Computer Integrated Manufacturing System, or Computer Aided Design and Computer Aided Manufacture). We shall return to dialogue design later in this chapter.

Summarizing, then, a transaction is a sequence of actions initiated by some event or by a desire for information. If it is simply a desire for information, then the transaction is concerned with *data retrieval*. If an event is to be recorded and all the consequent actions taken, then the transaction is about *updating* (which includes *inserting* new data, *deleting* redundant data and *amending* existing data). A group of transactions may be collected into a batch for batch processing at some later and convenient time; or there may be a requirement for demand processing, giving a response within a short period. This section has described the collection of data about the event which initiates a transaction.

8.3 Updating serial tables by batch processing

Let's return to our cub-scout sports day. The cub-scout table looked like Figure 8.8. Clearly, a real table for a sports day would have many more entries than this, so we have shown just a part of the cub-scout table. Now let's suppose that there are some amendments to this table:

Simon Birch's date of birth is wrong; it should be 12-Aug-81.
Jason Hewitt is going on holiday, and won't be at the sports.
Jason is going to be replaced by William Clarke.
William's birthday is 27-Dec-81, and he is also 25th Bath.

We could prepare a transaction table holding the new data (Figure 8.9). If we are keeping these data in *serial files* then we need to merge the transaction table with the original cub-scout table. Don't worry about the use of the word 'file'. Traditionally, a data store has been described as a file. We shall treat 'table' and 'file' as synonymous.

A serial file is a file in which every record is written immediately after the one before it. To get at any record on the file, you have to start at the beginning of the file and work through all the records until you get to the one you want. We shall treat a record and a

CUB SCOUT TABLE		
Cub-Scout Name	Date Of Birth	Pack Name
John Bates	3-Apr-82	2nd Bath
Simon Birch	12-Sep-81	2nd Bath
James Cumming	5-Dec-80	15th Bath
Jason Hewitt	12-Jan-82	25th Bath

Figure 8.8 The cub-scout data table

CUB-SCOUT TRANSACTION TABLE			
Cub-Scout Name	Type Of Transaction	Date Of Birth	Pack Name
Simon Birch	Update	12-Sep-81	Unchanged
Jason Hewitt	Deletion	-	-
William Clarke	Insertion	27-Dec-81	25th Bath

Figure 8.9 The cub-scout transaction table

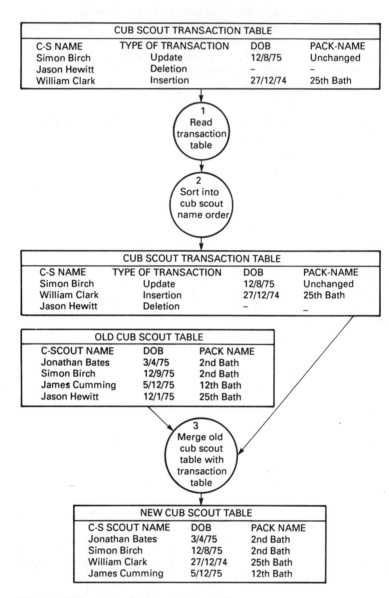

Figure 8.10 The cub-scout table-updating run chart

row of a table as synonymous. This means that you would have to start reading a serial table at the top row and read down until you reach the row you want.

The important thing to realize is that at the end of the updating process the *old cub-scout table*, the *new cub-scout table*, the *cub-scout transaction table* and the *sorted cub-scout transaction table* all separately exist. This means that if, for any reason, the new cub-scout table is found to be corrupted, or if the process fails before the new table is produced, the whole process can be repeated again from scratch. Traditionally, three versions of any table are kept:

The *grandparent table*;
The *parent table*; and
The *child table*.

Thus if the worst comes to the worst, we can go back to the last but one version of the table and do all the processing again to produce an up-to-date table.

A description of this process, such as that shown in Figure 8.10, is usually called a run-chart. Since the whole of the table which is going to be amended is processed together as a batch, we can call it batch processing.

Clearly each function bubble in Figure 8.10 can be enlarged into a rule. We'll develop function 2, 'sort into cub-scout name order'. There are many different sorting algorithms. The one we'll describe is laborious in processing, but doesn't require any extra tables to be created. 'Less than' or '<' implies that a name comes earlier than other names in the ordinary alphabetic sequence that you would find in a telephone directory. The sorting function finishes when all the rows in the table are arranged in cub-scout name order (Figure 8.11).

Number all the rows in the table from 1 to n.
Repeat while the value of a variable CHANGE is not equal to 'NO':
  Set CHANGE equal to 'NO'
  Set a variable i equal to 1
  Repeat while i < n:
    If the ith cub-scout name > the (i+1)th cub-scout name:
    Then
      Swop the ith row and the (i+1)th row
      Re-number rows so that the (i+1)th row is after the ith row
      Set CHANGE equal to 'YES'
      Increase the value of i by 1

Figure 8.11 A specification for a sorting function

8.4 Organization of data for batch processing

Necessarily, we need to organize data in a data table in such a way that we can easily retrieve particular data objects. The data table must have an *addressing structure*, just as the houses we live in all have postal addresses and an addressing structure which enable the postman to find the house.

In the previous section we looked at a run-chart describing a typical example of batch processing. We didn't simply add new data onto the end of the table. If we did that it would make data retrieval very difficult. Imagine updating a telephone directory by putting the new name at the end!

For any data table which is going to be updated with batches of transactions, one attribute, or a group of attributes, is selected as a key. The key of the cub-scout table is 'cub-scout name'. The key of the contestant table in Figure 2.3 is the 'race-number' and the 'cub-scout-name' taken together. Whether the data are arranged in ascending or descending sequence of the key is a matter of convenience. We are used to an alphabetic sequence from A to Z. We know where in that sequence any letter occurs. That is why, to take an obvious example, telephone directories are organized in alphabetic sequence of the subscriber's surname, with subsidiary sequencing on initials.

It doesn't matter whether the key is alphabetic or numeric. What does matter is that the sequence can be understood by a user or by a program updating the data table.

8.5 Dialogue design

Section 8.3 introduced the run-chart to describe the batch-processing way of updating tables. A run-chart specifies the way that the system changes status as processing progresses. Today a very large number of applications rely on processing of data immediately after a transaction occurs, with a rapid response from the information system. Booking air flights, consulting stock records, checking a customer's credit status all require that an answer be given immediately. The general label that we can put on this is demand processing.

Just as the run-chart describes the changing state of a batch-processing system, so we can speak of dialogue design for demand processing. Both the run-chart and the dialogue specify the changes of state of the computer system in its relationship with the outside world. It's likely (but not essential) that this dialogue will be conducted by a person sitting in front of a *terminal*, with a keyboard and a display screen (VDU). We shall return to the question of dialogue in Chapter 13, as a part of the whole question of Human–Computer Interaction (HCI). Essentially, we are speaking of the design of *information windows* by which information is passed between a person and a computer, and of the sequencing of these information windows[2,3].

Let's start by ignoring the constrains of current technology and by saying what we would like to do. This would surely be that we should like to treat the computer as we would an intelligent, completely reliable assistant. The relationship of the televison hero, Doctor Who, and his tame computer, K9, was affectionate and cooperative (subject to occasional sulks from K9 when his good advice was questioned!).

Whether the dialogue is by aural conversation or by use of a keyboard and VDU screen, the objects of the dialogue are still the same. We may wish to:

Locate and *retrieve* a particular data object in store;
Update a data object with new information;
Insert new data in such a way that we can later retrieve them;
Delete a data object already in store;
Use stored data and new data to reach a new conclusion.

Common in all these objectives is the need to locate the position of a data object in store using some addressing system. The difficult problem is to signal to the computer what data object it's looking for!

8.5.1 Natural language dialogue

This book is not the right place to discuss the problems of spoken communication between a person and a computer. We're going to discuss briefly the problems of using natural language, without worrying about whether that language is spoken or typed on a keyboard. We shall be ignoring the problems of homonyms (words that sound the same) and of different accents. We will discuss dialogue under just two headings, 'syntax' and 'semantics'.

Starting with *syntax*, generally, the more freedom a person is given to structure statements in an idiosyncratic way, the more difficult it will be to *parse* the statements and to program a computer to extract meaning and make appropriate responses. Fluidity and literary style are normally at odds with precision of meaning[2].

Conversation between two people is possible because they have a shared culture. If words are omitted, or are arranged in an unusual way, most of us are able to fill in the gaps. We are able to interpret the meaning of phrases even if they are considerably distorted and truncated. We can even get some fun from working out the meaning of the misprints in our favourite daily newspaper.

In order to do this it's necessary that we *understand meaning*. This is more than simply making appropriate responses. Weizenbaum[15] gives an example of a dialogue with the ELIZA system. The computer is programmed to recognize certain words and phrases and make programmed responses. The dialogue reported by Weizenbaum is between a young woman and a computer:

Woman: 'Men are all alike.'

The computer recognizes nothing and makes no response.

Woman: 'They're *always* bugging us about something.'

The computer recognizes 'always' and responds:

Computer: 'Can you give me a specific example?'
Woman: 'Well, *my* boyfriend made *me* come here.'

The computer recognizes 'my' and 'me', and repeats the statement in the second person:

Computer: '*Your* boyfriend made *you* come here.'
Woman: 'He say's *I'm depressed* much of the time.'

The computer recognizes 'I'm' as a state declaration and 'depressed' as bad. Its response is then:

Computer: 'I'm sorry to hear you're depressed.'

In experiments, people like the woman in the example behaved as if they were talking to an intelligent companion. In fact they were misled by receiving appropriate responses. In no way can ELIZA be said to have *understood* what it was being told. The response given by the computer is totally dependent on what the person has said.

Thompson[16] describes the DEACON military retrieval system[17]. This uses a set of rules to parse *and process* a retrieval request. For example:

'WHO IS THE COMMANDER OF THE 638TH BATTALION?'

In the DEACON system, words are classified in the system dictionary as *ring words* and *function words*. The ring words contain information defining the entities included in a search request. The function words define the processing required:

'WHO IS THE COMMANDER OF THE 638TH BATTALION?'
  F .F F   R   F F R   R   F

A set of rules which enables a search request to be parsed and responded to is specified by the system dictionary:

*'BATTALION' has a grammatical rule: $R1 + R2 \rightarrow R1$

                  Name of battalion   'Battalion'

Thus the result of the rule is:

'WHO IS COMMANDER OF THE 638TH?'

*'THE' $+ R \rightarrow R1$

Thus:

'WHO IS COMMANDER OF 638TH?'

*'COMMANDER' has a grammatical rule: $R1 + $'OF'$ + R2 \rightarrow R3$

     'Commander' A ring phrase or value Associated value

The result of the rule is:

'WHO IS JONATHAN M. PARKER?'

*Finally, 'WHO IS' $+ R + $'?'$ \rightarrow R$

Thus:

'JONATHAN M. PARKER.'

becomes the system's response to the search request.

The DEACON example given by Thompson does illustrate the requirements for talking to computers:

1. There must be a limited number of parsing rules. Thus the language used can allow only a limited number of relationships between words.
2. Only words included in the dictionary can be used. These words will therefore be unambiguous.
3. Each word must be distinctly stated. If speech is being used for the dialogue, there should be a clear gap between carefully articulated words.

The second requirement emphasizes the importance of *semantics*[4], or the meaning of words. Compare the meaning of 'looking for' in the following sentences:

'I am looking for the post office.'
'I am looking for a wife.'

or the meaning of 'nowhere' or 'anybody':

'Nowhere is more attractive than Bath.'
'We are on the road to nowhere.'
'Is there anybody at home?'
'Anybody can come to the party.'

8.5.2 Restricted dialogue

Because of these syntactic and semantic problems, the current approach to dialogue design adopts various devices to resolve any ambiguity in a search request or in a request to store or update data. Necessarily, the dialogue must establish uniquely which data object is being referred to and also what is required to be done to that data object.

The help and support given by a computer to a terminal user must be appropriate to that user's amount of training, technical knowledge, frequency with which the user works at a terminal and variety of different terminal tasks done. An experienced and dedicated user would become impatient with an overly supportive and *User Friendly* dialogue. At the same time, many existing dialogues could be described as *User Hostile!*

'Help' to a terminal user can be a well-written manual or the ability to do something which causes some explanatory text to appear on the screen. In either case, the presumption is that if a user is stuck, and doesn't known what to do next, he can ask for a helping hand.

To start with, we're going to concentrate on locating a data object. Every dialogue must attempt this, whether the objective is retrieval of data, updating, or finding the correct location in which to insert new data. We'll start simply and go through increasing complexity of dialogue.

System prompts and simple responses
The assumption here is that the computer system issues a prompt, which effectively says 'I await your instructions, master!' It is the 'computer system' rather than 'the computer', because each software package will have its own prompt. The Primos operating system will prompt 'OK!'; VAX VMS operating system prompts '$'; the Oracle SQL*PLUS system prompts 'SQL>'.

The response of the user must be *in the language which the computer system understands and must use symbols and words which the computer system understands.* For example, the response to Microsoft's MS/DOS operating system prompt 'C:\' may be 'WS', telling the operating system that the user wishes to use the 'Word Star' word-processing system.

If the user gives a response which isn't in the computer systems dictionary and doesn't conform to the syntactic rules which the system expects, then *the response will not be understood.* The response may be a single phrase or a program-like statement, but it must be within the computer system's lexicon.

Let's start with the simplest dialogue, and suppose that the computer system looks for a one- or two-word response to its prompt. In all our examples the user's response is underlined (Figure 8.12).

A user might be able to specify alternative search keys in a response. For example, in a library retrieval system it is possible that a potential book borrower might be able to respond to the system prompt by typing either the author's name or the title of the book he is seeking. Either input should result in a list of the qualifying books from the computer. Alternatively, a user may be able to specify more than one search key (Figure 8.13).

WHAT SYSTEM DO YOU WANT TO USE? <u>SPORTS RESULTS</u>
GIVE THE NAME OF THE CONTESTANT? <u>JOHN SMITH</u>

NAME	JOHN SMITH
PACK NAME	25TH BATH
DATE OF BIRTH	10TH AUG 1975
FIRST IN UNDER 12,	100 METRES
SECOND IN UNDER 12,	HIGH JUMP

Figure 8.12 Dialogue with a simple prompt and simple answer

NAME OF BOOK?	<u>DATABASE DESIGN</u>
NAME OF AUTHOR?	<u>WIEDERHOLD</u>
CATALOGUE CODE IS	001.WIE
NUMBER OF COPIES AVAILABLE IS	TWO

Figure 8.13 Simple prompt with multiple keys given by user

Somewhat more complex, and still in the area of library retrieval, the user may be able to give more than one subject description, for example:

WHAT IS YOUR SUBJECT DESCRIPTION? *MING/ CERAMICS*

to specify an interest in ceramics of the Ming Dynasty.

It's possible that the computer system may allow redundant words which make the request more intelligible to people but which the system ignores:

*PLEASE GIVE ME THE **SALARY REPORT** FOR THOSE **PEOPLE** WITH A **SALARY GREATER THAN $20 000***

Only the phrases in bold type are significant in the dialogue.

Let's finish this sub-section by noting *concept keys*. Perhaps the user can tell the computer system what he wants to do next by pressing a particular keyboard key ('next record', 'enter a query', 'I want help!', for example).

System prompts and more complex responses
We are assuming here that a user can respond to a system prompt by making 'program-like' statements defining his search request. The search request to some hypothetical legal database may be framed as:

S/'coal miners'/1940/A/DIS

which might be a request to a legal database to display abstracts of statutes since 1940 relating to coal miners.

The LEXIS legal database system allows search requests which include several descriptors and also provides for several different kinds of connectors to link the descriptors together into one statment[5]. Thus:

—(nuisance W/7 common OR public W/10 abat!)AND WRITTENBY (Denning)

would search for a case description in which either the word 'nuisance' is within seven words of the word 'common' or the word 'public' is within 10 words of any word beginning with 'abat' (e.g. abatement, abating, etc.). The cases retrieved would only be those in which judgment was given by Lord Denning.

The response to the Oracle 'SQL' prompt must be a statement beginning with one of a limited number of words such as 'SELECT', 'INSERT', 'COLUMN', 'HELP', and conforming to the strict syntactic rules of the SQL language (Figure 8.14). This would extract the specified attributes about John Smith from the three tables in the cub-scout sports day database (Chapter 2).

```
SQL> SELECT PACK NAME, DATE OF BIRTH, EVENT NAME,
                                              POSITION
      FROM CUB SCOUT, SCHEDULED RACE, CONTESTANT
      WHERE CUB SCOUT NAME = 'JOHN SMITH'
      AND CUB SCOUT, CUB SCOUT NAME = CONTESTANT.
                                      CUB SCOUT NAME
      AND SCHEDULED RACE. RACE NUMBER = CONTESTANT.
                                        RACE NUMBER;
```

Figure 8.14 A search request to an 'ORACLE' database

Search requests on multiple levels
The LEXIS legal database (and other systems too!) allows a search request to be progressively refined. Thus the search request:

-privacy

may retrieve several hundred references, each including the word 'privacy'. The user would then treat this as the *level 1* search request, and refine it by further levels:

-AND inva! OR infringe!

This would select from those references already retrieved only those in which any word beginning with 'inva' or 'infringe' appears. The user adds different levels of search request until a suitably small number of references is obtained.

System prompts which specify the available responses
If the syntax and semantics of the dialogue are problems then one way to overcome them is for the computer system to specify the range of responses which it can understand. For example,

IF YOU WISH TO CONTINUE WITH THIS REPORT, PRESS THE SPACE BAR. IF YOU WISH TO RETURN TO THE OPERATING SYSTEM, PRESS THE Q KEY, FOR 'QUIT'!

A more general form of this is the device of *menu selection*[3]. When the computer system is looking for guidance on the next state to move to, it displays the choices (Figure 8.15). If a user selects item 1, he could then be presented with another screen, which also asks him to specify the next stage that is wanted (Figure 8.16).

The example shows that the selection is not necessarily based on a single menu. There can be a hierarchy of menus. If a user selects

THESE SERVICES ARE AVAILABLE

1. THE LIST OF SCHEDULED RACES
2. DETAILS OF THE CONTESTANTS
3. DISPLAY OF RACE RESULTS BY PACKS
4. SUMMARY OF FIRST, SECOND, THIRD, AND TOTAL POINTS

ENTER THE NUMBER OF THE SERVICE REQUIRED

Figure 8.15 Menu selection screen

SCHEDULED RACES

RACE NUMBER	EVENT NAME	HEAT NUMBER	ESTIMATED START TIME
1	under 9, 80m	1	2.10pm
2	under 9, 80m	2	2.15pm
3	under 9, 80m	3	2.20pm
4	under 9, 80m	4	2.25pm
5	under 10, 3 legged	1	2.30pm

IF YOU WISH TO VIEW THE NAMES OF CONTESTANTS IN ANY RACE, TYPE IN THE RACE NUMBER.

IF YOU WISH TO UPDATE THE LIST OF RACES, PRESS THE 'U' KEY.

IF YOU WISH TO RETURN TO THE MAIN MENU, PRESS THE SPACE BAR

Figure 8.16 Combined data display and menu selection

option 2, he may still have the choice of inserting new data, deleting old data or updating existing data.

The problem of how many choices to put on one menu, and whether to introduce a hierarchy of menus, is really about clarity. If a user has to choose one among as many as ten available options, there is a chance of confusion. In these circumstances it may be better to allow fewer, simpler choices, and to add further menus to achieve the discrimination down to the *right* data object.

Menu selection leads into *Videotex*. There are several versions, but common to all of them is the ability to search through a 'tree' of possible screens displayed on a television type monitor or VDU. At any level, the choices available in the next level are displayed and the user asked to specify the option preferred (Figure 8.17).

In *any* menu system the designer must never drop the user out of the system! At any level, the option should exist either of going up one level or returning to the main menu. If all selected processing

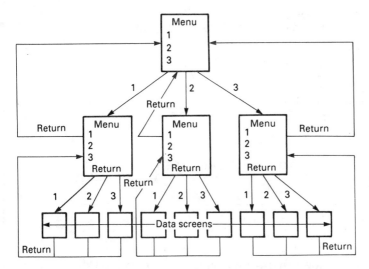

Figure 8.17 A state change diagram showing a hierarchy of selections

at any level has been completed, then again the computer system should return to the previous menu or to the main one. If a wrong response has been given by a user the system should give the user help in finding the correct response.

Figure 8.17, for obvious reasons of clarity, shows only a few of the possible return or error options. When the user himself wishes to sign off he should be given that choice on the main menu. Don't make the choice for him!

It's useful to combine the simple response to a prompt and menu selection. An example is a telephone directory system. The assumption is that the user is unsure of the proper spelling. The system produces a limited list, and the user then points (Figure 8.18).

A variation is the 'sounds like' list. If a user is unsure of a name, he may be given a list of candidate names which sound like his suggestion (for example, Brown, Browne, Braun, Braund).

In all the menu selection examples we've given we have provided for pointing to the required choice by specifying the row number. If the user's terminal is equipped with a light pen, it's possible for him to simply point to the option required. Alternatively, a user could 'point' to his chosen option by moving the screen *cursor* by means of cursor control keys or with a *mouse* attached to the terminal. Basically, what is required is that the user has a means of pointing to the selection he or she wants.

ENTER FIRST FOUR LETTERS OF THE REQUIRED NAME

>SZCZ

   1. SZCZECH, B.J.
   2. SZCZECH, Z.
   3. SZCZELKUN, A.
   4. SZCZELKUN, J.
   5. SZCZELTON, M.J.
   6. SZCZERBA, A.
   7. SZCZUTOWSKI, M.
   8. SZCZYGIELSKI, J.

ENTER THE NUMBER OF THE REQUIRED NAME OR THE
NUMBER WHICH ALPHABETICALLY PRECEDES THE REQUIRED
NAME.

Figure 8.18 A limited list, and the point

The selection by pointing still holds for the WIMP interface (*W*indows, *I*cons, *M*ouse, and *P*ulldown menus)[6]. The user can use the mouse to point to an icon (picture of a file) or a disc data store. The contents of that data store can be displayed in a window or overlay, either as a list or in icon form. As an example of an icon, the WIMP interface typically presents the 'delete' option as a picture of a dustbin. Again, a selection may be made by pointing with the mouse.

Input data and validation
Once we've found the required data object we may want to input new data (Figure 8.19). Concentrating on updating race details, it's appropriate that *one set of data is handled at one time*. In this example we would expect to input all the details of one race on one screen (Figure 8.20). Necessarily, we must provide for errors and for additional help. If the data which have been entered by a user are, for any reason, unacceptable, then an *exception report* must be given to the user. Briefly, this is a simple message, usually displayed either at the top or the bottom of the screen, telling the user what he has done wrong. Often there is a line on the screen set aside for exception reports, and that line isn't used for anything else.

A 'help' message is closely connected to the exception report. If a user is uncertain he may be able to press a 'help' key and have an explanatory message displayed in the exception report line. Alternatively, the help may be included in the text on the screen by adding format information (Figure 8.21). Again, the format

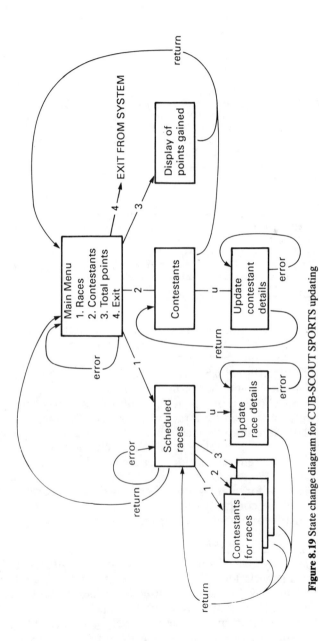

Figure 8.19 State change diagram for CUB-SCOUT SPORTS updating

```
            SCHEDULED RACE DATA
   RACE NUMBER            1
   EVENT NAME             UNDER 9, 80M
   HEAT NUMBER            2
   ESTIMATED START TIME   2.15 pm

   MOVE THE CURSOR FORWARD WITH THE TAB KEY, AND BACK
   WITH THE BACK TAB KEY. IF YOU WISH TO CHANGE ANY DATA
   MOVE THE CURSOR TO THE REQUIRED PLACE AND RE-TYPE.
   PRESS RETURN TO MOVE TO THE NEXT RACE RECORD; Q TO
   CANCEL THIS ENTRY; OR THE SPACE BAR TO RETURN TO THE
   LIST OF SCHEDULED RACES
```

Figure 8.20 A data input screen for scheduled races

```
   RACE NUMBER            9
   EVENT NAME             AAAAA 99,999'm'
   HEAT NUMBER            9
   ESTIMATED START TIME   99.99 A.A
```

Figure 8.21 Format data added to a screen

information may be superimposed on the space left for data entry, with the expectation that the data will be typed on the format.

Yet another possibility is that the user may be able to step through all the acceptable values which can be permitted at a particular entry point. When he gets to the one he wants he can confirm his choice. For example, a cub-scouts sports contestant could only be entered for a race which is actually being run.

One last point must be made. If we accept that we are going to handle the data which relate to one thing, on one screen, then we don't need different screens for inserting new data or for updating existing data. We should also be able to use the same screen layout for retrieval or for interrogation of existing data. What we need to do is to tell the computer system what we want to use the screen for, so that it can understand our messages.

'Query-By-Example' (QBE)
There is a number of similar systems; we are instancing QBE really as a generic term. In essence, the user is given a standard table format. This format can be used to define new tables and to add new data to already stored data tables[7].

The same table format is used for queries by the user typing examples of the data he is looking for on the standard table.

Search keys are typed into the appropriate columns and the database management system (DBMS) fills in the rest of the detail.

The system tries to get close to the way in which we might use a manually tabulated set of data. This gives it something in common with *spreadsheets*. The difference is that with a spreadsheet all the data are stored on a large matrix and the user can pan up and down and side to side on the matrix. His information window sees only part of the data at any one time. QBE, by contrast, is a system which allows the DBMS to identify the data object which the user requires, and then to do whatever the user wants.

More recent proposals[8] extend Query-By-Example to link database, word processing and electronic mail components of an integrated data-handling system.

Reports and documents

As a result of a dialogue between user and computer we can expect that either a report (summary of sales by sales people over the past quarter; list of cub-scout sports events with names of winners and second and third places) or a set of documents (customer invoices; wage advice slips; cub-scout sports certificates) will be produced. These reports and documents, and indeed the data input screens, are likely to be part of the requirements specified for the system but can also be seen as a part of the dialogue.

Reports may be displayed on the VDU screen or printed by the system printer. They may be in the form of tables or graphic displays of bar charts, 'pie' charts or any other pictorial representation of data. Documents will be printed on special stationery. Whatever medium is used, the same principles of clarity and good layout apply. There is a message to be put across, and the means of presenting that message should not get in the way.

8.5.3 Hybrid dialogues

We've mentioned natural language dialogue and restricted dialogue. The two are not incompatible. A restricted language is perhaps just a language with a very formal syntax.

Even with human conversation there are frequent misunderstandings which require explanation. We don't share a common culture with a computer! With any natural language dialogue we can expect that the computer will *reformulate the search request* and echo it back to the system user for *confirmation*. The reformulation will follow strict logical rules (first-order logic, for example) and must be unambiguous[9–13].

If the user rejects the formulation, or if the computer system is unable to interpret the user's meaning in the first place, then a *clarification dialogue* is required. We are back then with menu selection or pointing: 'Choose the interpretation which is closest to your meaning!' 'Closest' will still have to be refined to 'matches exactly'! As technical development stands at present, pointing systems appear to offer the most widely useful and user-friendly interfaces.

8.6 Organization of data for demand processing

The essential requirement of data organization is that a data object be stored in a place from which it can be retrieved when required. There must be an addressing system which facilitates this process. It does no harm to say that again.

Unlike the usual arrangement for batch processing, if a data table is to be updated on demand the table is updated *in situ*. It would take impossibly long to copy the whole of a large table every time one row in that table has to be changed. There are basically four methods of search:

1. Serial search
2. Sequential search
3. Indexing – which includes B trees
4. Hashing

8.6.1 Serial search

Serial search implies that the searcher starts at the beginning of a table and searches row by row through the table until he finds the required data object. It's unsophisticated, but, with a small set of data, may be the most sensible way of organizing those data. Most of us organize our address books with a separate page for each surname's initial letter. Within any one page we're unlikely to feel a need to put the names in any particular order.

It's possible that, with improvement of searching speeds, we should not concern ourselves with complicated addressing structures at all. If the time to search a whole table for desired data objects is sufficiently short, then we are not justified in carrying the overhead of an addressing structure designed to shorten it still further.

There is an updating advantage to serial search. If a new name is to be inserted we just add it on the end of the right page. Sequence is immaterial.

8.6.2 Sequential search

Sequential search requires that the data in the table be arranged in sequential order of a key. For example, cub-scouts may be arranged in ascending sequence of cub-scout name. The sequencing must be useful in isolating the desired data object.

Sequential search without using an index is not a usual means of retrieving data from a computer database. We might use it to search an alphabetically sequenced book catalogue by eye, to find a reference to a book by a particular author. A possible algorithm to guide this search could be a 'binary chop'. In Figure 8.22 we have specified 'median row or rows' simply because there may be an even number of rows in a data set.

Select the data set to be searched.
Until the required data object is found:

Find the median row or rows in the data set.
Note the key value of the median row, or values of median rows.
Select the case which applies:

Case 1: The median row contains the desired data object:
Carry out required processing and exit.
Case 2: The desired data object has a lower valued key:
Select the data set 'less than' the median row key.
Case 3: The desired data object has a higher valued key:
Select the data set 'more than' the median row key.

Report that the desired data object is not present.

Figure 8.22 Specification of a binary chop

It is unlikely that you would search a book catalogue by binary chop. If, for example, you know that the author's name begins with 'R', you will look for it about three quarters of the way through the catalogue. If you miss it, you will go a few pages forwards or backwards, and then try again.

Exercise
Can you write a specification for the search algorithm described?

8.6.3 Indexed searching

Essentially, the use of an index is a means of quickly reducing the size of the data set to be searched. The methods differ according to the density of indexing. If we have a low density, we require that the data table we are searching be sequentially ordered. This gives us an *index sequential* addressing structure. We quickly find an indexed row and then search sequentially until we find the row we want.

A telephone directory is a good example. The entries are in alphabetic sequence of surnames. The names in bold print at the top of a page tell us the first and last names on that page. These form an index to the directory.

The sequence doesn't have to be a physical sequence. In fact if we wish to have more than one *search key* for a table then the table cannot be in physical sequence of both these keys at the same time!

Figure 8.23 shows part of the cub-scout table. The names are physically arranged in cub-scout name order. There is also an index to cub-scout names. In addition, there is an index to pack-names, but the pack-name sequence can only be a *logical sequence*. Both cub-scout name and pack name can be indexed.

One clear advantage of logical sequencing is immediately obvious. Additions to the list of cub-scouts can be added to the end of the list and *chained in* by altering the 'next row number' pointer values. Since it may be time consuming to re-sort a list every time a new row is added, this gives an argument for always storing the 'next row number' for any key which is indexed. Overflow can then be accommodated until the next time the table is re-organized. Obviously, if you are using an index it's helpful to be able to follow a backward path through a sequence. This gives a case for storing the 'previous row number' as well.

Let's make a couple of qualifications. The first is that 'chaining-in' rows carries *high overheads of both storage and processing time*. Retrieval will be easier, at the expense of updating time, if updating alters the number of rows. If the number of rows changes quite frequently, it will be a mistake to index too many keys.

The second point is that 'row number', 'next row number' and 'previous row number' are not really part of the data. They are required only for manipulation of the data. Very probably, a database management system will perform this row-numbering task without the need for intervention by the system designer or user. Perhaps all the user has to do is to tell the DBMS to 'create an index'.

We can't leave indexed searching without mentioning *dense indexes* (Figure 8.24). Essentially, at least one index entry is made for every row in a data table.

Look at Figure 8.23. Let's suppose we have an index for 'date of birth', and for 'pack name'. Once the index has listed the

CUB-SCOUT TABLE				
Row number	Cub-scout name	Date of birth	Pack name	Next pack-name row number
1	John Bates	3-Apr-82	2nd Bath	2
2	Simon Birch	12-Sep-81	2nd Bath	13
3	James Cumming	5-Dec-80	15th Bath	8
4	Matthew Curley	3-Nov-80	25th Bath	7
5	Keven Curtis	5-Jul-79	9th Bath	6
6	Alun Davies	17-Feb-81	9th Bath	15
7	Stephen Davison	21-Dec-79	25th Bath	10
8	David Fox	13-Aug-81	15th Bath	18
9	George Frost	11-Apr-79	8th Bath	12
10	William Gardiner	8-Jan-79	25th Bath	11
11	Jason Hewitt	12-Jan-82	25th Bath	?
12	Carlos Lopresti	26-Mar-80	8th Bath	17
13	Sean O'Brien	20-Jan-80	2nd Bath	13
14	Rohit Patel	19-Apr-82	2nd Bath	5
15	Mark Pickford	5-Feb-79	9th Bath	16
16	Nicholas Pickford	30-Sep-80	9th Bath	3
17	Josef Szczech	22-Oct-80	8th Bath	1
18	Simon West	31-May-82	15th Bath	4

CUB-SCOUT NAME INDEX	
Cub-scout name	Row number
Jonathan Bates	1
Kevin Curtis	5
George Frost	9
Sean O'Brien	13
Josef Szczech	17

PACK-NAME INDEX	
Pack name	Row number
2nd Bath	1
8th Bath	9
9th Bath	5
15th Bath	3
25th Bath	4

Figure 8.23 The cub-scout table indexed on cub-scout name and pack name

DATE OF BIRTH INDEX	
1-Jul-78 to 30-Jun-79	9, 10, 15
1-Jul-79 to 30-Jun-80	5, 7, 12, 13
1-Jul-80 to 30-Jun-81	3, 4, 6, 16, 17
1-Jul-81 to 30-Jun-82	1, 2, 8, 11, 14, 18
1-Jul-82 to 30-Jun-83	–

PACK-NAME INDEX	
2nd Bath	1, 2, 13, 14
8th Bath	9, 12, 17
9th Bath	5, 6, 15, 16
15th Bath	3, 8, 18
25th Bath	4, 7, 10, 11

Figure 8.24 Dense indexes to cub-scout table

cub-scouts in 7th Bath there is no longer a need to put the pack name into the cub-scout table. Indeed, if every non-key attribute is indexed the only thing needed in the cub-scout table is the table primary key – the 'cub-scout name'. The term that describes this situation is that we have set up an *inverted file*.

You can take it further still. If the primary key is written into the indexes instead of the row number, *you don't need the cub-scout table at all!* The situation becomes rather like a library catalogue. The object of the search is actually outside the database.

Question
What could be the problems of updating an inverted file if the data stored change frequently? What will you need to do to reduce the time that it takes to follow 'next row' keys through lots of insertions?

It would be a mistake to suppose that dense indexes are necessarily linked to inverted files. It's much easier to sort data which can be held in a computer's memory ('Random Access Memory', or RAM), rather than to sort data held in a computer backing store. This makes life difficult if a data table is too large to go into memory.

A possible solution is to hold the data table in any order in backing store *with a sorted index in memory*. Each index entry contains only a row key and a pointer to the correct row of the data table. If new data are added, only the index needs to be resequenced!

8.6.4 B-Trees, and variants of B-Trees

In spite of what was said in the previous section, it's unfortunately likely that the set of all key values plus pointers to the main data table *won't* fit into memory if the data table is very large. In other words, the index is too large for the memory.

Once it's accepted that the index is also likely to be held in backing store, then the speed of data retrieval depends on the number of data store accesses that need to be made to locate the desired data object. If the data table is indexed, then all but one of these accesses can be to rows of the index. A danger of traditional 'chaining-in' methods of inserting new rows into sequential lists is that some access paths get very long indeed, with many backing store accesses. The access paths in data organized as a *B-Tree* are *balanced*, so that all routes from the *root* to the *leaves* of a tree are of equal length [14].

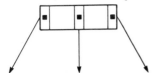

Figure 8.25 One node of a B-tree of order 1

We'll assume that a data table is organized into a B-tree *with no index*. We'll also assume that the B-tree is of *order 1*. This means that each *node* contains either one or two keys and the dependent data, but can't contain more than two keys! In general, each node of a B-tree of order d contains, at most, $2d$ keys, and $(2d+1)$ pointers to other nodes of the B-tree (Figure 8.25).

We'll start with an empty list and add key values one by one. At all times, the route from a particular node takes one of three paths, depending on the key sequence values. Always, an attempt is made to insert a new value into a leaf node. If the leaf node is already full, it is split and the middle value is promoted to the parent node. If the parent node is full, then that is also split and the middle value promoted. If a root node itself is full, then this too is split and a new superior root node created (Figure 8.26).

Note that all access paths to a root node are of the same length. With a little work, we could show that the number of nodes in each path with a tree of degree d and n keys stored is:

$$\log_d \left(\frac{n+1}{2} \right)$$

or, generally, that it grows as the log of the file size. The longest path in an unbalanced tree with n entries could be n nodes.

Deletion is an unwinding; the same process in reverse. If a deletion is made in a non-leaf node then an adjacent subordinate key must be swapped into the vacant position. Deletion could leave a leaf mode with no keys in it. The response should be to rearrange the data so that keys are evenly divided between two neighbouring nodes. If there are fewer than two keys in the two nodes, then they should be *concatenated* or joined. If you read Figure 8.26 from the bottom up as a set of deletions, you'll get the feel of it!

If the B-tree is an index, then instead of keys and dependent data, nodes are going to contain keys and pointers. On the face of it, this seems of little value, since it just adds on one more backing store access.

New key value   **Node key values**

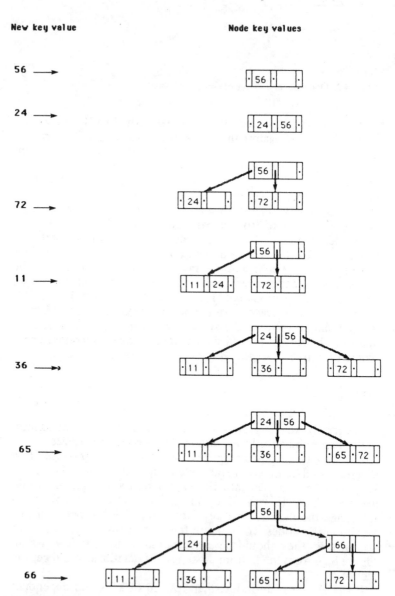

Figure 8.26 Insertion of new data into a B-tree of order 1

Let's consider a variant of the straightforward B-tree, which does provide for index nodes separately from data nodes. In a *B+ Tree* all data reside in the leaves. The higher values form an index. This may result in the same key value appearing in both an index and a leaf node (Figure 8.27). The assumption must be that the leaf nodes are in a physically contiguous data store. This gives a real advantage if sequential processing of a whole data table is ever required.

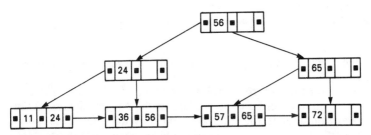

Figure 8.27 A B+ tree with a leaf entry for each key

8.6.5 Hashing

Exactly as for indexing, hashing reduces the size of the data set which must be searched to find a desired data object or quickly identifies the proper place to store new data. Viewed in a simple way, several separate storage places are provided for one set of data. A data table is divided into a number of parts. We'll call each one of these storage places a *bucket*.

To find in which bucket a particular row of a table belongs, some algorithm is performed on the value of the key for that row. Since the alogorithms are usually arithmetic, we'll assume that the key is a numeric attribute.

Let's recast the cub-scout table with the assumption that each cub-scout is identified by a cub-scout number (Figure 8.28). The choice of algorithm and key values should be made so that whatever additions and deletions are made to the table, and however, rapidly these changes occur, the number of rows in each bucket remains approximately equal. This should occur naturally without any need for a Database Administrator to intervene.

The simplest method of structuring the table is to give each row a key which identifies the storage bucket. Cub-scout 1 data are stored in bucket 1; cub-scout 2 data in bucket 2; and so on. The

CUB-SCOUT TABLE			
Cub-scout number	Cub-scout name	Date of birth	Pack name
103	John Bates	3-Apr-82	2nd Bath
104	Simon Birch	12-Sep-81	2nd Bath
106	James Cumming	5-Dec-80	15th Bath
101	Jason Hewitt	12-Jan-82	25th Bath

Figure 8.28 The cub-scout table, with a cub-scout number added

implications if cub scouts leave and join very frequently are obvious!

Getting a little more complex, we can divide the key by some constant number and use the *quotient* as the bucket address. If that constant number is 100, the effect on our cub-scout table is that cub-scout data 1 to 99 are stored in bucket zero; cub-scouts 100 to 199 in bucket 1; cub-scouts 200 to 299 in bucket 2; and so on. Effectively, this amounts to an indexing system. For what kind of data would this addressing structure be appropriate? What happens if the data are very volatile, with cub-scouts constantly joining, getting new numbers, but dropping out after a couple of weeks?

The last structure we are going to describe requires that the key be divided by some constant number and the *remainder* used as the bucket address. The number of buckets used will be the same as the value of the constant number. If we have seven buckets, a set of cub-scout data for cub-scout 101 would have its home bucket identified by:

$$\frac{101}{7} = 14 \text{ with remainder equal to } 3$$

Bucket 3 is therefore the home bucket (Figure 8.29).

A great deal turns on the choice of the number of buckets. There is a sound argument (which we won't explore here!) for this being a prime number, but that still means it could be 7, 251 or 1019 (for example).

If there are few buckets then the bucket contents will proportionally be fairly close to the average bucket contents. This means that *overflow* (trying to get new data into buckets that are already full) will not be much of a problem. The disadvantage with

CUB-SCOUT TABLE				
Bucket number	Cub-scout number	Cub-scout name	Date of birth	Pack name
1	106	James Cumming	5-Dec-80	15th Bath
	113	Simon West	31-May-82	15th Bath
2	107	Rohit Patel	19-Apr-82	2nd Bath
	114	Kevin Curtis	5-Jul-79	9th Bath
3	101	Jason Hewitt	12-Jan-82	25th Bath
	108	Mark Pickford	5-Feb-79	9th Bath
	115	Josef Szczech	22-Oct-80	8th Bath
4	102	Carlos Lopresti	26-Mar-80	8th Bath
	109	David Fox	13-Aug-81	15th Bath
	116	William Gardiner	8-Jan-78	25th Bath
5	103	John Bates	3-Apr-82	2nd Bath
	110	Matthew Curley	3-Apr-80	25th Bath
	117	Sean O'Brien	20-Jan-80	2nd Bath
6	104	Simon Birch	12-Sep-81	2nd Bath
	111	Stephen Davison	21-Dec-79	25th Bath
	118	Alun Davies	17-Feb-81	9th Bath
7	105	Nicholas Pickford	30-Sep-80	9th Bath
	112	George Frost	11-Apr-79	8th Bath

Figure 8.29 The cub-scout table divided between seven buckets

few buckets is that there will still be a lot of data to search to find the required data object, even after the correct bucket is found. If there are many buckets then the problem is reversed. Once you find the right bucket, there will be relatively few data in the bucket but the bucket contents will be very variable, causing overflow problems.

The methods of handling overflow vary. Taking the simplest first, we can just let overflow flow into the next bucket (Figure 8.30) or we can have a single overflow bucket into which all the buckets deliver (Figure 8.31). We can also temporarily chain in extra overflow buckets to particular, already full, ones (Figure 8.32). Just to complete the picture, we can make each of the home buckets so large that overflow never occurs.

Whichever of these methods we use, we still need the same administrative discipline. *When there is room in the home bucket, we need to sweep up all the overflow and put it back in the home bucket.* If we have temporarily attached overflow buckets to home

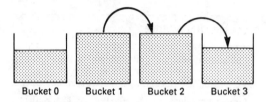

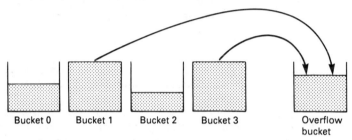

Figure 8.30 Hashing – data overflow into the next bucket

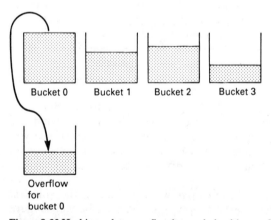

Figure 8.31 Hashing – data overflow into an overflow bucket

Figure 8.32 Hashing – data overflow into a chained-in overflow bucket

buckets we also need to detach them and put them back into the
bucket store when they are no longer needed.

Let's be clear. Most systems analysts will be able to do their jobs
quite happily without knowing about bucket organization. *You
can leave it to the database management system*. We discuss it here
only so that analysts and users better understand the system they

are using. If it's necessary to fine tune a data storage system, the Database Administrators will have to think about bucket size, hashing algorithms, overflow bucket size and the protocol for dealing with overflow.

8.6.6 Mapping the data model to the database

We have been describing access to the database in terms of access to a single file or table. If you want to list the event name, and the name and date of birth of each contest in race number three of the cub-scout sports day (Figure 2.3) then it is necessary to retrieve data from three different tables.

Creating normalized database tables, following the guidelines we set out in Section 7.5, is a perfectly reasonable strategy. It eliminates redundant storage of any data which are not part of a foreign key. By removing that redundancy, it makes better use of the available storage space, and it reduces the burden of updating the database to reflect any changes in the real world. Above all, the fact that there is only one copy of any data object makes the task of maintaining a consistent database immeasurably easier.

Normalization isn't, though, the answer to everyone's prayer! It could well be that in the cub-scout database we *never* retrieve data from the SCHEDULED RACE table without also retrieving appropriate data from the CONTESTANT table. If, in those circumstances, the data are stored in two separate tables then we incur needless extra processing cost from joining these two tables every time we access them. The proper action would be to store the rows from the CONTESTANT table *close to* the rows they relate to in the SCHEDULED RACE table. 'Close to' means that the whole set of rows from both tables may be retrieved with the smallest number of accesses to the database.

Everything we do has a cost. If we do disperse the rows of the CONTESTANT table as just suggested, then an attempt to retrieve the whole of the CONTESTANT table from the database could only be executed by joining all these rows together again!

Any indexes that we create on columns in a database table are there to speed up retrieval of the data, like the index at the tops of the pages in a telephone directory. It would therefore be rather pointless to create an index on a column of a database table which we have decided to disperse 'close to' rows of other tables.

The points we have just made are all about 'tuning' a database to improve the performance. Creating an index on a column of a table is done to improve the performance. Because of this, we must always be mindful of the costs of indexing. An index speeds up retrieval of data but it enormously slows down updating a database. Consider the re-compilation of the index which is necessary if we add an extra hundred names to a telephone directory!

In summary, if the content of a database is very stable and most of the accesses are for retrieval of data, then heavy indexing is justified. If updating of the database is fairly frequent, then indexing should be carried out with discretion. Probably the only indexes will be on primary keys and on the foreign keys by which tables will be 'joined' in response to a query such as for our cub-scout above.

Most database management systems commercially available today do allow a designer to make decisions of the type that we have outlined in this section.

8.7 Summary

- Data relate to some event. We need to capture the data quickly and with minimum transcription.
- Mark reading, character recognition, magnetic ink character recognition and (more recently) bar code recognition and 'smart cards' are all designed to facilitate data capture. Smart cards can, in addition, receive and store data for subsequent retrieval.
- The normal mode of working when a large number of similar transactions must be processed and the response time is not critical is batch processing. This requires an original data table, a transaction table which is then sorted into the same sequence as the data table, and finally a merging of the two tables to produce a new data table. The original data table still exists at the end of the process.
- If we wish to work to a 'short response time' then the mode of working is demand processing.
- There should be a preference for addressing our demands to a computer in natural language. This presents considerable syntactic and semantic problems.
- We are likely to resort to a restricted dialogue. The options available include:

    Simple system prompts, which can be responded to in a variety of ways;
    System prompts or 'menus', which specify the range of options open to a user.

- Menu selection can lead a user into other system states. We urge the use of a state change specification to define the navigation possibilities.
- It is becoming popular for selections to be represented by 'icons' or meaningful pictures (for example, a dustbin for throwing away files).
- Additional help may be provided by explanatory comments on the screen; by 'Help' screens; and by clarification dialogues.
- A particular form of providing a 'user-friendly environment' is 'Query-By-Example'. A user relates to the stored data by presenting the computer system with an example of what he is looking for.
- The organization of data for demand processing falls into four general categories:
  1. Serial search – look at everything!
  2. Sequential – look at everything in sequence;
  3. Indexed search; and
  4. Hashing.
- Both indexed searching and hashing rely on using some mechanism which rapidly reduces the size of the set of data which must be searched to locate the desired data object. Both methods require identification of a particular search key.
- Any data table which is updated, and which is used for demand processing, must have a mechanism for coping with data overflow. The more volatile the contents of the database, the more sensitive to overflow the system becomes.

Discussion points

8.1 In what circumstances would you be satisfied to update data tables by batch processing?

8.2 'The intervention of people in data collection introduces an error-prone element in what could otherwise be an efficient process.' Discuss.

8.3 If you offer data retrieval on demand, and update by a batch process after close of business for the day, how do you obtain the back-up data necessary to allow you to recover from a database failure during business hours?

8.4 What are the problems of inserting new data into an inverted file? Suggest suitable applications for an inverted file.

8.5 Suggest suitable applications for a hashed data table.

References

1. Barry Lee, *Data Processing Methods*, Hutchinson, London (1984)
2. James Martin, *Design of Man–computer Dialogues*, Prentice-Hall, Englewood Cliffs, NJ (1973)
3. Ben Shneiderman, *Designing the User Interface: Strategies for Effective Human–Computer Interaction*, Addison-Wesley, Reading, Mass. (1987)
4. William Kent, *Data and Reality*, North-Holland, Amsterdam (1978)
5. *Lexis Handbook*, Butterworths (Telepublishing), London
6. Cary Lu, 'Computer pointing devices: living with mice', *High Technology*, January (1984)
7. M. M. Zloof, 'Query-By-Example', *Proceedings National Computer Conference*, Anaheim, California, May (1975)
8. M. M. Zloof, 'Office-by-Example: A business language that unifies data, word processing, and electronic mail', *IBM Systems Journal*, **21**, No. 3 (1982)
9. E. F. Codd, 'Seven steps to RENDEZVOUS with the casual user', *Proceedings IFIP TC-2 Working Conference on Database Management Systems*, Cargese, Corsica, North-Holland, Amsterdam (1974)
10. L. R. Harris, 'The ROBOT system: natural language processing applied to database queries', *Proceedings ACM Conference* (1978)
11. 'INTELLECT' is available from Artifical Intelligence Corporation, 100 5th Avenue, Waltham, MA 02254, USA
12. E. F. Codd, 'How about recently? (English dialogue with relational databases using RENDEZVOUS version 1)', in *Databases: Improving Usability and Responsiveness*, edited by B. Shneiderman, Academic Press, New York (1978)
13. J. D. Hill, 'Wouldn't it be nice if we could write computer programs in ordinary English – or would it?' *BCS Computer Bulletin*, June (1972)
14. D. Comer, 'The ubiquitous B-tree', *ACM Computing Surveys*, June (1979)
15. J. Weizenbaum, 'ELIZA – A computer program for the study of natural language communications between man and machine', *Communications of the ACM*, **36**, January (1966)
16. F. B. Thompson, 'English for the computer', *AFIPS, Full Joint Computer Conference*, Vol. 29, 349–356 (1966)
17. J. A. Craig, S. C. Berezner, H. C. Corney and C. R. Longyear, 'DEACON – Directed English Access and Control', *AFIPS, Full Joint COmputer Conference*, Vol. 29, 365–380 (1966)

Chapter 9

System evaluation

9.1 The problem

Where are we at? What are we trying to do? Where do we want to be? These are the first and most important questions before we make any attempt at system evaluation. Unless we have a clear idea what our goal is, and what the purpose of the system is, we aren't going to make any progress with system design.

How can it be done? What are the possible actions which we can take? We can never hope to have considered every possibility. We must make sure that with the limited time and resources which are available to us we have identified as many feasible actions as we can.

What benefits and costs are associated with each action we can take? Both benefits and costs must be related to our judgement about what we are trying to do. It's right and proper to revise our goals as our expectations about what is possible change. It is neither right nor proper to parade a list of costs and benefits which bear no relation to our stated purpose.

How shall we do it? Which of the available actions do we choose?

It isn't our intention to be simplistic about system purpose. We suggested in Chapter 1 that the way a system is designed is completely dependent on the judgement about what the system is for. For the moment, we are assuming that a clear statement of intent can be made.

9.2 Simplification

As a first step, assume that all benefits and costs can be expressed in money units, and that there is a purpose which can easily be related to money units (for example, 'maximize the payoff'). An appropriate structure for analysis is the *pay-off table*. We draw up a table which describes the net monetary benefit which is estimated for each possible *action* and for each possible *state of the world*. 'Actions' are assumed to be *conduct over which we have total control*. Possible 'states of the world' are events *over which we as individuals have no control*. The pay-off table shows how much richer or poorer we may be if we take particular actions in different states of the world.

Example
The actions available to the Careful Manufacturing Company are to buy the 'With Bells On' universal production control system; to buy the 'Spartan' basic system; or to do nothing. The pay-off depends on whether the Prodigal political party or the Skinflint party wins the forthcoming general election. The company directors believe that if they do nothing, the wealth of the company will be unaffected, whichever party wins the election.

A pay-off table has been constructed for Figure 9.1. The pay-offs may be in thousands of dollars, or hundreds of pounds, or lacs of rupees. It doesn't make any difference to the analysis. We aren't at this stage questioning the accuracy of the pay-offs. They may have been obtained by detailed research or by consulting the company president's horoscope.

	Prodigal wins	Skinflint wins
Buy 'With Bells On'	100	−50
Buy 'Spartan'	20	25
Do nothing	0	0

Figure 9.1 A pay-off table for an investment by the Careful Manufacturing Company

The Careful Company has to choose an action which is the most appropriate to the company purpose or what the company is trying to do. For this we need a rule for making decisions, or *decision rule*. We'll discuss two:

1. The *pessimistic* decision rule. This says that for each possible action we decide which is the worst possible pay-off (−50, 20 and 0). We then choose the action for which this worst possible pay-off is the highest. The highest worst pay-off is 20; *therefore we buy Spartan.*
2. The *expected value* decision rule. For this we need to know the probablility of each future state of the world. Let's suppose that there is a 40% chance that Prodigal will win and a 60% chance that Skinflint will win.

Then:

> Expected pay-off of choosing 'With Bells On' = 40% of (+100)
> + 60% of (−50) = **10**
> Expected pay-off of choosing 'Spartan' = 40% of (+20) + 60%
> of (+25) = **23**

The decision rule tells us to choose the action for which the expected pay-off is the highest. The conclusion is *that we buy Spartan.*

Several other decision rules could be framed, but these two will do for our purpose. In the Careful Company's problem, both rules give the same answer. If we get such consistency, it must add weight to the credibility of the conclusion.

A last word on decision rules; *if it's obvious from the numbers which action to take, don't waste time agonizing over which decision rule to use.*

9.3 Coping with uncertainty

If we use the pessimistic decision rule then we have to try to get the pay-offs as right as we can. If we use the expected value rule, we need estimates of both pay-offs and probabilities. In practice, the use of probabilities could well reflect our uncertainty about pay-offs. Perhaps the Careful Company believes that there is a 40% chance of a pay-off of 20 if they buy Spartan and a 60% chance of a pay-off of 25. The two possible outcomes reflect different possible states of the world. Those states of the world don't have to have labels like 'Prodigal wins the election'. They may just be the worst and the best anticipated outcomes.

Our guesses about the chances of Prodigal or Skinflint winning may be quite wild ones. We can try to improve the guesses by commissioning opinion polls to measure what the electorate is currently thinking, but they may not help us much in predicting what the electorate will think *next* year.

Quite often we can judge the probability of future events, or states of the world, because they are a continuation of the past. There is well-founded expectation of the distribution of heights and weights of seven-year-old children. If a manufacturing process has consistently produced 5% defective product in the past, it's likely to go on doing this in the future. If you are interested in the probability of success for a borehole in prospecting for oil, then the records of previous boreholes in similar ground will be helpful. If we are interested in oil exploration, the oil does actually exist underground. A judicious programme of sampling can yield more and more information about what the true state of the world is. Sampling cannot tell us much about events that haven't yet happened.

It's when records of the past don't give a particularly good guide to the future, and there is little opportunity to improve knowledge of the state of the world by sampling, that prediction becomes very subjective. If it's the first time a particular problem has been addressed, then there isn't very much by way of guidance available for us to use. Perhaps the best we can do is to rely on the judgement of informed people.

Even then, we can't expect such a person to be able to attach a 43% probability to the chance of Prodigal winning. The estimate is very precise, but the accuracy is entirely spurious. Translating judgement into informed estimates requires responses to such questions as:

'Is the probability of Prodigal winning more or less than evens?'
'Are the odds against Prodigal winning more or less than two to one against?'
'Are the odds against Prodigal winning more or less than ten to one against?'

We all find binary (less than or more than) comparisons like this easier to respond to than a straight declaration of probability.

Question
If the answers to the above questions are 'less than', 'less than' and 'more than' what can you deduce about the probability of Prodigal winning the election?

9.4 Sensitivity analysis

If an informed person is going to make judgements about future events it is much more likely that the person will be able to estimate a *range of probabilities* than that he will be able to state a single probability value. Suppose that such a person estimates the probability of Prodigal winning the next election as between 30% and 50%:

Probability of Prodigal winning = 30%

Probability of Skinfint winning = 70%

Probability of Prodigal winning = 50%

Probability of Skinfint winning = 50%

Expected pay-off choosing 'With Bells on' = 30% of (+100) + 70% of (−50) = −5
Expected pay-off of choosing 'Spartan' = 30% of (+20) + 70% of (+25) = 23.5

Expected pay-off choosing 'With Bells on' = 50% of (+100) + 50% of (−50) = 25
Expected pay-off of choosing 'Spartan' = 50% of (+20) + 50% of (+25) = 22.5

Similarly, if the probability of Prodigal winning is 40%, then the expected pay-offs of choosing 'With Bells on' and 'Spartan' work out at 10 and 23 money units, respectively.

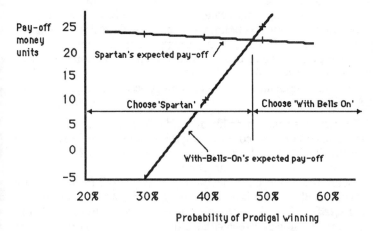

Figure 9.2 Sensitivity of Careful's choice of action to the probability of Prodigal winning

Figure 9.2 illustrates *sensitivity analysis*. It suggests that the choice between 'With Bells On' and 'Spartan' *does* depend on the estimate of Prodigal's probability of winning the election. It also suggests that the cut-over point from one decision to the other is at about 48% probability of Prodigal winning. This changes the crux of the decision to be made. It's now the binary decision: Is the probability of Prodigal winning less than or greater than 48%? If it's greater, then we must choose 'With Bells On'. If it's less, then we must select 'Spartan'.

If our 'informed person' is unsure whether the probability is above or below 48%, then the best estimate must be to presume that the probability isn't far from 48%. This must surely mean that the cost of making the 'wrong' decision is low, and it can't matter too much which choice is made.

9.5 Cash flow analysis

We've said earlier that the pay-off is the net monetary benefit. To arrive at an estimate of what that net monetary benefit is we will probably attempt *cash flow analysis*. Suppose that the cash flows associated with buying 'With Bells On', in the circumstances that Prodigal wins the election, are as shown in Figure 9.3. Negative cash flows represent *payments*, positive cash flows *receipts*.

The total of all the cash flows within a three-year planning horizon is the 100 pay-off that we wrote into the pay-off table for Careful shown in Figure 9.1. The length of the planning horizon, the distance into the future that we attempt to look, must depend on the situation which is being analysed. If it's a stable system not subject to outside threats, then perhaps a ten-year horizon would be appropriate. If the future is obscure, then perhaps one year is as far as it is wise to look.

Two quite important reservations must be made about this cash flow analysis:

1. The first reservation again depends on sensitivity analysis. If the conversion cost could be anything between −50 and −150 and if the 240 benefit per year could be 25 lower or 25 higher within the limits of estimating error, then we need more research. At one extreme the positive pay-off from choosing 'With Bells On' disappears altogether. At the other the *expected value decision rule* makes 'With Bells On' the preferred choice. Recalculate the table in Figure 9.3 for yourself with these changes! We aren't speaking of different possible states of the world but of *estimating errors*. The sensitivity of decision making to these errors should always be explored.
2. The second reservation is that there is a generally held assumption that a cash flow at some period in the future *is of less value than a cash flow now!* Would it be a good idea to invest £100 in a project if all you could expect is that you will get your £100 back in one year's time? In the biblical parable[1] the man who travelled into a far country and left a single talent with his servant gave him scant sympathy when the servant returned to him that same talent. Indeed, the servant had taken from him the single talent he had, and was cast into the outer darkness.

To allow for this decrease in the value of money with time all *future* cash flows are multiplied by a discounting factor before they are added together. The total of all discounted cash flows for

	Estimated initial cost	Cash flows in year 1	Cash flows in year 2	Cash flows in year 3	Total cash flows for three years
Investment	-300				
Training cost		-50			
Conversion cost		-100			
Operating cost		-20	-30	-30	
Benefits		150	240	240	
Total for year	-300	-20	210	210	100

Figure 9.3 The cash flow analysis associated with buying 'With Bells On' and a Prodigal win

Careful is therefore *less than* 100. The sum of all discounted cash flows is call the *net present value* (NPV).

The value of the NPV crucially depends on the discount factors used. These are based on the interest rates that a saver would get from a savings account. If an investment will earn 10% annual interest, then £1 invested now will amount to £1.10 in one year's time and to £1.21 in two years' time. For an investment to be worth £1 in two years' time, £$(1 \div 1.21)$ would need to be invested now.

Present value deals with this from the opposite view. It expresses the current value (or present value at this moment) of any future cash flows. With the above figures the present value of a cash flow of £1 in two years' time is £$(1 \div 1.21)$. The discount factor is $1 \div 1.21$, or 0.8264.

Sets of tables are available[2] which, for any specified rate of annual interest and for any number of years into the future when the cash flow is supposed to occur, state the present value of a future cash flow of £1. We've given an extract in Figure 9.4.

The decimal point is omitted from most published sets of tables: all entries are assumed to have a decimal point on the left. Figure

		Annual interest rate in %							
		5	6	7	8	9	10	11	12
Number of years into the future	1	9524	9434	9346	9259	9174	9091	9009	8929
	2	9070	8900	8734	8573	8417	8264	8116	7972
	3	8638	8396	8163	7938	7722	7513	7312	7118
	4	8227	7921	7629	7350	7084	6830	6587	6355
	5	7835	7473	7130	6806	6499	6209	5935	5674
	6	7462	7050	6663	6302	5963	5645	5346	5066

Figure 9.4 An extract from present value tables highlighting the 10% two-year discount factor

	Estimated initial cost	Cash flow in year 1	Cash flow in year 2	Cash flow in year 3	Net present value for three years
Total cash flow for the year	−300	−20	210	210	
Discount factor	1.0000	.9091	.8417	.7513	
Present value of cash flow	−300	−18.2	176.8	157.8	16

Figure 9.5 Discounted cash flows associated with buying 'With Bells On' together with a Prodigal win

	Prodigal wins	Skinflint wins
Buy 'With Bells On'	16	?
Buy 'Spartan'	?	?

Figure 9.6 Pay-off table for Careful showing the NPV of buying 'With Bells On' and Prodigal winning

9.3 can be re-presented with discount factors for a 10% rate of interest (Figure 9.5).

Question
Can you explain why the introduction of discount factors so significantly reduces the net present value? We've repeated this question in the self-assessment for this chapter.

Note that we have expressed the NPV to a precision of one part in one hundred! Any greater precision would be completely spurious. The NPV of 16 money units can now be used in the pay-off table (Figure 9.6). In the figure we have put question marks against combinations of buying 'Spartan' or Skinflint winning the election. A separate NPV calculation is required for each of these entries. (Try the self-assessment exercise at the end of this chapter.)

We have presented the calculation in detail, but virtually every financial analysis software package allows calculation of NPV for the whole range of cash flows to which the NPV is sensitive and for a variety of possible interest rates. This thorough sensitivity analysis is a vital part of any project evaluation.

9.6 Appraisal of the simple approach

We have outlined a very simple decision-making model. One simplification was the assumption that all benefits and costs can be expressed in money terms. We'll drop that assumption in the next section.

The real beauties of our simple model are that it encourages us to look for more than one *action* or solution; that it encourages us to speculate about what future (unknown) *states of the world* or *events* are in store for us; and that it encourages us to identify a *pay-off* for each action we could take. Necessarily, because time and money to research the environment, and to devise possible solutions, are limited our set of possible future events may miss the real future which will eventually unfold. The set of possible actions will be incomplete. We just have to do our best with what we can afford!

We suggested a net present value calculation to estimate the pay-off. There is a deceptive simplicity about this which needs to be qualified. The first qualification is about the glib use of a 10% annual interest rate. The interest rate that should be used is the *cost of capital*, or the overall interest rate that a firm must pay to all its sources of capital funds combined. It isn't reasonable to suppose that if a firm borrows money from the bank to finance a project at 10% then its cost of capital is also 10%. The fact of borrowing may well have depressed the value of the firm's shares on the Stock Exchange, and therefore reduced the firm's ability to obtain money for investment. We won't explore cost of capital any further here, but there are useful readings[3,4].

Next, we need to comment on the interest structure. We've assumed a building society deposit account type of investment, growing at a steady rate each year. This assumes that cash flows far into the future are taken into account but are heavily discounted. It might alternatively be a firm's policy to look for a return on an investment in the immediate future, and to ignore any cash flows more than three years distant. This should require a discounting pattern different from the one we've described. In particular, if future cash flows are clearly uncertain then it might be prudent to discount them more heavily, so that they have less effect on the decision.

One of the principal sources of uncertainty about future cash flows is the effect of inflation, or the depreciation in the value of money. This is much too complex to be described here, but again there are readings[5]. Generally, the effect of inflation will be to increase the size of future cash flows without increasing their true value. If discount factors are included at all it isn't necessary to assume any further cost of servicing debt. This is exactly what the discount factors are supposed to do for us.

There is still another qualification. If there is any shortage of resources we don't simply need to choose between several different ways of doing the same job, we also need to decide which of several jobs we are going to do. If we decide to do job A, then we incur the *opportunity cost* of not doing job B.

We have oversimplified in another way. The reality of decision making is often that the choices open to a decision maker are not different ways of doing the same job. One option may perform tasks A, B and C, another option may perform tasks A, B and D. In all cases *the decision taken should be the one which produces the greatest increase in the firm's wealth.* We attempt to estimate that wealth by using the net present value.

Throughout this chapter we've spoken of discounting to estimate a net present value. This means of bringing in the relationship of money and time is not the only method of investment analysis. A variation on NPV is the 'internal rate of return'[6]. Other methods of evaluation are the 'pay-back period'[6] and 'MAPI' (Machinery and Allied Products, Inc.)[7]. We believe NPV to be the most appropriate approach to the problem of evaluation.

9.7 Non-monetary pay-off

It isn't realistic to assume that all the costs and benefits which accrue from a particular action can be expressed in money terms. If hardware or software is to be bought, then some possible costs are:

1. Equipment purchase cost, including the cost of *expandability, reliability, flexibility, modularity* and *security.*
2. The cost of *unreliability* if the system fails, either for a brief period or disastrously.
3. The cost of *lost transactions* when capacity is inadequate to meet the demand.
4. *Conversion* cost from old equipment to new, including *retraining* cost.
5. The cost of *servicing a loan*, normally catered for by the discount factors described in reference 5.
6. The cost in the *quality of life* of those employees whose jobs become more tedious as a result of the action.
7. The cost of making some employees redundant, both in *severance payments* by the firm and in the *distress* to the employees themselves.

Conversely, some possible benefits are:

1. Ability to handle *more business* with the same staff by both the productivity of the income-earning staff and that of their supporting staff.
2. Reduction of *staffing levels* to do the same job.
3. Reduction in *elapsed time* before customers are invoiced, with a consequent increase in the flow of cash available to the firm.
4. Reduction in *inventory levels*, due to a faster response to customer demand.
5. Increased *customer goodwill*, due to quicker and more reliable deliveries.
6. Increased *customer goodwill*, due to faster response to customer enquiries.
7. More detailed and more timely *breakdown of costs* and of *time usage*. This might be used to improve knowledge of the cost of specific jobs (job costing) or to improve the estimating of prices for future work.
8. *Increased sales*, due to a greater sensitivity to the market.
9. *Expandibility, reliability, flexibility, modularity* and *security*. There is a cost of providing these but there is also a benefit from having them.
10. Improved *management information*, providing feedback to a firm's decision makers about how effectively the firm's policies are being carried out.

Let's comment on some of the items on this list. Several of the costs are written in twice. We have noted the cost of *unreliability*. Clearly, if a hardware device or a software package was worth buying, there must be a cost of losing it through breakdown. One way to estimate this cost is to estimate the cost of the resources of every kind that must be employed to make sure that *a breakdown doesn't happen*. If there is a chance of breakdown then the cost of that breakdown has to be estimated. This can involve lost sales, customer ill-will and expensive emergency arrangements.

If we are interested in reliability of purchased software then there are some defensive actions we can take[8]. Some of these will increase the cost:

1. Assure ourselves of the financial viability of our software suppliers. We will be on our own if they go out of business!
2. Check that the software is being successfully used by firms similar to our own.
3. Insist on obtaining all the documentation of any software we buy, so that our own people can amend the software as required.

4. If possible, make arrangements so that in the event of the supplier going out of business the software documentation becomes our legal property.
5. Specify our requirements very closely and exhaustively test the software to make sure it meets these requirements.

All these arrangements will be costly. They may preclude us from buying the cheapest product. Together they enhance the reliability of the software. It is in the interests of the supplier to make us come back to him to buy any after-sales service we need. It's in our interest not to be dependent on our supplier.

We can put a similar argument for *flexibility* and *modularity*. We cannot accurately predict what the future holds. Perhaps the best we can do is to invest in flexibility. The price of that flexibility is that software must be written in a way that makes alteration easy. One means of doing this is to make sure that any application software is divided up into reasonably self-contained modules. Each module has a clearly defined interface with the environment and with all the other modules. If we have to make an alteration to an 'order entry' module we can be confident that the alteration won't harmfully spread its effects into the 'invoice processing' or the 'stock table amendment' modules. Anything designed for flexibility will be more expensive than something designed for one specific task.

Security, too, is expensive. It requires redundancy of processing, of storage and of communication capacity. All the extra items that must be calculated must be stored and transmitted and increase both the initial and the running costs of any application.

Management information is extraordinarily difficult to value. We can approach an estimate by supposing that a firm's management have *no* information with which to conduct the firm's business. They don't know whether inventory levels are going up or down; how much is being sold; what the sales revenue is; or how long the firm's customers are being kept waiting for deliveries. Clearly, it would be a nonsense to talk about management at all!

Management information, then, is something we must have. It can differ in quality, and we must then judge the value of these qualitative differences. We can try to estimate the costs of providing the information with different system designs.

9.8 Utility

Some of these costs and benefits are readily expressed in terms of money. Others are much more intangible. In the previous section we suggested that we may be able to make an estimate of the value of an intangible benefit (for example, 'reliability') by trying to measure the cost of not having it. If our interest is in measuring the 'quality of life' of the employees then we would be hard pressed to put a value on that in money units!

Sometimes, although the benefit which we are trying to measure can be quantified, it can't easily be quantified in dollars or pounds. Let's suppose that the Production Manager of the Careful Manufacturing Company has complete reports of the previous day's operations on this desk by 11 a.m. each day. He believes that this is too late to be able to make any effective response by making changes in the production schedules for the current day. Ideally, he would like the reports on his desk when he starts his day at 8 a.m. This would allow him to control manufacture more closely, but would be very costly to achieve.

Perhaps there is some intermediate time between 8 a.m. and 11 a.m. which would be satisfactory. We can measure the time it will take to produce the production report, given different levels of investment. What is more difficult is to estimate the relative value of early or late delivery.

What we do know is that delivery at 8 a.m. is *the best possible outcome*. Earlier than this would be of no extra value because the manager wouldn't be there to see it. Delivery at 11 a.m. is *the worst possible outcome*, because it is already being achieved and there can be no advantage in a new system which is worse than this. We can give these 'worst possible' and 'best possible' outcomes *utility values*, or indicators of the relative satisfaction or dissatisfaction which we feel with that outcome[9].

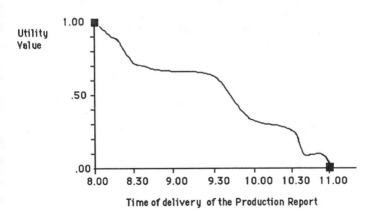

Figure 9.7 Two points on the Production Report utility curve

Quite arbitrarily, we will give the worst possible outcome a utility value of 0 and the best possible outcome a utility value of 1. We could equally well make the limits 0 and 100, or -100 and $+100$. With these two values we can make two entries for a *utility curve* (Figure 9.7). We have no idea of the shape of the utility curve between these two points!

One way of resolving the utility curve for one particular decision maker is for an analyst to sketch freehand some utility curves and to ask the decision maker whether the curve represents his utility preferences. *It can only be a curve for that particular decision maker*. If decisions are a group responsibility, then the whole group needs to meet to work out its utility preferences.

Some people suggest that a decision maker's utility curve can be estimated by a *lottery dialogue* between the analyst and the decision maker. Let's illustrate it by a supposed dialogue between the Careful Manufacturing Company decision maker and a systems analyst.

Analyst: Well, we've worked out two points on your utility curve. Now let's try and fill in the bit in between! I want you to suppose that I have designed a system which gives you an *even chance* of having the report at 8 a.m. or at 11 a.m.

DM: Sounds a strange system; but OK! I'll go along with it!

Analyst: Let's call that 'System A'. I can also offer you System B which will give absolutely guaranteed delivery of the Production Report, every day, at 9 a.m.

DM: If I'm going to wait that long I might as well have an even chance of having to wait until 11. I'll go for A!

Analyst: I'm afraid the situation has changed. System B can deliver the Production Report at 8.30 a.m.

DM: That's a bit more like it; B!

Analyst: System B will deliver at 8.45 a.m.

DM: No, too late! I'll switch back to A.

Analyst: 8.40 a.m.

DM: Well, that's a bit difficult. I think I'm indifferent between the two options.

Analyst: I'm going to change System A. The system will give you an even chance of delivery of the Production Report at 8.40 a.m. or at 11 a.m. System B will deliver at 9 a.m.

DM: System B!

Analyst: 9.15 a.m.

DM: Still B!

Analyst: 9.30 a.m.
DM: I'll change to A.
Analyst: 9.25 a.m.
DM: Well that seems to be the point where it doesn't matter either way!

We'll stop the dialogue there and see where it has got us. The decision maker was indifferent between A and B when A gave an even chance of delivery of the Production Report at 8 a.m. or at 11 a.m. and B gave delivery at 8.40 a.m. Therefore:

Expected utility of delivery at 8.40 a.m. = 0.5 × Expected utility of delivery at 8 a.m. + 0.5 × Expected utility of delivery at 11 a.m. = (0.5 × 1.0) + (0.5 × 0) = **0.5**

We can add this value to the decision curve (Figure 9.8).

After the analyst changed the definition of System A, so that it offered an even chance of delivery at 8.40 a.m., or at 11 a.m., the decision maker was indifferent when B promised delivery at 9.25 a.m. We already know the expected utility of delivery at 8.40 a.m.!

Expected utility of delivery at 9.25 a.m. = 0.5 × Expected utility of delivery at 8.40 a.m. + 0.5 × Expected utility of delivery at 11 a.m. = (0.5 × 0.5) + (0.5 × 0) = **0.25**

We can now plot four values on the utility curve (Figure 9.9). The utility curve suggests that our decision maker's satisfaction decreases rapidly with any delay after 8 a.m. On the other hand, his dissatisfaction doesn't get much greater between 10 a.m. and 11 a.m.

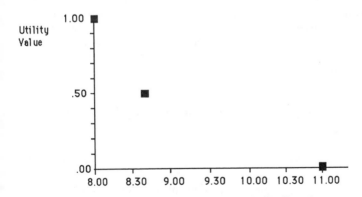

Figure 9.8 Three points on the Production Report utility curve

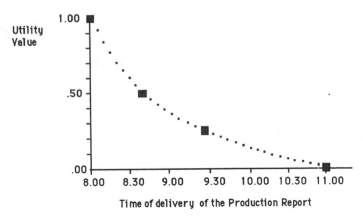

Figure 9.9 Utility curve for the Careful Manufacturing Company Production Manager's attitude to delivery of the Production Report

The dialogue between the decision maker and the analyst would continue longer than we have suggested. As well as establishing more points on the curve, the analyst would attempt to obtain cross checks on points already estimated. Eventually, the analyst and decision maker will, between them, have estimated *the value that the decision maker puts on the whole range of delivery times for the Production Report.*

The idea of utility is not novel. In an earlier section we explored the use of discount factors to estimate a net present value. The NPV is a measure of the satisfaction that a decision maker feels about a set of cash flows, and is therefore in all respects a utility measurement.

There is a good case for saying that all cash flows should be translated into utility terms, as well as the less tangible factors of a firm's performance. A fairly small loss could tip a firm into bankruptcy. A similarly sized gain is likely to be much less crucial to its fortunes.

9.9 Estimating the reliability of our suppliers by using an expression

If we are purchasing software it may be quite crucial to judge the chance that our suppliers are going to remain in business. Should they not, then any guarantees they have given about correcting errors in the software, modifying the software to meet changed conditions, or supplying improved versions of the software are valueless. This is particularly important with a product like software. No large capital investment is required to set up in business. The supplying company may consist of two software builders, a secretary and the proverbial dog.

A company's annual accounts (if we have access to them) should tell shareholders and potential customers of the company a great deal about that company's health. Rate of gross profit, turnover, creditors, bank overdraft and excessive debt are all cited as important indicators, probably in combination. Argenti[10] quotes a golden rule that no company should have one single project that it could not afford to write off. In the same book Argenti suggests that a small company which appears to have little budgetary control and inadequate records is suspect. He refers to the need to judge the image that the company gives to people who visit it, and the degree of trust that, as potential clients, we may feel for its officers as individuals. Small, highly technically oriented companies do not have a good record of survival.

As for external signs, a company which is cutting prices, pressing customers for payment and delaying paying its own bills almost certainly has cash flow problems. Poor cash flow, an inability to pay due bills, is the usual immediate cause of a company's downfall.

Altman[11], using data relating to American companies, suggests what is truly a utility measurement of company health. He acknowledges that a company is more likely to fail during hard times, and therefore starts by calculating the change in the failure rate (the number of failures per 10000 existing firms) from one quarter to the next. His failure rate is computed as a weighted sum of the change in the Gross National Product, the change in the Stock Exchange Index, the change in the money supply, and a constant term. It is only for the same period, when the same failure rate applies, that comparison between companies can be made.

Altman's final equation to determine an index, Z, of a company's health, is:

$$Z = 0.012\ X_1 + 0.014\ X_2 + 0.033\ X_3 + 0.006\ X_4 + 0.010\ X_5$$

where

X_1 is the ratio of working capital to total assets. Working capital is the difference between current assets and current liabilities. Total assets is, according to the US definition, the sum of fixed assets plus current and other assets. This is not reduced by current liabilities, as it would be in Britain;

X_2 is the ratio of retained earnings to total assets;
X_3 is the ratio of earnings before tax and interest to total assets;
X_4 is the ratio of stock exchange market value to total debt;
X_5 is the ratio of sales to total assets.

If for a specific company Altman's Z comes out as less than 1.8, then it is extremely likely that the company will fail. If it is more than 3.0 then the company almost certainly will not fail. In the American environment, Altman's Z does seem to have some validity.

All the measures of company reliability which we have considered are, in effect, binary ones, such as we discuss in the next section. Either we have confidence in the company's survival or we don't.

9.10 Binary utility measurement

Before we leave utility there is one extremely useful utility measurement to mention. This is the binary measurement that distinguishes between 'good enough' and 'not good enough'. Perhaps instead of helping to prepare a utility curve the Careful Company's Production Manager might have said that he *must* have the Production Report by 8.30 a.m. Anything later than this is of no value!

The process is often called *satisficing*[12]. There is some threshold of performance which is acceptable and anything short of that threshold is unacceptable. There is no particular merit in doing better than the threshold.

If we are concerned with reliability perhaps we can demand that the system is available for use for 95% of peak usage time (or 99%, if that is deemed by the people who own the problem area to be more appropriate). For system performance, we may demand that there be a response to new transactions within ten seconds, or that the system will handle 1000 transactions an hour.

The threshold chosen will probably be somewhat arbitrary. Perhaps ideally we would prefer to specify requirements, and measure performance in dollars, pounds or utility units. If we decide that we can't do that then we are bound to choose a satisficing level which we believe to be in the best interests of the firm.

Some measurements we may wish to make are, by their nature, binary. If we are interested in whether a supplier of software makes all the documentation about the software available, then either it is available or it isn't! There isn't a half-way house.

9.11 System evaluation with multiple purposes

If all the purposes of a system can be described in the same unit of measurement (dollars or pounds, for example), then evaluation is no more difficult than with a single purpose. All we have to do is to represent each possible action in terms of that unit, and then choose the action which gives us the best total value for the pay-off.

Inventory models express *stock holding cost, ordering cost, lost sales cost* and *salvage cost* of stock surplus to sales requirements, in money units. The preferred action is the one which minimizes the total of all these costs[13]. In this section we shall consider cases which are less straightforward[14].

We'll assume that the Careful Manufacturing Company is pursuing four purposes:

1. It wishes the Production Manager to receive a report of the previous day's production;
2. It is concerned about the time at which the report is delivered each day;
3. It wishes to minimize the cost, subject to the other purposes being achieved; and
4. It is concerned about the reliability of the software product it is buying.

The company is considering two products, the 'Spartan' and the 'With Bells On', which we have already met. The two products each have both hardware and software aspects. Both products are capable of producing the required production report and therefore the first purpose isn't contentious. The utility curve for delivery time is displayed in Figure 9.9.

In Figure 9.10 we show, a utility curve for system cost. We have assumed that the utility, or satisfaction that the decision maker feels about the cost is, up to a certain limit, roughly inversely proportional to the amount in dollars or pounds. Above that limit (perhaps when the departmental cost budget is exceeded) the utility goes down very fast!

After long discussion, the Careful Company have decided that an appropriate measure of reliability is the number of similar systems which have been supplied to other firms by the supplier in question. The utility curve is displayed in Figure 9.10. The real benefit to the firm is linked with the ability to deliver a daily production report. In addition, the firm wishes to obtain the benefit cheaply, sufficiently early each day, and reliably. The appropriate estimates for the two contending systems are as shown in Figure 9.11.

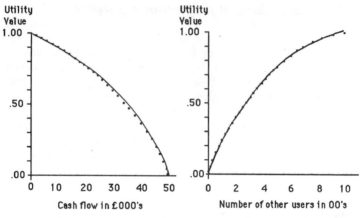

Figure 9.10 Careful Manufacturing Company's cash flow and reliability utility curves

	With Bells On		Spartan	
	Estimated Value	Utility Value	Estimated Value	Utility Value
Daily delivery time	8.00 a.m.	1.0	8.30 a.m.	.6
Cost of the system	£45000	.2	£30000	.6
Reliability	75 users	.2	700 users	.9

Figure 9.11 'With Bells On' and 'Spartan' utility values

There would not be any particular difficulty about postulating different 'states of the world' if this is appropriate to the real problem. We are still concerned with converting data such as those we have just set out into a form which we can enter into a pay-off table. Four of the six approaches that we outline below do that by producing a single scalar value.

9.11.1 A weighted sum of utility values

If we were to add the three utility values together for each of the two competing systems, we would be back with a single measure of satisfaction. We would choose the system with the highest utility score, out of a maximum of 3.0. Since we have considered each of our four purposes in isolation, it's very unlikely that that would give us the answer we are looking for. Necessarily, we have to make a judgement about the *relative* importance of delivery time, cost and reliability.

We'll suppose that by a dialogue such as that in Section 9.8 we've established the decision maker's indifference between two options:

Option 1: Delivery time – 11.00 a.m., giving a utility value of 0.0
         Cost   – £0,   giving a utility value of 1.0
         Reliability   – 500 users, giving a utility value of 0.75
Option 2: Delivery time – 8.40 a.m., giving a utility value of 0.5
         Cost   – £50 000, giving a utility value of 0.0
         Reliability   – 500 users, giving a utility value of 0.75

In addition, we've established the decision maker's indifference between two further options:

Option 3: Delivery time – 8.30 a.m., giving a utility value of 0.6
         Cost   – £45 000, giving a utility value of 0.2
         Reliability   – 500 users, giving a utility value of 0.75
Option 4: Delivery time – 9.00 a.m., giving a utility value of 0.4
         Cost   – £30 000, giving a utility value of 0.6
         Reliability   – 500 users, giving a utility value of 0.75

Since the reliability measurement is constant for all the options, we can leave it out of the comparison. If we compare the options on the other two system purposes we must conclude that *the decision maker regards the delivery time as twice as important as cost!* Will you check that conclusion as a self-assessment?

We'll assume that by a similar set of comparisons we've established that the decision maker regards reliability and delivery time as equally important. Answer the self-assessment questions at the end of the chapter to be sure that you appreciate this. Evidently, the weightings that the decision maker gives to delivery time, cost, and reliability are 2, 1 and 2, respectively (or 10, 5 and 10, if you prefer those).

Now we can take those weights into the comparison of 'With Bells On' and 'Spartan' (Figure 9.12). This gives us the comfortably preferred choice of 'Spartan'!

	With Bells On			Spartan		
	Utility value	*Weighting*	*Total*	*Utility value*	*Weighting*	*Total*
Delivery time	1.0	2	2.0	0.6	2	1.2
Cost	0.2	1	0.2	0.6	1	0.6
Reliability	0.2	2	<u>0.4</u>	0.9	2	<u>1.8</u>
			2.6			3.6

Figure 9.12 Evaluation of 'With Bells On' and 'Spartan' by weighted utility

9.11.2 Combination of several utility curves into a single utility function

If we are going to produce a single utility function the extreme points are quite easy to fix. The highest utility is a delivery time of 8 a.m., a cost of zero and a reliability of 1000 other users. The three utility values are all 1! Similarly, the lowest utility is where the delivery time, cost and reliability all have utility values of zero. As always, it's fixing the utility values between these extremes which is the difficult part.

The indifference comparisons between options 1 and 2 and between options 3 and 4, described above, could be extended over the whole possible range of utility values, for all three of the system purposes. It's conceptually possible to identify 'contours' so that the decision maker is indifferent between any points on any one contour. The difficulties standing in the way of doing this seem to be immense.

The first problem is that the number of comparisons that the decision maker would be called on to make is extremely large, with a very small chance of maintaining consistency over the whole range. The second is closely related. The amount of effort involved in producing the utility function is large and the product is ephemeral. A small change in the environment can change the decison maker's decision preferences and make it necessary to repeat the whole process.

The third difficulty is less serious. It's easy to display a utility curve if we have a single purpose. If our purpose has two dimensions then it's more difficult. Anything above that is harder still. We don't want to exaggerate this point, because it can be overcome by using a computer to store the utility function and display the combined utility value. In spite of the attraction of producing a single utility value to plug into a pay-off table, we don't recommend this approach to evaluation[12].

9.11.3 Other examples of weighted formulas

It is in fact extremely common in decision making that a set of utility measurements is made, and these are then combined together by some kind of weighted formula, as in Section 9.11.1. We give a few examples below.

In many games the purpose is to get a ball between goalposts, or through a net or over a line. Rugby football is more complicated. A player earns merit by scoring a try, by converting a try into a goal, by scoring a penalty goal, or by scoring a dropped goal. Each of these desirable actions is rewarded by scoring a different number of points. Presumably a try is of more utility than a penalty goal, because (in the Rugby Union game, at least) more points are awarded for a try. To determine who has won a match you add together the number of tries multiplied by the points scored per try, the number of conversions multiplied by the points scored per conversion, and so on. It is a sum of weighted utilities.

Many Football Association teams compete in a league. In some leagues a team scores three points for winning a game, one point for a draw and none for losing. The points for all the games they play in a season are added together to give their total season's points.

In most examinations sat by students, the marks available for each question vary according to the supposed difficulty of or time required to complete that question. The student's examination mark is obtained by adding together the marks awarded for each question.

Some well-known retail stores offer their customers 'charge cards', provided those customers are deemed to be 'creditworthy'. The measurement of creditworthiness is based on the answers the customers give to questions on an application form. The questions asked are along the lines of:

'Do you own your own house?'
'How long have you lived in your present house?'
'Put a tick against the range which includes your present annual income.'

Each response a customer gives is scored. The total of all the individual scores determines the customer's creditworthiness.

If you should go on a railway journey or stay in an hotel you may be asked to fill in a questionnaire, giving a rating from 1 to 5 on, for example, the quality of the food, the cleanliness, the helpfulness of the staff, or whatever else appears to the questionnaire designer to be an appropriate purpose that you may have. The individual scores you give will be summed and used as an assessment of customer satisfaction.

Employee-appraisal schemes often require an employee's supervisor to complete an appraisal form[15]. The form will have such questions as:

'Is he punctual?'
'Do his staff maintain a good standard of dress?'
'Is the workplace clean?'

The employee's eligibility for promotion or salary enhancement may depend on the appraisal score obtained.

Our theme is that utility measurement is an almost indispensable part of decision making; that the measurements used are often arbitrary; that the utility measurements often relate to several different purposes or to a purpose that has several dimensions; and that arbitrary means are used to combine these measurements into a single total utility.

9.11.4 Non-monetary costs and benefits as tie breakers

If all the cost and benefits can be translated into cash terms and entered into a pay-off table, then the simple approach outlined in Section 9.2 will be quite adequate. One method of evaluation requires that the evaluation be made on tangible cash costs and benefits alone. Any other purposes that the decision maker may have and which cannot be expressed in cash terms are ignored. Only if there is a tie between two possible actions are the non-monetary costs and benefits brought in as tie breakers.

Clearly, this strategy emphasizes the monetary purpose. It should not be rejected out of hand. If a firm operating in the marketplace fails to meet its monetary objectives it will go out of business. There is an unavoidable imperative about that.

Monetary purpose isn't necessarily only about profit. A redesigned inventory control or invoicing system is probably justified by a consequent reduction in working capital. This will reduce interest payments and therefore will be reflected in the pay-off table, but the benefits to the firm will be greater than just a reduction in interest payments. The firm's earnings will relate to a smaller total investment, to the benefit of the health of the firm. Investment which did not produce an income will have been removed, leaving funds available for other purposes. The equity-to-debt ratio may be more healthy. We don't, then, remove the need to think about the utility of an action simply because we confine ourselves to money!

9.11.5 Satisficing, with several system purposes

Satisficing was described in Section 9.10. Only one assessment is made against each purpose. Either the required level of performance is reached or it isn't! This offers us an effective means of combining several different system purposes.

Satisficing does alter the nature of the decision rule. It may be that we require that the satisficing level be reached on all the various system purposes. The converse of this is that all the available actions which reach these satisficing levels are each equally acceptable.

With our Careful Manufacturing Company case study we could, for example, specify that the Production Report must be produced; that it must be produced by 8.30 a.m. each day; that the cost should not exceed £30 000; and that there should be at least 300 other similar users of any selected product. If you look at Figure 9.11 you will see that this will result in selection of the 'Spartan' basic system.

A variation of this decision rule is to set satisficing levels for all but one of the system purposes, and to maximize or minimize on the remaining purpose. The Careful Company could properly set their production report, delivery time and reliability requirements as constraints. They would then choose the action which met all the constraints with the least cost.

An alternative variation is to fix satisficing levels for each constraint and to choose the action which achieves the highest number of passes. This must be a crude decision rule, and our preference is strongly for the method illustrated in the next section.

9.11.6 The 'squash ladder' or 'bench mark' decision rule

This method is, in many ways, the most satisfactory. Basically it is a *satisficing* method, but with interesting variations.

First, we list the purposes which *must* be achieved. In Figure 9.13 these are:

	Purpose	With Bells On	Spartan
Essential	Produce a Production Report	✓	✓
	Deliver the Report by 9.00 a.m. each day	✓	✓
	Initial cost not more than £30,000	✓	✓
	Good quality documentation provided	✓	✓
Desirable	1. At least 300 other users of this software		✓
	2. Deliver the report by 8.30 a.m. each day	✓	✓
	3. Graphical display of data	✓	
	4. At least 1000 hours mean time between failures.		✓
	5. Supplying firm appears to keep good records		✓
	6. Supplying firm has at least five employees		✓
	7. Deliver the report by 8.00 a.m. each day	✓	
	8. Enhancement of the system not necessary for at least two years	✓	

Figure 9.13 The 'squash ladder' method of evaluation

1. To deliver the production report;
2. To do it by 9.00 a.m. each day;
3. To limit the cost to £30 000; and
4. To obtain good-quality documentation from the suppliers.

Necessarily, we must be able to show that any proposed action meets these purposes.

Second, we list below these essential purposes, the purposes *we should like to achieve*. Further, *we list them in order of importance*. This is the key part. It means that agreement must be reached by all those involved in the decision about *what we are trying to do*, without being too heavily influenced by the actions which are actually available. (Although there can be no guarantee that a decision maker who already has a preferred action won't bias the list of purposes towards that preferred action!)

A very important point is that although all the purposes have satisficing criteria, there is nothing to prevent a purpose being entered twice:

1. Production Report delivered by 9.00 a.m.,
2. Production Report delivered by 8.30 a.m.

The second entry is a more stringent requirement. Conversely, there is nothing to prevent two different utility measures being used, even though the purposes to which they relate are broadly similar.

Thus for an assessment of the chance of the company supplying the product remaining in business the following information is required:

1. Rate of gross profit of the supplying company for the last financial year;
2. Whether the supplying company appears to keep good records;
3. Whether the supplying company has at least five employees;
4. Value of Altman's Z greater than 3.

If one of the four is deemed more significant than the others it will be promoted to a higher position in the list of purposes. You will see that we have not included all these measures in Figure 9.13.

In addition to the purposes previously listed (delivery of a production report, delivery at an appropriate time, limitation of cost and good-quality documentation), the other purposes we may try to meet are:

1. Reliability;
2. Enhanced performance of the product, such as graphical display of data;

3. The ability of the system to recover after failure;
4. The ability of the system to expand to cope with growth;
5. The continuing viability of the supplying company.

The option always exists of subsuming any of these purposes in a monetary pay-off *if the translation into cash terms is feasible*. Thus reliability may be measured by mean time between failures or by the expected annual cost of non-delivery, if it is feasible to assess that cost.

Once the essential and the desirable purposes have been set out and a record made of whether or not a proposed action satisfices that purpose, as in Figure 9.13, evaluation can proceed. To qualify for selection, any candidate action must meet all the essential purposes. In general, the action will be chosen which satisfices *furthest down the list of desirable purposes*. Subjective choice must remain. In Figure 9.13, 'With Bells On' reaches further down the list of desirable purposes than 'Spartan' but it has some failures high up the list.

What is important is that the decision maker has a clear way of comparing the anticipated performance of the competing actions. This can be done by the 'squash-ladder' approach which we have outlined. It could be done by listing the purposes and rating each possible action against these purposes by awarding one, two or three stars. With both methods we are trying to evaluate the relative utility of the competing actions.

9.12 Review of methods of evaluation

We started this chapter by suggesting the pay-off table as the mechanism for choice. That remains our position. The pay-off table requires us to identify the available actions. Without that there can be no choice. If different possible future states of the world exist, they can be catered for. What is required is that estimation of pay-off is repeated for each proposed action and for each possible state of the world.

It is unlikely that a pay-off will be a single scalar quantity. Much more likely is that it will be vector of several values, each relating to a different system purpose. One of those purposes is likely to be the maximization of monetary benefit or the minimization of monetary cost. Apart from monetary cost or benefit, other values will be expressed in units of utility or satisfaction. The selection of units which express the level of satisfaction is perhaps the most difficult part of the whole evaluation process.

Any uncertainty which we feel in estimation of pay-off values should be tested by sensitivity analysis. If the decision choice made by the decision maker is robust and not sensitive to changes in the pay-off values, then we can have a lot of confidence in that decision. If the decision changes as we change pay-off values, then more searching judgement is required about where the value actually lies. The time and expense that we devote to this search will depend on our judgement of the cost of being wrong.

Somehow, we have to combine the vector of utility values in a way that allows us to choose between different pay-offs. If we are contemplating a future with only one assumed state of the world, then the decision rule is designed to choose the most attractive pay-off vector. If we contemplate several possible states of the world, then the decision rule must take account of this uncertainty. If the decision maker is unable to guess what the possible states of the world may be, then the situation is one of risk, with no real basis for any analysis of this risk. If none of the actions we are examining meets the requirements of the decision rule, then we must either revise downwards our statement of what we are trying to do or invest more time and money into the search for more acceptable solutions.

Finally, let's repeat a rider that we put in earlier. There is no point in complicated analysis for its own sake. If it is obvious which action should be taken, don't waste time chasing complexity. We round off this section with a statement from a well-known industrialist: 'If you need a sophisticated technique to show that something is worth doing, it probably isn't worth doing!'

9.13 The relationship with subsequent design stages

If we select one action in preference to other actions we are doing so because of the assumed benefits of that action. It is important then that those benefits are actually realized. The performance which we have assumed for our chosen action against the defined system purpose (the statement of *what we are trying to do*) must eventually provide the basis for system testing of the completed and packaged new system. It must also be the basis of any audit that we carry out on the implemented system. If we find that the action we have chosen *doesn't* result in a system that corresponds to the benefits that we assumed for it, then we urgently need to overhaul our evaluation methods.

9.14 Summary

- We must be clear about the problem. What are we trying to do? Where do we want to be at?
- The basis for analysis is the pay-off table. This is a set of available actions from which one must be chosen. Different pay-offs will result from each action. The pay-offs depend on the future (unknown) state of the world.
- Our choice of action depends on the decision rule that we use. The pessimistic rule assumes that whatever action we choose, the pay-off will be the worst possible. We then maximize these worst possibles.
- The expected value decision rule requires that we have an estimate of the probability of each state of the world. We then choose the action with the highest expected value.
- Whenever a pay-off analysis is made, the sensitivity of the solution to assumptions about pay-off values and probabilities should be tested.
- If we are performing our analysis on cash flows the value inserted into the pay-off table will be the net present value (NPV) of these cash flows.
- Many of the costs and benefits of any action are non-monetary and non-tangible. If a benefit can be expressed as an equivalent monetary amount, and a cost can be expressed as the cost of avoiding it, then there is no real need to change the simple approach.
- For other non-tangible costs or benefits we can attempt to estimate the utility or satisfaction which is linked with that cost or benefit.
- Estimates of utility might be by a subjective judgement, by a lottery dialogue or by using an expression based on previous research.
- A particularly useful approach is satisficing, or binary utility.
- If several different purposes are being pursued, then these must be reconciled. We describe:

    A weighted sum of utility values;
    Combination of utility values into a single utility value;
    Using non-monetary costs and benefits as tie breakers;
    Satisficing on each of the different system purposes;
    The 'squash ladder' or 'benchmark' decision rule.

- We regard the last of these as the most useful. It separates the purposes which are essential from those which are merely desirable. It requires an attempt to rate the desirable purposes in order of desirability.

Discussion points

9.1 We suggest two decision rules; the pessimistic and the expected value. Do you consider that an individual person will always be either a pessimistic or an expected value decision maker?

9.2 'Pessimistic decision making is a recipe for inaction.' Discuss.

9.3 A well-known industrialist is quoted as saying 'if you need a sophisticated technique to decide whether something is worth doing, it probably isn't worth doing'. Discuss.

9.4 Why does the introduction of discount factors tend to cause a large decrease in the net present value?

9.5 If a company commissions software development by an outside contracting company then the cost of that development will clearly be the price charged by the contractors.

If the software development is carried out by an internal department of the same company, which is itself a profit centre, then presumably the situation is similar to that of the outside contractors.

The internal department carrying out the development may be a cost centre which is not required to show a profit but is required to keep its costs within its departmental cost budget. The last situation is that the software development is done internally but by a group of people who are regarded as a necessary overhead (for example, the Treasurer's department) and who do not charge for their services.

Discuss these several arrangements for carrying out development work, with regard to:

> Work being done which should not have been done;
> Work not being done which should have been done;
> The likelihood of achieving a design matching the user's requirements;
> The 'efficient' use of the company's resources.

In the case of the internal development department operating as a profit centre, should external contractors be allowed to compete with this department?

9.6 'Whenever assumptions are made about the real world, these assumptions should be tested for sensitivity.' Discuss.

9.7 'The imperative of the marketplace is that to stay in business a firm must make adequate profits. Therefore any investment must be examined in terms of monetary profitability.' Discuss this statement.

9.8 'Utility measurement is an integral part of almost all routine decision making.' Discuss.

References

1. The Gospel according to Matthew; Chapter 25, verses 14–30
2. J. Murdock and J. A. Barnes, *Statistical Tables for Science, Engineering, Management, and Business Studies*, Macmillan, London (1974)
3. F. Modigliani and H. Miller, 'The cost of capital, corporate finance and the theory of investment', *The American Economic Review*, June (1958)
4. H. Bierman and S. Smidt, *The Capital Budgeting Decision*, Macmillan, London (1958)
5. *Accounting for the Effects of Changing Prices: a Handbook*, Issued by the Accounting Standards Committee of CCAC Ltd, London (1986)
6. C. West, *'SWOT' (Success Without Tears) – Investment Appraisal*, Financial Training Publications, London (1987)
7. G. Terborgh, *Business Investment Policy*, Machinery and Allied Products Institute (1958)
8. K. Bedall Pierce, 'Computers and information technology', *Financial Times* (1984)
9. Prepared for the course team by Lyn Jones, The T341 course units 9 and 10, Decision Analysis, Open University (1975)
10. John Argenti, *Corporate Collapse: The Causes and Symptoms*, McGraw-Hill, Maidenhead (1976)
11. Edward Altman, *Corporate Bankruptcy in America*, Heath, Lexington, Mass. (1971)
12. S. E. Bodily, *Modern Decision Making*, McGraw-Hill, New York (1985)
13. H. V. Wagner, *Principles of Operations Research*, Prentice-Hall, Englewood Cliffs, NJ (1969)
14. P. G. Moore and H. Thomas, *Tha Anatomy of Decisions*, Penguin, Harmondsworth (1976)
15. J. Tiffin and E. J. McCorwick *Industrial Psychology*, Allen and Unwin, London (1971)

Part 3

Management and control

Chapter 10

The data dictionary

10.1 What is a data dictionary?

We have referred to data dictionaries many times in earlier chapters, and in Chapter 2 gave some examples relating to the cub-scout sports day. A conventional dictionary records *how words are used*. A data dictionary records *information about data*. Writers often speak of *meta-data* to describe this information.

We'll deal with synonyms first. The terms *directory* and *catalogue* are often used. It is tempting to adopt both terms, and to use them for different meta-data. For simplicity, we shall stick with data dictionary but commend Everest's description of a data dictionary as an *information system resource catalogue*[1].

The data we are interested in include any *data object*. A data object can be a table in a database or any column of that table. We are also using data object to cover a named entity type or any attribute of that entity type. We are considering a screen definition or a program to be a data object. In brief, anything which has a *structure* which we can describe and a *context* in which to place it is a data object.

Let's give some examples of context data:

1. Frequencies and volumes of data flows. (Cub-scout sports day *entries* are made once a year for each of five packs and comprise data on 100 to 150 cub-scouts. Separate entries will be received from different cub-scout packs, spread over about two weeks.)
2. Frequencies of execution of functions (*Line up at start* occurs once for each of the 30 scheduled races included in the cub-scout sports day.)
3. Volume of data in a data store (SPORTS PROGRAMME stores one instance of general header data, plus data about 30 races, with from four to eight contestants in each race).
4. A description of the meaning and purpose of the data and why it is kept[1].
5. Some subjective expression of the reliability of the data[1].

Apart from queries relating to the data just described, others on context data might be:

1. Has a proposed name for a data object already been used to identify a different data object?
2. It has been realized that a firm's stock inventory is excessive. What synonyms exist for the same stock item?
3. Which programs require access to a particular data object?

Structural data define the data object and the data object's role as a part of larger data objects. A program's structure is defined by listing the program itself. The structure of a data model is recorded by describing the entity types, relationships and attributes which make up that model and the integrity rules which govern its use.

A program can be seen as a set of rules. Similarly, a screen definition may include integrity rules as an integral part of that definition. This makes sense if you are using software which enforces integrity rules as data are entered through a VDU screen. In this chapter we shall assume that integrity rules are a part of the data model, and will not separately list programs or the integrity rules within a screen definition.

The data objects on which we shall concentrate in our study are data models, entity types, attributes, base tables, views, columns of tables and relationships. We have earlier (Figure 2.2) suggested a description of data flows and we shall return to them later in this chapter. The great majority of the meta-data that we shall present will be structural data. Some examples of queries posed on structural data might be:

1. Do we record the colour of cub-scout's eyes?
2. What attributes describe the CUB-SCOUT entity type?
3. Must a cub-scout be enrolled in a cub-scout pack?
4. If we delete a cub-scout pack from the database what do we do about the cub-scouts who are enrolled in that pack?

Finally, there are some meta-data which are best described as *administrative data*. The date on which a data table was last modified, the name of the person who made the modification and that of the person currently responsible for that data object come in this category.

The context data and the administrative data are both principally *data for designers* and *data for database administrators*. The structural data are, of course, of great interest to designers, but this is not their main function. If an application is going to exist at all, then the integrity rules must be enforced. We assume that these integrity rules will in some sense be stored with the data and invoked to ensure the integrity of those data.

Let's end the section by suggesting queries which would require access to the database rather than to the data dictionary:

1. How many customers do we supply?
2. Which of our sales people works in the Great Missenden area?
3. Who came third in the under-9, 80-metre race?

10.2 What do words mean?

In this section we are going to discuss words in general rather than words that you would look for in a data dictionary. We'll then concentrate on data dictionary words in the rest of the chapter.

Some of the words that are essential to the processing of data are those that are defined in a language manual (COBOL, FORTRAN, CODASYL data definition language, etc.). As in ordinary speech, the *grammatical words* are needed in order to put together intelligible 'program' statements, but they don't contain any information.They include the propositions (to, in, from); the words introducing clauses (if, then, while, until, else); and adjectives (next, last, prior, current). The role of these words is similar to that of punctuation. Perhaps a grammatical rule will decree that a conditional statement must start with 'if' and end with ';'.

Next, there are *imperative verbs* (print, read, write, assign, open, close, goto). They imply manipulation, change of state or change of control. In some sense they will be used in any processing language. Any change of state requires the use of *operators* (plus, minus, divided by, union, negation). Most of the operators will be written as symbols rather than as strings of characters, but that doesn't alter the argument in the least.

There are also words or groups of words that predicate something. Basically, these are verbs, possibly but not necessarily qualified by other words. These verb groups will be recognized by processing languages as *relational operators* (is less than, is equal to, is less than or equal to). When we produce data models the relationship names also predicate something about the relationship between the entity types (includes, is entered as, places, makes payment for).

Function names are also verbs (line up at start, judge heats, cut kit, manufacture moulds). They assert some action by a subject. If the function we are identifying includes several activities, we prefer to use a gerund (a verbal noun, ending in 'ing') as a function name (accounting, manufacturing, purchasing). There is a real difficulty here. When an analyst attempts to draw up a physical data flow diagram the first cut at functions may be an identification of what departments do. The function names are then the names of those departments (Accounts, Stores, Mould Shop, Inventory, Sales). These names probably won't conform to our linguistic convention.

The last group of words are *nouns*. These come at several levels. At the highest level are the *structural terms* which are the basis of any language in which we make models of systems. If we want to describe the components of a real world system, we can do it in terms of entity types, attributes, relationships, data flows, functions, and sources or sinks of data (just as we did for the cub-scout sports day). If we want to describe the data storage requirements it may be in terms of files, tables, columns, record types and data items. Because the meaning of words is often ambiguous, we may use 'attribute' to describe something both about the real world and about data storage.

If we look for particular *examples* of entity types we can identify CUB-SCOUT, CONTESTANT, CUSTOMER, PRODUCT. If we want examples of attributes we can identify CubScoutName, DateOfBirth, Position, CustomerName, Description. These entity type and attribute names are nouns too. It is to find out the meaning and use of these names, and, of course, of relationship names, that we resort to a *data dictionary*. To find out the meanings of the structural terms themselves we need a good technical dictionary, or perhaps this book itself can give adequate understanding!

Attributes have instances (Sean O'Brien, 9th Bath, J. Smith & Son, 5th December 1981, Widget). Some of these instances are also nouns. In many cases, they are proper nouns. If we want to know the values or instances of attributes *it is the database itself we must consult*, not the data dictionary.

In a convential dictionary we expect to read different things about different kinds of words. A verb like 'run' is fairly easily described. A noun such as 'Islam' may need many pages to give an inkling of its meaning derived from many centuries of experience. A verb (and a function) is about *doing*. A noun (and an entity type) is about *being*, with all the accumulated history of having things done to it. Similarly, with a data dictionary you will want to know things about an entity type different from those you want to know about a function.

We believe that an essential part of information system design is rigorous use of the proper words. Sloppy specification causes sloppy design.

In Chapters 6 and 7 we set out the structural rules for a variety of situations. In the sections following this one, we repeat the rule statement. So far as possible, we shall present the rules as tables. By doing that, we preserve the same structure that we have adopted for the display of data. Most of the attributes that we suggest are about structural data.

The sections following this discuss particular kinds of data objects. We shall return to the subject of naming conventions after we have discussed these data objects.

10.3 What we want to know about tables

If we go back to the cub-scout sports day data tables of Figure 2.3 there are four data dictionary entries which are *table descriptions*. We show these as a table (table about tables!) in Figure 10.1. We also include tables based on the Careful Manufacturing Company data model of Figure 6.3 and use the convention adopted throughout this book of naming both entity types and tables with upper-case or capital letters.

The first point to make is that we are talking about *database tables* not entity types. As we progress, both types of data object must, of course, be accommodated. We have also included tables relating to two different data models. Neither design nor computer operation is ever exclusively concerned with one *application*.

We haven't included the 'table description' table in the table. There really is no reason why we shouldn't. It has to be described somewhere! It would be part of the data dictionary database.

table description					
Database Name	Creator Name	Table Name	Type	Date Last Modified	Name of Modifier
C-S SPORTS	SGB	SPORTS	Base	12-Dec-88	SGB
C-S SPORTS	SGB	SCHEDULED RACE	Base	6-Jun-88	SGB
C-S SPORTS	SGB	CONTESTANT	Base	6-Jun-88	SGB
C-S SPORTS	SGB	CUB-SCOUT	Base	9-Sep-88	CYP
C-S SPORTS	SGB	PACK	Base	10-Sep-88	SVB
CAREFUL	CYP	CUSTOMER	Base	5-Jan-89	CYP
CAREFUL	CYP	ORDERS	Base	10-Jan-89	CYP
CAREFUL	CYP	LINE	Base	11-Jan-89	EMM
CAREFUL	CYP	PRODUCT	Base	17-Jan-89	EMM

Figure 10.1 Tables relating to the cub-scout sports day and the Careful Company

The table suggests that there are certain things we want to know about tables. These things are the *atributes* of a class of things called *table descriptions*. These attributes will appear in the data dictionary as *columns*. Our list of attributes is somewhat arbitrary, but reasonable!

It may be that the name of the table creator is required for unique table identification. We have not carried that assumption through this set of tables. 'TableName' is assumed to be unique.

The tables we have described are all *base tables*. The other obvious table type is a *view*. We shall assume that in all respects, save the actual storage of data, a view can be regarded as a table.

The 'DataLastModified' and 'NameOfModifier' are obviously administrative data. These attributes could be included for every data object in the data dictionary. Having made the point once, we shall not show them again.

We have not identified the table key. A table key is still a column of a table, and there are several different roles a column can play apart from being a key. We have shown *key* status in the column description table.

10.4 What we want to know about columns

There are three structural things we want to know about columns. We want to know which columns are included in a table. We shall call this *aggregation*. We want to know what role the column performs in the table. In Figure 10.2 we have labelled this *status*. Finally, we want to know what values we can legitimately write into a column of a table. We shall label this set of values a *domain* but postpone exploring this until later in this chapter. From this we arrive at our first version of column descriptions in Figure 10.2.

We have named the columns as they were orignally presented in the cub-scout sports day tables and the Careful Manufacturing Company data model. The convention that we adopt is to name columns in lower-case letters, with an initial capital for each word and no spaces between words.

Column names must be unique within a table. We do permit duplication of column names between tables but any ambiguity must then be resolved by including the table name in any reference (for example, as 'CONTESTANT.RaceNumber').

'Status' is starred as needing some explanation. 'Key' is fairly self-explanatory. 'Ka' means that the data in the column are a key *attribute*, but are not enough to uniquely identify one row of the table. 'F' designates a foreign key; therefore 'Ka & F' indicates a

column description				
Creator Name	Table Name	Column Name	Status *	Index Name
SGB	SCHEDULED RACE	Race Number	Key	raceindex
SGB	SCHEDULED RACE	Event Name	Attribute	
SGB	CONTESTANT	Race Number	Ka & F	contindex
SGB	CONTESTANT	Cub-Scout Name	Ka & F	contindex
SGB	CONTESTANT	Position	Attribute	
CYP	CUSTOMER	CNo	Key	cusindex
CYP	CUSTOMER	CName	Attribute	
CYP	ORDERS	ONo	Key	ordindex
CYP	ORDERS	CNo	F	
CYP	ORDERS	ODate	Attribute	
CYP	LINE	ONo	Ka & F	lineindex
CYP	LINE	PNo	Ka & F	lineindex
CYP	LINE	OQ	Attribute	
CYP	LINE	DelQ	Attribute	
CYP	MAXNUMBER	NewSeqNo	Attribute	

Figure 10.2 Some of the columns in the cub-scout sports day and the Careful Company's data tables

key attribute, which is also a foreign key in some relationship (so far unspecified!). If any column were a part of a foreign key, then it would be labelled 'Fa' as a foreign key attribute. 'Attribute' is any other undistinguished column!

'IndexName' indicates that an index has been created for that column. We have written about indexes in Chapter 8. The purpose of declaring an index on a particular column is to speed up retrieval using that column. We could have an index on every column, which would give us fast retrieval using RaceNumber, EventName, Cub-ScoutName or any other column in the database. The cost of doing this would be that updating would be slowed down by the need to alter all the indexes.

We deliberately don't present the tables with the entries in any particular sequence. Sequence is really a matter for *how we want to present the data to a human reader* rather than how we want them stored. This means that sequence specification belongs in a view. The logical action that we take to tell the database management system that we want fast retrieval on a particular column is by declaring an index for that column. How the data are arranged to give that fast retrieval is a matter for the database management system, not for the application system designer.

Before we leave column definition there is more to be said about complex data objects. The tables we have presented so far have all been *flat tables*, with all columns of equal standing and one data entry for each row and column intersection. Figure 10.3 gives an

CUB-SCOUT TABLE						
Pack name	Leader's Name	Cub-Scout Data				
		Cub-Scout Name	Date Of Birth			Address
			Day	Month	Year	
2nd Bath	John Miles	Rohit Patel	19	Apr	82	10 North Road
		Simon Birch	12	Sep	81	3 Evelyn Road
25th Bath	Jean Rooke	Jason Hewitt	12	Jan	82	7 George
15th Bath	Edna Collins	David Fox	13	Aug	81	101 Bristol Road
		Simon West	31	May	82	47 Eagle Road
		James Cumming	5	Dec	81	13 High Street

Figure 10.3 An alternative layout for the cub-scout data

alternative arrangement of cub-scout data, with much intra-table rather than inter-table complexity.

Clearly, this doesn't conform to the structural description of Figure 10.2. The difference is that in the previous structure the only levels we allowed to exist were tables and one level of column. Figure 10.3 demonstrates *aggregation* into several more levels of data object than that. We give a revised column description table in Figure 10.4.

The two notable changes are that different levels are introduced and that two more instances of 'Status' appear. A *repeating group* is a group of attributes which is repeated several times. Thus 'Cub-ScoutData' is repeated twice for the 2nd Bath, once for the 25th Bath and three times for the 15th Bath. We could reasonably have added the number of occurrences of the repeating group, or alternatively the maximum number of occurrences of the repeating group, to our column description.

A *vector* has a strictly prescribed number of elements. 'DateOfBirth' always consists of a 'Day', a 'Month' and a 'Year'.

We have not shown any column having the status of *key*. This is because the data in Figure 10.3 are *not normalized* and there is no column which fits our definition of a key. There is no God-given necessity about normalizing data. Since this book is not about designing a data store we shall not discuss whether you should or shouldn't. If for good design reasons you decide not to, then you will need a column definition such as that in Figure 10.4. The effect of this must be that there will be a difference between the *conceptual data model*, describing the real world, and the *storage data model*, describing the database. For the remainder of this chapter we assume normalized data storage and the column definition of Figure 10.2.

column description						
Creator Name	Table Name	Column Name	Level	Higher Level Column Name	Status	Index Name
SGB	CUB-SCOUT	Pack Name	1	CUB-SCOUT	Attribute	
SGB	CUB-SCOUT	Leader's Name	1	CUB-SCOUT	Attribute	
SGB	CUB-SCOUT	Cub-Scout Data	1	CUB-SCOUT	Repeating group	
SGB	CUB-SCOUT	Cub-Scout Name	2	Cub-Scout Data	Attribute	cubindex
SGB	CUB-SCOUT	Date Of Birth	2	Cub-Scout Data	Vector	
SGB	CUB-SCOUT	Day	3	Date Of Birth	Attribute	
SGB	CUB-SCOUT	Month	3	Date Of Birth	Attribute	
SGB	CUB-SCOUT	Year	3	Date Of Birth	Attribute	
SGB	CUB-SCOUT	Address	2	Cub-Scout Data	Attribute	

Figure 10.4 Revised column description

10.5 What we want to know about domains

We referred to a domain as the set of values which we can legitimately write into a column of a table. If two columns belong to the same domain then they are allowed to accept *the same set of values*. A foreign key must obviously belong to the same domain as the primary key to which it points in a different table. More generally, there is no point in repeating a domain definition for several attributes when that definition can sensibly be written just once. We discussed this in Section 7.3.

Figure 10.5 sets out some domain definitions for the Careful Manufacturing Company. Our convention is that the last word in every column name is the domain name. It follows from this that two columns in different tables with the same name *must belong to the same domain*.

To distinguish domain names from column names we always write the domain names with lower-case letters. Since we are

domain description				
Domain Name	Data Type	Data Width	Picture	Values
no	integer	4	'9999'	no between 1 and 1000
name	character	20	'20A'	
date	date	9	'DD-Mon-YY'	date between '1-Jan-1901' and '31-Dec-2000'
q	integer	4	'9999'	q between 1 and 9999
description	character	30	'30A'	

Figure 10.5 Domain descriptions for the Careful Manufacturing Company

assuming normalized data storage, the one data model provides a mapping between the real world and the database, and our domains apply to both.

The data types are the ordinary conventional ones. A domain definition creates a more restrictive data type. In our example we have created a domain ('date') which has the same name as a conventional data type. This could cause some unnecessary confusion and is best avoided. There is a certain amount of redundancy in specifying the width, the 'picture', and the value description for a domain. We don't consider this redundancy harmful.

The conventions we have used in the Picture column are:

9   A decimal digit. If a group of 9s constitute a number, then any zeros at the beginning of the number would be dropped. A negative number is preceded by '-'. Decimal points are indicated by '999.99'.

A   An alphabetic character or a space. The '30A' means that up to 30 such characters are allowed.

N   A decimal *character* or blank character. Although this looks like a decimal digit, it is really part of a string of characters. You cannot add, subtract or divide with it or do any other arithmetic operation.

'th' A literal or string of characters. Thus '8th Bath' would be a legitimate value for PackName.

Different domains will appropriately be defined in different ways. The set of legitimate pack names in the cub-scout sports database could best be defined by a domain with values given as a set:

{ '2nd Bath', '8th Bath', '15th Bath', '25th Bath'}

Domain definition is never easy. We would all be able to say with fair accuracy whether a particular person's name is a woman's name or a man's name. It would be very hard indeed to write a definition of the two sets that a computer could understand.

By implication, *every domain includes a null value*. The null means that there is nothing stored at that position.

We do not, in this book, go into great detail about database integrity. It is enough to say that a system cannot operate at all unless an adequate level of integrity is maintained. Domain definition is a very desirable tool for achieving integrity.

10.6 What we want to know about relationships

The relationships we are describing here are one-to-many relationships between tables. Thus each relationship, its *owner* table and its *member* tables constitute one *A-set type*. It is helpful to list some of the things we might want to know about a relationship. It will be found that we can't easily include them all in one data dictionary table:

1. The name of the relationship;
2. The name of the owner table;
3. Whether or not every row of the owner table must be related to at least one row of a member table (ownership rule);
4. The name or names of any member tables;
5. Whether or not every row in a member table must be related to a row in the owner table (membership rule).

It is the fact that many tables can participate as members of a relationship that makes if difficult to squeeze all this information into one data dictionary table. Figure 10.6 displays information largely about the *owning* table. The DegreeOfMembers tells us about the ownership rule. If the degree is 'none or more' then the owner row in the owner table is allowed to exist with no member rows related to it. A cub-scout pack is allowed to be recorded in the database even if there are no records of member cub-scouts 'enrolled' in the pack.

OwnerDeletion provides a binary rule governing what happens if an attempt is made to delete a row in an owner table. Either the member rows will be deleted by cascade or deletion of the owner

relationship description					Owner Deletion
Arc Name	Owner Table	Relationship Name	Degree Of Members	Owner Deletion	CACSC =
	SPORTS	includes	one or more	CACSC	'Delete
	SCHEDULED RACE	has	none or more	CACSC	members
	CUB-SCOUT	is entered as	none or more	CACSC	on deletion'
	SPORTS	brings together	one or more	CACSC	
	PACK	enrols	none or more	RESTR	RESTR =
order arc	CUSTOMER	places	none or more	RESTR	'Exception
order arc	CUSTOMER	is invoiced for	none or more	RESTR	report if
order arc	CUSTOMER	makes payment for	none or more	RESTR	members
	ORDERS	includes	one or more	CACSC	exist'
	PRODUCT	is ordered in	none or more	RESTR	

Figure 10.6 Relationship descriptions with emphasis on the owner table

row will be restricted if any members exist. If a cub-scout is deleted from the CUB-SCOUT table, then any rows in the CONTESTANT table recording races for which that cub-scout 'is entered' are also deleted. On the other hand, a cub-scout pack cannot be deleted from the PACK table if any cub-scouts 'are enrolled in' that pack.

The ArcName relates to Figure 7.11. An order for a product is allowed one of three relationships with a customer:

1. The customer places the order, or
2. The customer is invoiced for the order, or
3. The customer makes payment for the order.

A customer and an order must be in one of these relationships but *cannot be in more than one at the same time.* We would like to go further, and display the transition possibilities which exist. In this case, an order must pass from 'places' to 'is invoiced for' and finally to 'makes payment for'. These transition possibilities would be a part of the arc description, which we have not presented.

The above paragraph presented integrity rules in terms of real-world entities. The same rules must, of course, be enforced in the database.

Figure 10.7 fills in the missing information about relationship members. The table specifies which column in the member table acts as a foreign key. Obviously, this is a strictly database consideration, and is not part of the data model.

The last column tells us whether or not a row in the member table *must* be related to a row in the owner table. The mechanism for allowing a member row not to be related is to permit a null

relationship member description			
Relationship Name	Table Name	Foreign Key	Maybe/ Mustbe
includes	SCHEDULED RACE	null	Mustbe
has	CONTESTANT	Race Number	Mustbe
is entered as	CONTESTANT	Cub Scout Name	Mustbe
brings together	PACK	null	Maybe
enrols	CUB-SCOUT	Pack Name	Mustbe
places	ORDERS	CNo	Maybe
is invoiced for	ORDERS	CNo	Maybe
makes payment for	ORDERS	CNo	Maybe
includes	LINE	ONo	Mustbe
is ordered in	LINE	PNo	Mustbe

Figure 10.7 Relationship member descriptions

value for the foreign key. The notion of *referential integrity* (Section 7.3.2) is implicit in all the relationships we define.

10.7 The data dictionary data model

It is time to pull all these tables together and present a *data model of the data dictionary*. So far, the only things we have described in the data dictionary have been database tables and the relationships between them. Our first attempt at a data model will include just those.

Let's summarize where we are. To a very large extent, what we have suggested as the data dictionary contents duplicates what we have learned to draw on the ERA data model diagram. As a specification tool, the only things gained from the data dictionary is closer definition of column contents and the owner deletion rules. If we had included an arc definition we would also have recorded some transition possibilities within arcs.

Both the owner deletion rules and the arc transitions relate to what we called *transition integrity* in Chapters 6 and 7. Our data dictionary appears to be a rather better means than an ERA diagram of recording transition integrity rules but, so far, not much else.

An *active data dictionary*, which can be invoked by applications as they are being executed for real, guarantees that integrity rules are being consistently applied to all users of a database. An active data dictionary helps designers. It frees them from the burden of re-specifying consistent integrity rules for every screen they design and for every program.

Outside of the scope of an active data dictionary the benefits of the data dictionary must lie in the ability it gives to designers to interrelate all the different components of design; entity types, tables, attributes, columns, domains, relationships, views, integrity rules, etc. and to maintain the essential consistency of definition without which design becomes impossible. It is that interrelationship that we shall try to present in the remainder of this chapter.

We start in Figure 10.8 with the data model of the data dictionary as we have so far developed it. The data model attempts to show that a database table aggregates many columns, and that some of those columns are key attributes; that tables can be owner tables of relationships, and also member tables of relationships; that a relationship can have many member tables; that a column can sub-aggregate subordinate columns; and finally that columns belong to specific domains.

Data Dictionary

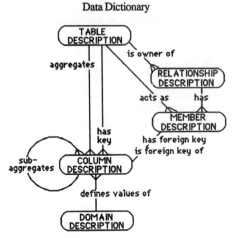

Figure 10.8 A data model of a data dictionary database

We emphasized in Chapter 7 that the integrity rules are a part of the data model. The domain integrity is defined by the combination of the domain description and membership of domains by columns. Table integrity is defined by the column description. We have not yet pinned down transition integrity, apart from the *owner deletion rule* within the relationship description. Figure 10.9 goes a little way towards meeting this by including a rule for *default values* which would be used during input of new values to table columns.

The default values defined are precisely those outlined for the Careful Manufacturing Company in Section 7.7. Keeping to the argument of Section 7.7, there are likely to be transition integrity rules which don't fit easily into our tabular framework. An example is the rule **Roe1** in Section 6.3:

Pre-Insert ORDERS Update MAXNUMBER set NewSeqNo = SeqNo + 1;

In Section 6.3 we suggested that typical descriptions of these rules are 'pre-insert' (like **Roe1** above) or 'pre-delete' or 'pre-update'. We must necessarily record these rules. Figure 10.10 serves to emphasize provision for transition integrity in the data dictionary.

The relationship 'is governed by' is many-to-many, as you will see by examining rule **Roe1** above. We have omitted to label the relationship in both directions.

column description							
Creator Name	Table Name	Column Name	Status *	Index Name	Domain Name	Null ?	Default
CYP	CUSTOMER	CNo	Key	cusindex	no	not	
CYP	CUSTOMER	CName	Attribute		name		
CYP	ORDERS	ONo	Key	ordindex	no	not	MAXNUMBER.NewSeqNo
CYP	ORDERS	CNo	F		no	not	
CYP	ORDERS	ODate	Attribute		date		SystemDate
CYP	LINE	ONo	Ka & F	lineindex	no	not	:orders.ono
CYP	LINE	PNo	Ka & F	lineindex	no	not	
CYP	LINE	OQ	Attribute		q		
CYP	LINE	DelQ	Attribute		q		min(:oq, owner PRODUCT.AvlQ within 'is ordered in')

Figure 10.9 A revised column description, taking account of default values

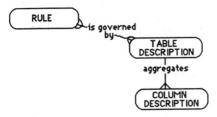

Figure 10.10 Provision for transition rules in the data dictionary

The last modification to the COLUMN DESCRIPTION table is the column headed 'Null?' This recognizes that whether or not a column takes a null value is nothing to do with the domain it belongs to. It is part of the role of that attribute within a table or *table integrity*.

10.8 The relationship between an application and the database

An implemented application must be related to some of the database tables. The application might update them, delete data or insert new data, or simply retrieve existing data. We are going to subsume all these things as 'update', for the purpose of presenting a data dictionary data model. It is quite likely that some of the tables 'updated' will be views. These are usually restrictions on a user's ability to update a database through a view, but that is outside our scope. Essentially, we are seeing a view as either a device for restricting access to the database or a device for defining how new values are calculated from source data (Section 7.8). Any application must be bound by the integrity rules of all types: domain, table, and transition.

Applications will be intimately related to data flows. Some of the data flows will be documents; some will be VDU screens; some will be reports generated by the application. We gave a very sparse outline of a data flow definition in Figure 2.2. Data flows can be very complex data objects. Precisely the structure of attributes, relationships and domains that we have outlined for the database applies to the data flows.

We are still striving for a simple picture. We assume that each data flow is divided into *fields* and that each field relates to exactly one database column. The field must belong to the same domain as the column. Data flows must be related to other data flows (documents to VDU screens, for example) and data flows will have sub-parts which aggregate several fields. We are omitting these niceties. From this we get our next revision of the data dictionary data model in Figure 10.11.

We've already spoken of leaving out most of the complexity of data flow structure. We have also omitted detail of database relationships and of domains. You would also expect to see some link between data flows and tables, just as 'is linked with' relates data flow fields to database columns.

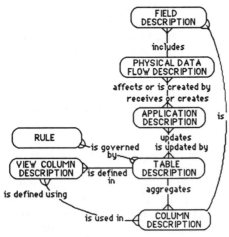

Figure 10.11 Data dictionary data model including application menu-data

10.9 Global data dictionary data model

We need now to present an overall view. We have been putting together a data model describing the data dictionary information about databases. The data dictionary itself is a database. So far, we have presented it as a database about databases. Information about databases isn't the only kind of meta-data that designers need. They also need information about data models and also about how the constructs which model the real world in the data model map to the constructs in the database. Does the entity type CUB-SCOUT map exactly to the database table CUB-SCOUT, or are there perhaps two database tables carrying data represented by just the one entity type?

Our data dictionary must contain data about both databases and data models and our data dictionary data model must try to represent this. We show our (simplified) data dictionary data model in Figure 10.13.

For teaching purposes we have broken some of our cherished rules. All the links between related constructs in the data models and in the databases have been labelled 'maps'. We have given the same entity type name to descriptions of relationships in the data models, and to descriptions of relationships in the databases. Corresponding relationship names in the two halves of the data model are the same. A data dictionary data model which we proposed to use to guide the design of a real data dictionary would require all these names to be distinct.

The segmentation of the data dictionary data model is shown by the thick lines. To illuminate what they mean we have drawn the introductory diagram in Figure 10.12. The 'domain' segment we consider to be independent of both data model and database. If the data dictionary is meta-data then the data model of the data dictionary must be meta-meta-data.

Function description	Application description
Data model description	Database description
Domain description	

Figure 10.12 The global data dictionary data model structure

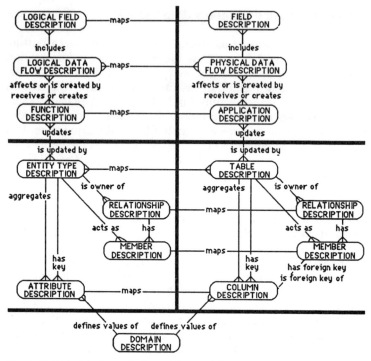

Figure 10.13 A global data dictionary data model

10.10 Naming conventions and synonyms

At the beginning of this chapter we discussed what words mean. We noted that the names of data objects may be different parts of speech, depending on the type of the data object. We also noted that designers must be interested in any synonyms which exist to name the same data object. Subsequently, we explained our own conventions for naming tables and entity types, columns and attributes, and domains.

We want now to emphasize the importance of a consistent naming policy for an organization. It is because of the enormous mass of data that designers must contend with that they need a device such as a data dictionary. If there is no consistent naming policy some of the support that a designer can get from a data dictionary will be lost.

Carter[2] suggested a possible set of guidelines:

1. Use one abbreviation per word ('num', or 'no', but not both).
2. Use the same abbreviated name consistently.
3. Form abbreviations by dropping characters at the end, not in the middle ('Del' for 'Delivery' rather than 'Dlvry').
4. An abbreviation should be at least three letters shorter than the original word.
5. Different words should not have the same abbreviation ('Del' for both 'Delivery' and 'Deletion').
6. An abbreviation for one word should not be confused with a possible abbreviation for another ('q' might be thought to represent 'question' or 'query').
7. An abbreviation should not be another full word ('no' for 'number' or 'ORDER' for 'CUSTOMER ORDER').

10.11 The last word

The data dictionary is a tool for managing size and complexity. An active data dictionary which is in some sense stored with the data is for ensuring consistent enforcement of integrity rules. A data dictionary is used by people, whether they are designers or administrators, to find out what is available, what it means and how to get it[1].

10.12 Summary

- We are interested in any data object, whether it be a database table, a column of that table, a screen definition or a program.
- For each data object, we identify context data, structural data and administrative data.
- We want to know different things about different kinds of words (grammatical words, imperative verbs, predicates, nouns). The words that we expect to be defined in a data dictionary are those such as table names, column names, relationship names.
  We again want to know different things about each of these classes of names.
- For a table description we look for the database name, the creator name, the table type, the date last modified and the name of the modifier. Some of these data are structural and some are administrative. We could additionally define context data.
- Tables may easily be more complex data objects than those we describe in this book. If they are more complex, then a more complex description is required.

- For a column description we look for the table name, the column name, the status, the name of any index defined in that column, the name of the domain that column belongs to, whether the null values are allowed in that column and the default on insertion rules.
- The column status describes the particular role within the table of the entries in that column.
- For a domain description we look for a definition of the set of data allowed in any column belonging to that domain. The set always includes a null value.
- For a relationship description we separate out the description of the relationship members. For the relationship generally, we need the relationship name, the name of the owning table, the degree of members and the rule governing what happens if we try to delete a row in the owning table.
- For a relationship member description we need mainly to know whether that member *may-be* or *must-be* a member.
- If we have defined any arcs we also need an arc description.
- Owner deletion rules and arc transition rules are about transition integrity. Transition integrity usually requires formulation of rules additional to these.
- A passive data dictionary is of value to designers and to database administrators. An active data dictionary is in some sense stored with the data in the database and seeks to guarantee that the integrity rules are consistently enforced.
- A data dictionary must record data not only about the database but also about the data model (or models), the data flows and functions, and the applications which are implemented. We attempt a global picture of this.
- If a data dictionary is to fulfil its purpose we must enforce a consistent set of naming conventions.

Discussion points

10.1 Which of the following queries would you expect to answer by reference to a data dictionary?

Which of our students have blue eyes?
Do we know what training courses our employees have attended?
How many database tables contain personal data about students?
How many students are under 18 years old?

10.2 Should we keep context data, structural data and administrative data in the same data dictionary table?

10.3 What are the relative merits of storing data in normalized flat tables or in tables which are more complex data objects?

10.4 Is there any advantage in using domains to define column contents, apart from the convenience of defining the set of data just once?

10.5 If we are principally concerned with the specification of information requirements what advantages are there in inserting the rules as data dictionary entries rather than recording them on the data model diagram?

10.6 What benefits, if any, do you see from an active data dictionary?

10.7 What advantage, if any, do you see from recording all data object definitions in a single data dictionary?

Exercises

10.1 Make appropriate data dictionary entries in a table description table, a column description table and relationship description tables for the Sellemkwik Garage case study in Chapter 5.

10.2 Suggest a suitable way of recording in a data dictionary how a view is defined. Draw an appropriate data dictionary data model describing this.

10.3 What context do you envisage for a function entry in a data dictionary? Would this context be different in form from the context of the RULE table in Figure 10.11?

References

1 G. C. Everest, *Database Management: Objectives, System Functions, and Administration*, McGraw-Hill, Singapore (1986)

2 B. Carter, 'On choosing identifiers', *ACM SIGPLAN Notices*, May (1982)

3 The M352 course, Computer based information systems, Block 4 – data management, Open University (1980)

Chapter 11

Project management

11.1 Background

We must first decide what it is that we are attempting to control. We suggest:

1. That the artefact we are creating is suited to its purpose.
2. That the work is done within the budgeted limits of development time.
3. That the work is done within budgeted cost.

These aspects are highly correlated. It is easy to produce a list of projects where suitability to purpose was not initially clear, and which ran into a host of time and cost problems. Concorde, the Sydney Opera House and Brunel's *Great Eastern* are just three. If the scheduled development time is overrun, then fixed development costs will be incurred for a longer period and anticipated benefits will be postponed.

The requirements for control are easily stated, and correspond to the three points above. We must be quite clear what the thing we are constructing is supposed to do; we must know what resources we need in order to create it; we must know how long it 'should' take. Unfortunately, we cannot be sure of any of these things until our artefact is virtually complete. If we know what it is that we are trying to design before we design it, then it doesn't need designing! Each step forward increases our knowledge of the design needs and the cost of achieving them.

Even when we are reasonably clear about the purpose, and about the time and cost to achieve that purpose, we need to measure the extent to which the purpose is achieved and to monitor the actual expenditure of resources. Crucially, we should not have to postpone this measurement until completion of the project. All along the line from the first conception to the time when our artefact is fully operational, we should be able to measure whether we are achieving design suitability and are meeting time and cost budgets. We should be able to decide whether to increase the allocated resources, to accept delayed implementation, to abort or to change the purpose of the project.

11.2 Partitioning

A necessary part of any control methodology is the ability to partition the project. With anything but the simplest system, control is difficult (if not impossible) if the project is viewed as a single whole. The difficulties are threefold. First, if progress requires the intellectual cooperation of a group of people it will be difficult for more than about five people to contribute to a single task. Beyond that, attempts to communicate will generate so much noise, and occupy so much time, that little energy will be left over for useful work. The second difficulty is that the larger and more complex the task, the harder it will be to make sensible estimates of the time and cost requirements. Third, it is difficult to monitor partial completion of work. After one month a project may be half finished; after two months three quarters finished; after three months 90%, and after four 95%. It's asymptotic. It gets closer and closer but never actually arrives! The only useful measure of one *work package* is binary. It's either finished or it isn't.

There are clear implications, then, for designing a work package:

1. Its boundary must be clear.
2. Its interface with other work packages must be defined.
3. We must know what it's for.
4. We must know how it contributes to the purpose of the whole system.
5. We must expect completion of the package in a reasonably short period.

The boundary and interface requirements ensure that the 'thing' which is being built can be worked on in relative isolation, and that when it is finished it will slip relatively easily into its place in the great scheme of things. The work packages which follow it will get all the design information they need; no function will be unnecessarily duplicated; no function will be left out by mistake.

A happy by-product of being clear about the boundary and interface of a module produced as one work package is the ease of *application maintenance* which it buys. If the module proves to be unsuitable, or if the demands placed on it change, the outcome should not be disastrous. One implementation can be removed and another slotted in!

It is quite feasible to set up design objectives for work packages (define what the package is for) and to achieve those objectives. Weinberg[1] found that by giving groups of programmers explicit objectives which were different for each group, each group ranked first on the achievement of its own objective. The objectives in Weinberg's experiment were minimum store usage, output clarity, program clarity, minimum number of program statements and minimum hours of development time. The conclusion is that objectives should be clear and explicit. Lacking goals, a group of workers may make their own assumptions, and these assumptions may be in conflict with one another. One of the skills of design management is to ensure that the design objectives for partitions of the system are compatible with the objectives of the system as a whole. Eventually all the separate pieces have to be bolted together and work together!

If we can expect completion of a work package in a short period then there is no need to agonize about what proportion has been completed. At the due reporting time the analyst or programmer is simply asked whether the package is finished. We believe that the estimated length of one work package, at whatever stage it occurs, should be not more than two weeks. For most design projects that is sufficiently short to avoid disaster if thing go badly wrong.

We suggest that partitioning of projects should be both *vertical* and *horizontal*. Let's define what we mean by those two words.

11.2.1 Vertical partitioning

An inherent partitioning exists in the stages of a project. Figure 4.1 suggested that the design process consists of:

Survey
Analysis and specification
Functional construction
Database construction
Hardware study
Implementation
Audit.

Later figures in Chapter 4 showed how these functions could be sensibly sub-divided, but the list is enough to support our argument.

We characterized *completion* of any of these functions as the production of a set of documents or products. The *control milestones* which indicate how far design has progressed up to and including functional construction are:

1. Feasibility document;
2. Functional specification, acceptance test plan, state change specification, global data model, physical requirement specification, budget and schedule;
3. Completed software, training and changeover plan, test plan.

All of these, except for 'completed software', are documents. The 'feasibility document', 'functional specification' and 'completed software' all initiate a three-part decision:

1. Is this thing that has been produced good enough for us to make a decision about what to do next?
2. Do we continue to the next stage, re-do the last stage, or abort the project?
3. If we continue, what resources do we allocate to the next stage of the project?

We will need an up-to-date estimate of how long it's going to take and what it's going to cost us. We listed the budget and schedule as a documentary output of functional specification. These documents are particularly important because they are the resource allocation for the rest of the project. They may be the basis on which we are going to be paid, and they include all the assumptions we are currently making for estimating the cost of future jobs. In addition, *every stage of the project* must produce:

1. A revised time and resources estimate for completion of the project;
2. A detailed time and resources estimate for *the next stage* of the project.

The by-product of comparing the budget and schedule with the actual resources used to complete any task is that *we improve our estimating database*. The more reliable this gets, the more realistic all our future estimating of project cost and duration is going to be.

We are not going to include a long list of rules of thumb for estimating. Some of the classics ('a programmer can complete ten lines of tested code in a day') are becoming outdated by the growth of programmer aids, 'fourth-generation languages' and 'application generators', all of which we believe to be about improving system builders' productivity rather than devices to allow users to do their own system design.

What is important is that any group of people engaged in system design should adopt a *structured approach* such as that outlined in this book, and that they should *standardize* their procedures among themselves. Partitioning is a nonsense if each small part is going to be executed in a different way. The Sistine Chapel's ceiling would look quite different if each section had been executed in a different artistic style!

We emphasized the design decisions as each stage is completed. If decisions have been made, they may need to be re-examined when the system is audited. It is a very important point that not only the decisions *but also the evidence on which those decisions were made* are recorded. A *project history file* recording both the progress from stage to stage and the documentation of *solutions which weren't adopted* is a necessary part of system design. We shall return to this later in this chapter.

11.2.2 Horizontal partitioning

If we are going to adopt 'do it in a fortnight' as the guideline for partitioning then there is an immediate problem. A project for which we can write a feasibility document in two weeks may need two months for analysis and specification and six months to build the software package. Implementation, or the actual changeover to a working system, may be scheduled to be complete in a fortnight or may be staged over several weeks or months.

Necessarily, the *scope* of each work package may be less than that of the package which preceded it. If we have a 'Sales' project for the Careful Manufacturing Company (Figure 6.1), then the scope of the feasibility study may be exactly that. Analysis and specification may be separately carried out for each of the functions 'create customer', 'terminate customer', 'order entry', 'despatch', 'invoicing' and 'process payment' (Figure 6.2).

Once the functional requirements specification for 'order entry' has been written, a test database established, and a view or local data model established for 'order entry', then construction can begin. The function doesn't need to be built in one piece. We could decide that 'order insertion' (Figure 6.5) is a suitable work package. Alternatively, generating the basic input screen may be one work package and building in all the necessary protection may be the subsequent one.

Anything which is decomposed must be put together again. If 'order insertion', 'order update' and 'order deletion' are separate construction work packages, then there is a need for a work package to fit them all together and to test that they actually work together.

It's implicit in the above three paragraphs that an essential part of any work package is to make decomposition necessary for any *dependent* work packages. You cannot know exactly what you mean by 'order insertion' until you have worked out exactly what you mean by 'order entry'. Just as importantly, the 'order entry' work package must make it clear how the 'order insertion' work package is going to be tested to make sure that it does what it's supposed to do! We spoke above of the boundary and interface requirements of a work package. We are now saying that those requirements must be specified within the next senior work package. The design and execution of each work package is a microcosm of the design and execution of the whole system development.

11.3 Naming work packages

Naming of vertical decompositions is relatively easy. If the function we are designing is 'order entry', then we can designate 'oe.survey', 'oe.analysis' and 'oe.construct' or 'oe.build' as design steps. Similarly, the documents resulting from these steps can unambiguously be named as 'oe.feasibility document', 'oe.functional requirements specification', and so on. The requirement for naming follows from the requirement to be able to report how far we have progressed and therefore how much still remains to be done.

Naming horizontal decompositions is more complex. *It is necessary to connect one work package to all its dependent work packages.* If we know the expected time necessary to complete 'order insertion', 'order update' and 'order deletion', and we know the expected resources to complete these three things, then the expected completion time for 'order entry' cannot be shorter than the longest of the three. The expected resources to complete 'order entry' cannot be less than the sum of the resources we need for the three.

An obvious way of making this connection is by some naming convention. We've assumed an hierarchical naming convention in Chapters 2 and 5. Thus Figure 6.2 allows us to name 'order entry' as '1.3(oe)'. If we decide to use unique alphabetic names, such as 'oe', only for the lowest-level functions in the set of data flow diagrams, then we don't need to carry the '1.3' forward into the decomposition of the 'oe' function. We shall call these alphabetically named functions *'applications'*. Figures 6.5 and 6.7 both demonstrate precise naming of quite small partitions of the 'oe' application. These names are all unique identifiers of sub-applications.

All our naming so far has been hierarchical. In Figure 6.5, 'oe123' and 'oe161' are both described as 'Update Product.Av1Q'. If the same function is used in two places, it's absurd to design and build it twice. This is the old 'program sub-routine' idea. It does mean that we need to have a special name for any function that we can use in several contexts.

Fundamentally, every data object is named. If it isn't, then we can't refer to it. We've just described naming applications. Entity types and attributes, tables and columns, and domains too, are all going to be uniquely named. Views and local data models come in a rather special category. One important purpose of both is to record the data needs of a particular application. Thus Figure 6.3 needs to be described as 'oe.local data model'.

With the two small caveats in the above two paragraphs we have described a *top-down* naming convention. This is a comfortable bedfellow with top-down functional analysis and top-down data analysis.

Let's try to summarize all that we have said so far in this chapter. We are trying to preserve the coherence of the whole system and at the same time provide a means of monitoring progress at the basic level. To do this we suggest a progressive decomposition into work packages. Each work package should be of such a size that one or more people (but not more than five people!) *can do it in a fortnight*.

11.4 Reporting plans and results

We choose to describe how data are to be presented before we discuss their collection. We aren't considering who receives these reports. It can as well be the individual analysts and programmers or system builders themselves or the design manager. The information we expect to be reported is:

1. The initially scheduled completion time for each application, and each work package;
2. The current best estimate of completion time for each application and work package;
3. The initially budgeted resources for each application and work package;
4. The current allocation of resources to each application and work package;
5. The work packages into which any one work package or application has been partitioned.

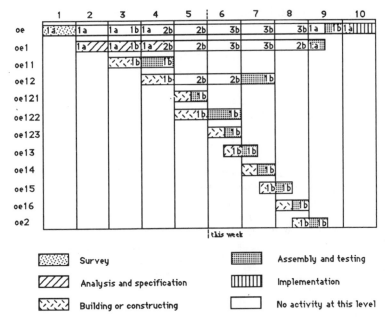

Figure 11.1 Planning display for the order entry project

Visual display is always powerful and we suggest appropriate charting. We are not saying whether the chart should be screwed onto the wall, in a binder or displayed on a screen driven by a computer. Any of these could be the medium for Figure 11.1.

Each bar displays the chronological sequence of each project or sub-project, with the sub-projects below the project. Each vertical column represents one time period, probably one week. The display relates to the *planning* phase of project management, with the assumption that the last level of decomposition has taken place. Thus it attempts to project forward for five weeks from the current week.

For this display we have assumed that the only resources that we have to dispose are people, and that people come in two kinds. There are 'analysts', designated by 'a', and 'builders', designated by 'b'. The quantity of each resource that we need for a particular task is shown within the bar for a particular week. The resource requirement at any level includes all the sub-levels. We assume that 'survey', 'analysis', 'specification' and 'implementation', are analysts' tasks and that builders build. 'Assembly' and 'testing' are things which could be the responsibility of either role at different levels.

Precedence rules apply! If a task must logically follow on behind another task, then that is how we show it. Assembly and testing of 'oe1' cannot start until all the sub-projects have been individually built and tested.

The actual reporting medium adopted by an organization must depend on the circumstances of that organization. We are simply suggesting a suitable method of display of *planning data*.

Necessarily, we must also display progress data, showing the completion of each stage of work and the resources devoted to that stage. Without that, planning the remainder of the project is not possible. There is no imperative that this must be displayed with the planning data, but we have taken that approach in Figure 11.2. For a part of the 'order entry' project the figure adds on a lower bar for each project, identified by the horizontal arrows. The data to the left of 'this week' record the tasks completed and the resources expended. To the right of and including 'this week' the bar shows the resources currently projected to complete the project or sub-project.

The specific information needs must always depend on the particular circumstances. A likely set of information needs in addition to the figures above is:

1. A list of how people are allocated to projects and sub-projects;
2. The projected work schedule for individual people, allowing for holidays and training;
3. Performance of individuals in completing work packages of varying complexity.

Whatever the task, the information required by different levels of management varies. Project management is no different. In

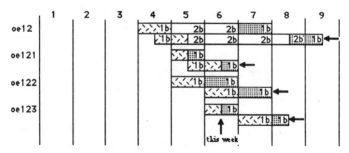

Figure 11.2 Addition of progress data for the order entry project

terms of Figure 3.5 we have talked about the information required for management of the 'technical core' of the design activity. At the 'organizational level' a broader brush is required. There is too much detail in the displays we've presented. We attempt to give an organizational level picture in Figure 11.3.

The unbroken line in the figure gives a cumulative week-by-week budgeted *variable* cost. This is based on the work packages scheduled for completion each week and the required resources to complete each work package as displayed in Figure 11.1. We have made assumptions about the cost of 'analysts' and 'builders' which need not concern us here. We have ignored the cost of computer time.

The *fixed costs* of office space and other company costs are not taken into account. The chart simply shows how much we have to pay to employ people to design and implement the 'order entry' project. The broken line in Figure 11.3 shows the *actual costs* incurred up to week six and the projected costs on from week six to give a best current estimated cost of completing the project.

Point A shows the budgeted cost of the work packages scheduled for completion by the beginning of week six. Point B occurs some time during week six, and shows the actual cost of *the same work packages*. It appears that we haven't paid out any more than we expected to, but we are about three-quarters of a week late.

The variable v_t, just above A and B, is the *time variance* in week six. By week six, we should know a lot more about the cost of

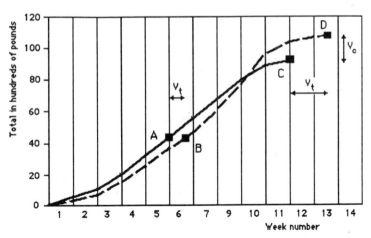

Figure 11.3 Budgeted and actual cost and degree of completion against week number

completing the project than when we started. The line to point D is the best estimate that we can make during week six of the eventual cost, and completion time. v_t and v_c, below and to the right of C and D, are the *estimated time variance* and the *estimated cost variance*.

11.5 Data flows, data analysis and the data model

There must be some *collection* of data before it is possible to produce the reports we have just described. We won't be far off the mark if we suggest that this must include data about:

1. New projects and new sub-projects;
2. New estimates of completion times, and of the resources required in order to complete;
3. Allocation of analysts and builders to projects and sub-projects;
4. The elapsed time analysts and builders actually spend on projects, and what they accomplish while they are spending this time.

Before we tackle the question of what form these input data take we shall attempt the *data analysis* and suggest a data model. We are treating project management *as a system which we have to design!* Initially, let's look at the relevant data flow diagram (Figure 11.4).

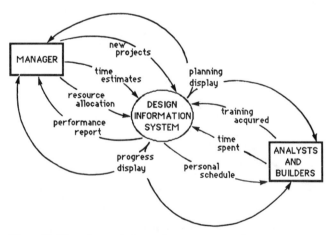

Figure 11.4 Data flows relating to the management of design projects

We aren't going to produce a full functional requirements specification. The details of the *HCI* (human–computer interaction) must depend on the particular circumstances of the organization. Both the input data and the various reports may be processed in *batch mode* or *on demand*. We have suggested some *report formats* above. In the next section we outline some formats for *data collection*. Most of the data flows on the DFD will occur with a *frequency* of the order of once weekly. *Volumes* of data will be determined by the number of projects being handled by the organization at any one time.

'Managers' on our DFD don't provide any information about themselves. There is no need to see them as an entity type which we want information about. We are quite definitely interested in 'Analysts and Builders'. They are the only resource we are using in the design process. Apart from their personal details, we need knowledge of their skills before they can be effectively allocated to tasks.

Analysts and builders could become separate entity types. We consider that it is necessary to know *the same kinds of things* about both groups of people and prefer to treat them as a single group: entity type DESIGNER. This allows for the situation of a person possessing both sets of skills. The possibility does exists of creating two sub-types of DESIGNER for the two groups, but we see no advantage in that solution. Managers may themselves be designers, and as designers, we need information about them. If designers are trained in many skills; and skills are possessed by many designers, then part of out data model comes out as Figure 11.5.

The next basic entity type must be PROJECT. We know that a project consists of sub-projects and that each project or sub-project uses many skills (survey, analysis, building, assembly, and testing). If a sub-project produces software that can be used in many projects, then the 'consists of' relationship will be many-to-many. For simplicity, we shall disregard that.

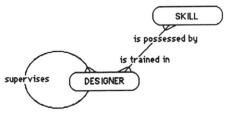

Figure 11.5 A relationship between designers and skills

A designer may be allocated to one or to many projects. A designer also records time spent on any one project. Whenever a designer spends time on a project, a skill is used on that project. Designers can be employed in one of two categories (analysts and builders) and each category is charged for at a different rate (Figure 11.6). It's interesting that the only 'mustbe' membership rule is that designers must be employed in a particular category. There aren't any 'mustbe' ownership rules.

Each of our entity types is a basic entity type with a unique key. There are no relationship entity types so far. The relationships 'is allocated to'/'has allocated' and 'is trained in'/'is possessed by' probably have attributes which we are interested in. The relationship 'uses'/'is used by' certainly has an attribute telling us how much of that skill is expected to be used for that particular project.

The relationship which demands more exploration is 'records time spent on'/'is used on'/'is advanced by'. Clearly, we do need to know how much time a designer records, using a skill and advancing a project. Additionally, at present we have apparently no means by which a designer can record time spent in any other way than advancing a project (Figure 11.7).

The TIMESHEET entity type is a recognition of the interrelationship between functional and data analysis. If designers are required to complete a weekly timesheet, then this is a

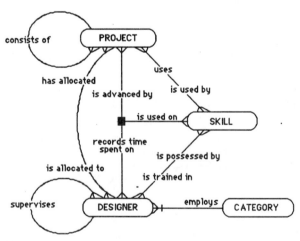

Figure 11.6 The basic project management data model

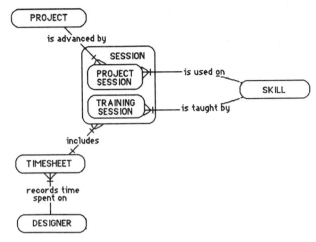

Figure 11.7 Detail of the relationships between DESIGNER, SKILL and PROJECT

piece of information which must be modelled. One timesheet includes many sessions. We have not specified the length of a session. Our opinion is that it should be half a working day or four hours. Any greater precision than that is pointless.

SESSION has two sub-types. These sub-types are exclusive. A session must be devoted either to training or to a project, not both. There is a possible use for the arc concept here, although it isn't quite the same situation as the one we described in Chapter 7. We also wish to allow a session to be devoted to a task which is unrelated either to SKILL or to PROJECT; 'pastoral care of staff' or 'sales conference' could be examples.

It is interesting that now we have introduced the relationship entity types it is easier to see that some membership and ownership rules are *mustbe*. The 'is taught by' relationship could be revised a little more. If the organization is interested in details of training courses then we should recognize an entity type COURSE (Figure 11.8).

Figure 11.8 Revision of the 'is taught by' relationship

11.6 Data collection for project management

We have listed appropriate reports to be produced by a project management system. In this section we are therefore considering only the *collection* and *input* of data. There is no reason to suppose that decisions are going to be made as a result of studying the data at this stage. That's what the reports are for!

The people originating data could be entering them directly on a VDU screen or writing them on a paper document so that someone else can subsequently enter them on a VDU. The choice is a part of the human–computer interaction which we mentioned earlier. HCI includes the design of the screen and the document, if one is used. If a screen is going to be used with a document, then they must surely correspond closely to each other. All this must be a part of the functional requirements specification.

In this section we shall suggest a format only for the collection of data about the way designers spend their time. This has been shown in the data model as TIMESHEET for the 'header' data and SESSION for the detail. We said above that we believe half a day to be an appropriate length of one session.

The left-hand version of Figure 11.9 assumes that a separate entry is made for each half day which elapses, whether it is a morning (am), an afternoon (pm) or an evening (even). This means that the actual start and finish of tasks is detected, but many data have to be collected rather unnecessarily. The right-hand version records less data, but doesn't allow work to be allocated to any period shorter than the reporting interval (one week in the figure). The right-hand version also implies that the designer is keeping a separate 'back of an envelope' record of the way time is spent and then totals it on this form.

Whether they are defined as part of the definition of a screen, as a part of a program, or as entries in a data dictionary, the integrity rules must be enforced. If there are exceptions, corrective action should be taken as new data are collected and put into the system. There are obvious rules, such as *domain integrity* and *referential integrity*. In addition, we would expect to enforce the following rules:

1. No designer works more than the time available.
2. A designer only works on a project to which he or she has been allocated.
3. A designer only undertakes tasks for which training has been given.
4. Each project must pass through the recognized cycle of tasks.

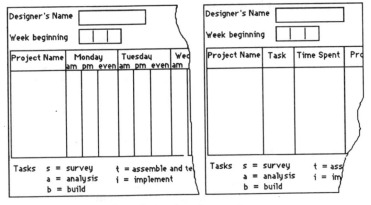

Figure 11.9 Possible designs of a timesheet document

11.7 Work measurement and estimating

So far, we have described a work package as 'do it in a fortnight'. If it is going to be useful as a marker, we must be able unambiguously to describe the work included in a work package and measure whether it has been done. We said that the rule of thumb specifying that a programmer can write and test ten program instructions in a day is rather outdated. This may be true, but it is an excellent model of an estimating rule. A suitable equivalent today may be that one builder can construct one VDU screen in a day or design a report in a day.

The more creative and innovative an activity is, the more difficult it will be to estimate it in advance; which is the ancient problem of 'how do you manage a research activity?' However true this may be, there are always many routine and time-consuming tasks which are more amenable to control. If as system designers we are going to retain the confidence of users, *design must be managed*.

We repeat here an earlier assertion. If we make understandable and unambiguous definitions of work units, monitor the completion of the work unit and record the result in an accessible form in our estimating database then we have the data to allow us to achieve the targets that we set out at the beginning of this chapter.

The best summary we know of what estimating is and what it isn't are the eight rules for estimating given by de Marco[2]. One quotation from this, which says most of it, is 'most people . . . understand an estimate to be the most optimistic imaginable result which is not demonstrably impossible'.

11.8 Clients and managers

The only people we have recognized so far have been designers and managers. That ignores the client. The client is the most important person or group of people in the whole enterprise. The client is the *problem owner*. The only *quality assurance* that is relevant is that the client be satisfied.

The client may be the same person as 'the user'. That isn't our concern here. We have written about participation and the need to win the commitment of users elsewhere. If the commitment of users is not won, the client is unlikely to be satisfied with what is delivered.

Regardless of whether a system designer is working as an internal employee of an organization or as an outside consultant, we recommend the client/consultant relationship. One of the authors believes that the proper way to get maintenance jobs completed around the home is to pay your neighbour to do them! Meanwhile, your neighbour can be paying you to do his jobs. Each job you do has a definite beginning and end, and you have an incentive to finish it.

If we are working with a client/consultant relationship then the design team will have a *contract* with the client. This always exists, but we urge that it be a formally agreed document. The project management data model that we suggested in Figure 11.6 is incomplete. It should provide for both CLIENT and CONTRACT. When a work package has been completed it is only the client who is able to say whether it is of the required quality. It is only the client who can say that the requirement specification defines what has to be done. It is only the client who can say that the completed work satisfies the requirement specification. We recommend that this approval be formal and that the client 'signs-off' each significant stage of project development.

Even if project implementation goes perfectly, there is still a need to review the progress of a project. It is much more likely that there will be omissions and mistakes. We spoke earlier in this chapter of the project history file. In all cases, a record of progress including all the documents that have been produced, all the system tests and results of the system tests, all the design decisions and all the formal acceptances by the client must be stored. Even the rejected plans should be kept.

There is an advantage if the client is one person. We have noticed that there are rarely implementation problems in small firms. The owner knows what he wants and is able to make sure he gets it. In a large organization there is the need to make sure that different managers' aims are compatible. One popular device to meet this need is the *steering committee*. A group of senior managers meets at regular intervals and is charged with overseeing system design and implementation.

Increasingly, organizations are coming to regard the organization's database as a corporate resource. This resource, and the applications which use it, must be planned as carefully as any other corporate asset. There is no room for idiosyncratic designer solutions.

11.9 Composition of the project design team

Completion of a design project requires many different skills. We've listed several of them in this chapter. In addition, there may be a need for accountants, people specializing in ergonomics, and specialists in industrial relations. There is also a need to win the commitment of the eventual users of the system. One way of doing this is somehow to include them in the design team.

The effect of all this is that the design team is multi-disciplinary. Broadly, there are two ways of bringing these different disciplines to bear. People may be organized on a basis of disciplines. The builders are grouped under the Chief Programmer, the analysts under the Senior Systems Analyst. The advantages of this are that specialist skills are concentrated and technical help is readily available.

The alternative method is to concentrate the members of the design team in a single organizational unit. The advantages are that the team members develop a commitment to the project and the delays caused by communications between departments are eliminated. There are two main disadvantages. One is that team members may feel locked into a particular area of work. An accountant in a design team may feel that he is left out of the mainstream of his promotion prospects. The second disadvantage is inflexibility. As the project develops, we shall need different skills. It may be difficult to change the membership of the team and still retain their commitment.

One possible compromise is the *military solution*. The army has many specialist corps. A signaller looks for his promotion and training to the Corps of Signals; an engineer to the Engineering Corps. Separately from this, both the signaller and the engineer look for day-to-day direction to the commander of their operational division. They can do this, confident that their promotion opportunities within their corps won't suffer.

11.10 Computer Aided Software Engineering (CASE)

Projects progress by designers undertaking and completing tasks, but there is far more to project management than storing data about what has been accomplished and what remains to be accomplished. We discussed recording decisions, the evidence on which those decisions were based, and the formal acceptance by clients of each stage of the project. If we want to design a *maintainable* system (which is really the same thing as a *usable* system) then there must be documentation which explains each separate part of the system: data models, data flow diagrams, procedural or non-procedural statements of rules, functional specifications, state-change specifications, and user manuals. All this must be recorded.

If more than one person is engaged in a project there is a pressing problem about consistency. Each component must fit into the whole. The set of assumptions being made must be consistent with those being made by other designers. We've frequently quoted the ceiling of the Sistine Chapel. Close control must have been necessary to ensure that each assistant used the right tint, that figures were painted to consistent size, and that each separate part of the whole fitted into its allotted space.

On top of all this, we can never expect that every task will be right first time. There will always be different versions of applications, of data models, of views, of screen designs, and indeed of any artefact we build. Perhaps our current version of order entry header update is 'oe13 (Version 4)'. It's obviously important to know that we are using the current version and that this has been formally approved by whatever mechanism has been legislated for. Consider the frustration of designing a screen to update a database table which no longer exists, or to accept data from a document which has been changed in some subtle but significant way. *Somewhere there must be a list of the current versions of every single data object.*

Prototyping, as a design method, turns multiplicity of versions into a virtue. We spoke of prototyping in Chapter 4. Essentially, a fairly crude version of an application is produced quickly, and the client is asked 'Is this what you want? If it isn't, then tell me what is wrong; we'll throw this one away, and I'll produce another version for you to try!' In no way does this alter the need for clear identification of version names.

It is probably the need to schedule new versions of applications and sub-applications that is the largest imponderable in projecting future completion of projects. Once we are clear about what something has to do, we are in a reasonable position to forecast the resources we need to build it. It is more difficult to be sure that the right questions are being asked than to produce answers to those questions.

Projects are progressed by project teams, but the membership of those teams may be constantly changing. A task may have been completed by someone who is no longer a member of the team, or the team which carried out a project may no longer exist.

For all these reasons, the management of a project is complex and requires decisions drawing on extensive and highly interactive data. Today we have a considerable development of CASE tools, as *Integrated Project Support Environments* (IPSEs). Support of this quality has always been necessary with complex projects and this is increasingly being provided by using computer-based information systems. At its simplest level, an IPSE may be just a means of keeping track of all documentation. More comprehensively, we may call on it for any of the recording and reporting functions described in this chapter.

We can reasonably expect integration between the design function and the whole project management function. When a builder undertakes construction of a new version of a sub-application he should have access to all the relevant design information. When the construction task has been completed then, implicitly, new design information has been created which must be available for subsequent design.

11.11 Team leadership

The ideal leader of a design team is the person who will eventually have to manage the redesigned system. If that isn't possible, then we should aim for a team leader who is an influential person among the users. No solution is ever ideal for all circumstances. If the designers belong to a firm of consultants with a strict contractual agreement with the client then the problems of integrating and making proper allowance for the cost of a team leader belonging to the client organization will be very difficult indeed. It is another case of the design compromises which necessarily have to be made.

Just as there were two alternative strategies for team organization, so there are for team leadership. In many organizations the team leader is typically a computer specialist. He will be strong on the technical computing requirements of the system but weak on practical knowledge of the user system; technical, political and sociological.

One danger of the team leader being a user of the system is that the distinction between the design team and the client may become blurred. If the danger is recognized it should not be a problem. The team leader should never be the person who 'signs off' the various stages of the project.

Again, a compromise solution has been tried by some organizations. They maintain a corps of professional project leaders. These people are specialists in the art of management, rather than either the user's or the designer's skills and technology. They report to a director, or vice-president, who is charged with responsibility for system development. We recognize the advantages, but declare our preference for management by an influential user.

Whatever source we recruit the team leader from, the task remains the same. We set out the requirements of project management at the beginning of the chapter and repeat them here:

1. That the artefact we are creating is suited to its purpose.
2. That the work is done within the budgeted limits of development time.
3. That the work is done within budgeted cost.

Design is a creative process. The team will succeed in these aims only if they are led in a way that allows all members to feel that they are being given space for the creativity of which they are capable within a coherent design framework.

11.12 Summary

- The basic purposes of the activity are:

    That the artefact we are creating is suited to its purpose;
    That the work is done within the budgeted limits of development time;
    That the work is done within budgeted cost.

- In order to accomplish this we partition into separate work packages with clear boundaries and clear uses.
- Part of the partitioning is vertical, into the various stages which any development project must pass through. Each stage is terminated by production of some milestone document.

- Additionally, we partition horizontally. The basis for partitioning should be that we can 'do it in a fortnight'.
- Work packages should be named so that their place in the order of things is clear from the name. The partitioning and naming must preserve the coherence of the whole system, and at the same time provide a means of monitoring progress at the basic level.
- Reporting of results requires a means, preferably visual, of presenting the plan of future work and of reporting progress against that plan.
- The reporting information needs will differ at different management levels. At the 'organizational level' the information need is an assurance that work is going according to plan (or not, as the case may be!).
- As well as reporting information needs, we need to identify the data capture data flows.
- The data model for the project management activity must identify DESIGNERS employed in various CATEGORIES; who are allocated to and spend time on specific PROJECTS; which PROJECTS may consist of SUB-PROJECTS. The DESIGNERS use and are trained in various SKILLS in order to advance PROJECTS.
- The relationship between a DESIGNER, a PROJECT and a SKILL is described by a relationship entity type called a SESSION.
- Work measurement is not simply to measure progress against an estimate. It is also designed to improve future estimating.
- The criterion for successful completion of a project is that the client is satisfied. There is no room for idiosyncratic designer solutions.
- Project development teams have members and are led. There is a variety of strategies followed in deploying team members and leaders.

Discussion points

11.1   We assert that if an artefact is not suited to its purpose then there will be a host of time and cost problems. Why should this be so?

11.2   Our insistence on being able to define 'do it in a fortnight' work packages is likely to result in a fragmented system, with unnecessary interference between different parts. Discuss this proposition.

11.3   We have suggested a hierarchical naming system for functions and work packages. We have been satisfied to name data tables and columns by a simple name with little connection with any other name. Is this differing practice justified?

11.4   If an organizational-level manager receives information suggesting the progress on a project is not going to plan what can he do about it?

11.5   What is a suitable length of a 'session'? To what level of detail should we be able to report what a designer is doing, what he is doing it to, and when?

11.6   De Marco[2] presents a situation in which your boss has asked you:

> 'Quick, give me an estimate for how long it's going to take you working full time without help to do such and such between now and this time next year.'

You have countered by saying you need fourteen months. Your boss insists it must be done in a year. What is your reaction? If the project comes unstuck, who is to blame?

11.7   The US Weather Forecasting Bureau attaches probability estimates to its weather forecasts. The British Meteorological Office makes firm predictions, on the argument that the public doesn't understand probabilities.
Should estimates of future project work durations be expressed as probabilities? How does an estimate of how long a job will take relate to our 'do it in a fortnight' prescription?

11.8   Is satisfaction of the client the sole criterion in executing a project? If the client wishes to have an efficient gas chamber designed to solve the 'Jewish problem', does the designer design the gas chamber?

11.9   Is it necessary when development of a project is undertaken by an internal design department that a contract be entered into and that all the stages of the project are 'signed off'?

11.10 Once a particular stage of project development has been started, should the designers close their eyes and ears to any demand for changes in the specification of that stage?

References

1 G. M. Weinberg, *The Psychology of Computer Programming*, McGraw-Hill, New York (1973)

2 Tom de Marco, *Structured Analysis and System Specification*, Yourdon Press, New York (1979)
3 Tom de Marco, *Control of Software Projects: Management, Measurement, and Specification*, Yourdon Press, New York (1982)

Part 4

Human factors

Chapter 12

Aspects of human–computer interaction (HCI)

12.1 Introduction

'A designer is someone who creates an agreeable environment', Terence Conran (designer). In Chapter 8 the issue of dialogue design was addressed and its importance assessed in determining the behaviour of the intended system. In Chapter 13 some specific aspects of user involvement will be described.

In this chapter we will examine in greater detail that aspect of system design which has the greatest impact on the user, but which is often overlooked or hurried – human–computer interaction. We will examine it from three perspectives: what it comprises; why it is important, and how an understanding of it can be used to best advantage in helping to ensure that our systems are comprehensible and usable.

As an editorial in *Computing* warned in June 1987[1]:

Failure of systems analysts and designers to make systems easily and comfortably usable by laymen is the most significant inhibiting factor in the future progress of the IT industry.

Rasmussen[2], a foremost worker in the HCI field, has said that:

To be effective, the design must be based on compatible models of human information processes as well as the functions of the control system.

Fortunately, there are signs that the Information Technology industry is beginning to take on board the importance of good human–computer interaction, and that academic researchers in HCI are addressing the major issues of commercial system requirements.

The main problem seems to be that system design is, in the early stages, a 'person-centred' activity, where a 'rich picture' emerges via modelling, structured walkthroughs and so on. In the later stages, as implementation approaches, the activity becomes much more 'computer-centred'. Knowledge of user characteristics is lost, or deemed irrelevant, leading to systems which behave in a 'brittle' manner, that is, they fail to respond flexibily to unforeseen situations.

In the final stages, the operation of the planned system is almost entirely computer-centred, with little opportunity for adaptation or flexibility in the user interface. As Shneiderman[3] has pointed out, systems generally:

1. Require users to remember too much;
2. Are intolerant of minor errors;
3. Are confusing to novices;
4. Use inappropriate command modes;
5. Force users to perform tasks in undesirable ways.

12.2 The nature of HCI

For many years, there have been disciplines which are primarily concerned with the design of systems which humans have to use: ergonomics, occupational psychology, etc. The scope of ergonomics is wide, and covers those aspects of system construction and operation which interact within human beings on a mainly physical level, such as the design and placement of controls, readability of displays, etc. An ergonomics expert would normally be consulted, for example, during the design of a new power station operating console or a new aircraft flight deck. The occupational psychologist is more concerned with the impact of working practices on individuals or groups in terms of their attitudes, and, if consulted at all, would normally be brought in prior to a major reorganization within a department.

For some time it was assumed that attention to these levels of interaction would suffice, and that higher-level aspects of interaction (the mental rather than the physical) were better left to medical experts or psychologists. As systems became more complex, and more demanding of human resources, it became apparent that many situations were arising that existing practice could not cope with. This was especially so with computer-based systems. Errors were occurring, and system designers could not say why. Users reported that systems were 'unusable' or 'unfriendly' but could not be more specific. Research on the problem began to indicate that the trouble often lay not with the physical aspects of system operation but with a tenuous, conceptual space between the human and the computer. The tenuous nature is best evidenced by the fact that there is no consensus on what this space should be called – it is generally termed the 'human–computer interaction', but the British Computer Society has recently favoured the 'human–systems interaction', which is arguably more acceptable.

The basic rationale for HCI, then, is that although the communication between humans and systems is ultimately mediated by physical devices such as keyboards or mice, the actual interaction takes place at a higher, cognitive, level. These two levels are interdependent – the physical level has to be correct before the cognitive can work; something as trivial as a 'sticky' key can result in a bad experience with the system, however good its logical design. A common problem, for example, has been the variable placement of the CONTROL key in various versions of PC keyboards. By the same token, an ergonomically sound layout cannot possibly compensate for a bad logical design.

HCI is therefore a broad discipline, spanning areas as diverse as *keyboard and display design, task analysis, formal grammars* and *affective* (i.e. emotional) aspects of system interaction. It is best viewed as a collection of related disciplines. What substantiates its claim to professionalism is the standards it brings to bear on all aspects of system design, and the applied research which is carried out by HCI workers in their drive to understand the complex processes within the interface. The aim, at all levels, is to understand and improve the usability of systems. This is accomplished by:

1. Discovering the constraints of *user behaviour, knowledge* and *performance*, and providing appropriate models; and
2. Using this information to build better systems.

Finally (and perhaps most importantly), the effect of HCI can be seen in the emergence of international standards for the design of such components as keyboards, displays (ANSI), interface managers (X-Window) and communications (the X400 messaging protocol). Figure 12.1 indicates the relationship of HCI to other disciplines concerned in system design.

12.3 Relationship of HCI to system design

In this section we will examine specific HCI topics, both theoretical and practical, and apply them to various activities which have been discussed in earlier chapters. Before we do this, it may be helpful to discuss a particular 'model' of HCI which we have found useful.

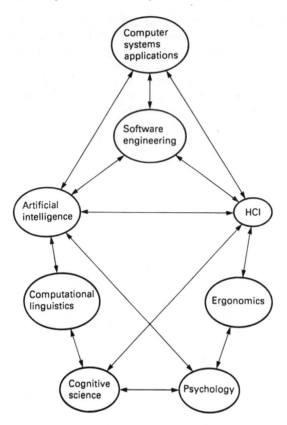

Figure 12.1 HCI and other disciplines

HCI could be seen as varying along two dimensions: *Weak–Strong*, and *Broad–Deep* (see Figure 12.2). For example, a person adopting a *'Broad–Weak'* HCI approach would assert that considering the user is generally a good idea at all stages of system design, from initial discussion to interface testing, whereas a *'Strong–Deep'* HCI worker would be involved in, say, basic psychological research into human short-term memory and would, moreover, insist that such knowledge was carefully considered before the system was designed. The particular approach we take will depend on the topic under consideration, but will lie broadly within the circle in Figure 12.2.

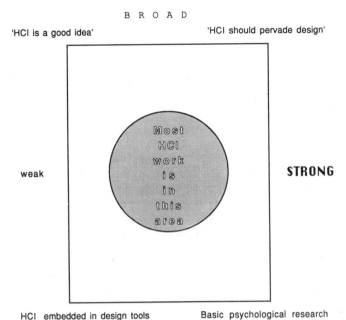

Figure 12.2 The scope of HCI

In discussing the various aspects of HCI, a *'layered'* approach will be adopted. This approach has been used in, for example, the definition of communications protocols such as the Open System Interconnect model of the International Standards Organization. To the extent that HCI is also about communicating, it is an appropriate treatment of the topic. The rationale is that each 'layer' depends on the layer below it for the reliable and error-free transport of information: and, in turn, is given tasks by the layer above it which are formatted in a way it can understand. In this way, the higher layers are not concerned with the low-level implementation details and the whole system can be designed in a modular way.

12.3.1 Physical layer

Input devices – the keyboard
Physical characteristics Shneiderman[3] has stated that 'The keyboard is an extension of the fingers', and it would seem

reasonable to ensure that the static and dynamic characteristics of the keyboard are well matched to the known properties of the *'user finger'*.

Static characteristics are to do with the size, shape and spacing of each key, and the angle at which the whole keyboard is used. Dynamic characteristics are concerned with how the key behaves while being used. The interaction of the two factors can be quite subtle, and very often the user can only report a preference for the *'feel'* of one particular type of keyboard.

Figure 12.3 shows the layout of the ANSI standard keyboard and Figure 12.4 the ideal dynamic behaviour of a single key. It will be seen that, on depression, the key displays increasing resistance, until it 'gives' (possibly with an audible click). On return, a definite 'closure' is felt, followed by a decreasing resistance as the key returns. A well-known example of this profile is the IBM Selectric typewriter, for which most touch typists express a preference.

Keyboard layout

It is probably true to say that the bulk of new information being input into computer-based systems is going in via a keyboard of some kind, and it is ironic to note that the most commonly used layout (termed *QWERTY*) was arrived at by its inventor, Sholes, as a solution to the problem of clashing typebars in early typewriters. The most frequently used letters have been placed far apart, thus increasing finger travel distances. This must be the world's only recorded instance of negative HCI!

Alternative layouts are the *Dvorak*, where the layout has been arrived at by using knowledge of letter frequencies; the *ABCDE*

Figure 12.3 The layout of the ANSI standard keyboard

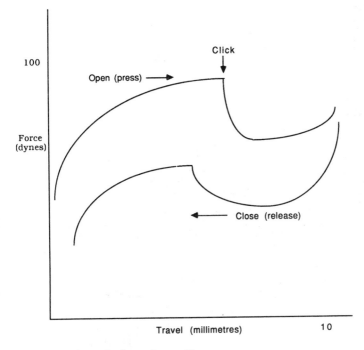

Figure 12.4 Keystroke depression profile

layout, where the natural alphabetic sequence is followed; and special-purpose devices, such as the *Microwriter*, which has only five keys and where the letters are formed by particular key combinations or 'chords'. In addition to the normal alphanumeric keys, a large number of special-purpose keys are generally to be found which have control purposes (SHIFT, CONTROL, ALT, BREAK) or whose use can be determined by an application program (ESCAPE, Function keys 1–12, PAGE UP, PAGE DOWN). There are also a number of *keypads* – groups of keys with a related function. The ANSI keyboard, for example, possesses a group of cursor keys, a numeric keypad and a block of six keys concerned with document manipulation.

Other input devices
As we have seen in Chapter 8, the range of input devices is increasing all the time and the choice available to the system designer is wide. Figure 12.5 shows a typical information system based on a *multi-media workstation* approach. Each of the input

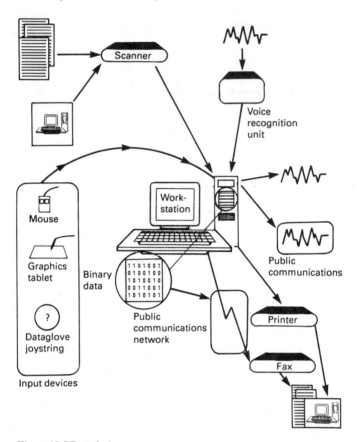

Figure 12.5 Data fusion

devices has its own particular characteristics and appropriateness for a particular task, and gives the HCI specialist a different set of problems. It is likely that some major rethinking will have to be done now that devices such as intelligent page scanners are available.

Such devices as voice-recognition systems may also be included at this level, although they will not be discussed in detail. In spite of the inner complexity of these devices (which may include an on-board computer system of considerable power), they may be regarded as functionally very simple – to provide an input of characters to a system which have been derived from the user's speech.

Pointing devices

This class of device offers the most significant alternative to the keyboard as a human input medium. It comprises *trackerballs*, *joysticks* and *mice*. Although the keyboard is indispensable as a means of inputting text to a system, it is arguably deficient when it comes to manipulating that text as an object rather than as a set of characters.

The functions of a pointing device may be summarized as follows:

Selection from a set of items (for example, a menu selection).
Location in a space (as when moving a pointer to a menu bar).
Orientation in a direction (for example, in a graphics package).
Valuation – supplying positional information (for example X–Y value).

The mouse

The design of this component has now been standardized to some extent. It comprises a hand-held body with a number of buttons. Two types of information are supplied to the system; the position of the mouse and the state of the buttons. The significance of each button depends on the number of buttons: in most professional systems a three-button mouse is favoured. In this case, the leftmost button is for SELECtion, the middle button for MENUs, and the rightmost button for ADJUSTment (for example, UNDO). This follows the conventions used in the original STAR system developed by Rank Xerox. As we will see later, the mouse is almost always used in conjunction with some kind of windowing software (for example, a 'desktop' manager).

Output devices

Displays Display technology has seen a rapid increase in functionality over the past few years. In 1983 the standard display device was a monochrome VDU with a text-only output of (say) 80 characters per line × 24 lines. Today, colour devices with both text and graphics capability are common. For example, the IBM Enhanced Graphics Adapter (EGA) standard provides for up to 256 colours on an APA (All Points Addressable) display of 640 × 350 points. Enhancements of this standard provide for up to 640 × 480 points in 256 colours. For very high quality application (text processing, for example) a monochrome screen is considered superior as it does not have the 'granularity' of a colour display. A typical resolution is 1280 points × 960 or 1024.

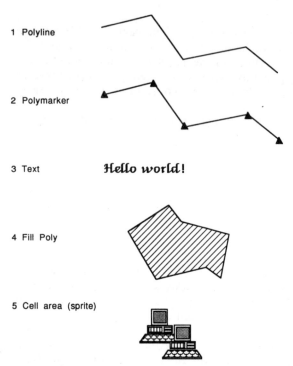

1 Polyline

2 Polymarker

3 Text   𝓗𝒆𝓵𝓵𝓸 𝔀𝓸𝓻𝓵𝓭!

4 Fill Poly

5 Cell area (sprite)

Figure 12.6 GKS primitives

Fortunately, standards exist which enable software to make best use of the performance of such displays. We will discuss one, the GKS (Graphics Kernel Standard), which has been adopted by most vendors. The GKS standard also includes input devices, so the discussion above on input devices should be borne in mind.

The GKS standard is intended to provide a convenient way of constructing arbitrarily complex displays from a set of simple shapes or *primitives* (Figure 12.6).

Usability of displays
The increased functionality of display devices should give the system designer great scope for improvement from an HCI point of view. Unfortunately, it has also given great scope for bad practices to develop. There is no correspondence to 'keyboard feel' when it comes to displays. Human beings seem to have less insight into the preferences of their visual system (which may be related to the fact that, from an evolutionary point of view, it is

very recent). The consequence is that some very poor displays have been produced, apparently driven by a desire on the part of the designer to make use of as many colours as possible. So, for example, an input field may have green letters on a red background despite the fact that these two colours are focused at different distances by the human eye. Add error messages in flashing cyan on magenta and you have a recipe for headaches, eyestrain and eventually a total aversion to the system!

12.3.2 Syntactic layer – command line interpreters

Despite recent advances in interface technology, such as windowing systems, the main method of interaction between humans and systems (especially large ones) is via some kind of command line entered via a keyboard. There are two kinds of demand on the user in this kind of task: remembering the set of possible commands and ensuring that they are typed in a way which is acceptable to the system. The first is basically a *vocabulary* problem, while the second is concerned much more with the *structure*, or *syntax*, of the command and its possible variations.

Overall, it could be said that the Command Language route offers a potentially very rich interaction between user and system, at the expense of a considerable overhead in the learning and maintenance of the syntax. Additional problems arise, of course, when training has been done on one system and the user changes to another. Many *negative transfer* effects have been observed where inappropriate commands are carried across from one system to another. Perhaps surprisingly (to non-psychologists), the greatest problems arise between systems which are quite similar in their syntax.

Shneiderman[3] has listed some of the pros and cons of command languages:

For	*Against*
Flexibility	Poor error handling
'Power users' like them	High learning load
Supports initiative	Syntax forgotten easily
Can build macros, aliases, etc.	Retraining necessary

We'll now examine a typical situation which, on the face of it, is quite simple: obtaining a directory listing of the files available to the user. Typing

DIR

is reasonable if the user knows about directories as a technical concept, but there is nothing unreasonable about

CATALOGUE

or

LISTFILES

both of which would fail on the VAX/VMS operating system. Equally well, it would be unlikely if a novice to the UNIX system hit by chance upon

ls

which stands for 'List Segments'.

Assuming now that the user has a list of commands to refer to, we'll examine a further complication of his or her task, using the BACKUP command of MSDOS as an example. The complication is that most commands, to be useful, require some kind of qualifier or modifier which conveys additional information to the command, either to limit its scope or to modify its operation in some way.

For example, to back up all the files in all the subdirectories which were modified after 23 June 1988 to drive A, the user should type:

BACKUP *.* A:/S/D: 06-23-88

There are several questions we could ask about the syntax of this command line. First, does the list of options have to follow the file specification (*.*)? Why could it not follow the command itself, especially as only one command can be issued per line? If the '/S' option means 'SINCE', why do we need an additional '/D' option? Why is this followed by a ':' rather than '='?

With regard to the date format, what is wrong with '23 June 1988' or, indeed, June 23 1988' or '23-6-88'? Most importantly, what are the aspects of this command which make it easy to remember its sytax?

Errors
This aspect of the interaction with a command language should not be overlooked; the need for an acceptable syntax works both ways. For example, how is a user to interpret the following message which occurs after issuing a 'DIR' command?

I/O Error 106: PC = 10FA0372

What is I/O? And of what significance is the number 106 unless there is a printed cross-reference available? What does 'PC' mean

– is it the PC at which the user is sitting? If Error 106 is looked up, and found to represent (say) 'Too many file handles', is the user any the wiser? Who is to blame? Many users experience guilt feelings when in fact the blame lies (as in this case) with the systems or applications programmer for allowing such a situation to develop. Would it be any less informative to display the following error message?

There are too many files open.
The system may have been configured wrongly.
Please consult your system manager or ring our help line.

Although it might seem that this level of friendliness panders too much to the novice, it is interesting to note that Shneiderman reported in 1982 that even expert users were, on average, using one-third of all commands in making or correcting errors. These questions will be examined further when we discuss natural language processing.

Although the examples have been concerned with operating system commands, the principles hold true for all situations in which a user is expected to remember a series of commands and their associated syntax – in an SQL dialogue, for example.

Overall, the perceived *quality* of an interface is often bound up with the command syntax. If it is quirky or unmemorable, it will not only be more difficult to remember (resulting in lost time every time a user returns to the system) but may even cause an aversion in the user such that learning is actively blocked. After all, people avoid other people who they perceive as difficult or capricious. Why not computers?

Window, icons, menus, pointers
There is an alternative way of solving the syntax problem: by avoiding it altogether. *WIMP* systems, employing a combination of advanced hardware and software, are a tribute to the intelligent collaboration of people involved in the diverse fields of hardware design, software design and psychology. The credit is due largely to the Palo Alto Research Centre (PARC) of the Xerox Corporation, where the STAR office automation system was developed. This forms the basis of most of the currently available WIMP-based systems.

The operation of a WIMP system is clear and unambiguous. Objects (files, programs) in the system are represented by *icons* in a *window*. The window is situated on a *desktop*. Several different windows may be open at once, and windows may be moved, resized, opened and closed. Objects are activated by selecting with the *pointer* (generally mouse-driven) and *double-clicking*; or they can be moved about in the window. Alternatively, a special kind of icon, with selectable items (a *menu*) can be *pulled down* from a *menu bar* at the top of the desktop. Operations such as file copying are achieved by selecting and dragging one icon over another; and all applications have to be written in a way which makes best use of the resources available.

The underlying operating system is similar in many ways to a conventional one (with, for example, a normal range of file-handling services), but has many enhancements to enable the various windowed operations to be handled. Output, for example, would not be to just a screen but to a uniquely identified *virtual workstation*. Input operations have to handle *events* such as the entry of a pointer into a window, or a resize operation. The operating system handles this by treating every event as a *message*. Applications can wait for, and interpret, these messages and act accordingly. An extensive set of graphics primitives is also implemented (see the description of the GKS above).

The significance of this *desktop metaphor* for the design of systems cannot be overestimated. As far as the user is concerned, there is a good match between the 'mental model' of the system and its physical appearance. Syntax errors are eliminated, so the only complexity lies with the application, not with the system interface. Most importantly, this kind of system provides a *generic* interface which can be made common to all applications.

For the designer, the advantages include rapid development, especially of the user interface; a 'prototyping' ability so that certain aspects can be fine tuned, possibly to individual end-user requirements; and an easy migration to the system, as the facilities are available from any high-level language which supports operating system calls.

Hypertext

Once the principle has been established that text and graphics can be easily mixed on a high-resolution display and that it is equally easy to access sound images, then it is a simple step to create sections of *active text*, or *hypertext*, which can be activated like an icon. On activation, an appropriate image, to which the hypertext has been linked, is called up via screen or loudspeaker.

When combined with the message-passing facilities of a WIMP operating system, a very large increase in functionality is conferred onto the system; such systems are now commercially available. The Hypercard system views the target system as a series of 'stacks' of cards. Cards can be cross-indexed in the usual way, but can also trigger events when accessed. The accompanying programming language, *Hypertalk*, is an 'object-oriented' language which 'drives' the card stacks.

Among the claims made for such systems are that the traditional development cycle is rendered redundant. Certainly, system designers have every reason to be disturbed by the experience of one department in a large organization where a system that had taken three years to develop in the traditional manner was outperformed by one designed, coded and tested in an afternoon!

Natural language processing
The most enthusiastic proponents of WIMP systems would not claim that they offer a totally general metaphor. There are some situations in which a command language has to be used. For example, copying or deleting a file is simple in a WIMP system, but specifying a group of files for deletion based on last-used dates or size is more awkward. Indeed, some WIMP users have reported that the system is so proscriptive of their actions that it 'gets in the way' of what they want to do.

Command languages, therefore, have a place; but do they have to be opaque, arcane and unmemorable? Is there indeed a command language which is transparent, well matched and memorable? There is – English (or French, German, Swedish, etc.). To return briefly to our command line example:

BACKUP *.* A:/S/D: 06-23-88

What this command line actually *means* is:

'Back up all files in all sub-directories created since 23 June 1988 to Drive A:'

There are two points to note here. First, the command is not so concise; and possibly as a result of this, it is ambiguous. Is it the files or the sub-directories which were created since 23 June? The problem with natural language is its richness and diversity. The ambiguity that results from an alternative choice of expression can only be resolved by referring to the *context* of the command. Do people want to back up files or sub-directories? It does not make sense to back up sub-directories by date, only their contents. So the difficulty is resolved by maintaining a 'knowledge base' of the likely situations, much like the 'world knowledge' component of the Maass model discussed elsewhere in this chapter.

Fortunately, software technology is now capable of providing the tools for building natural language *front ends* to systems. Here is an example of *restricted-domain* NL processing, using Bobrow's STUDENT program[4]:

(TOM HAS TWICE AS MANY FISH AS MARY HAS GUPPIES.
IF MARY HAS 3 GUPPIES, WHAT IS THE NUMBER OF FISH TOM HAS?)

The brackets are part of the syntax of the LISP language in which the program is written. The generated output is:

(THE EQUATIONS TO BE SOLVED ARE)
(EQUAL X0001 (NUMBER OF FISH TOM(HAS/VERB)))
(EQUAL (NUMBER OF GUPPIES (MARY/PERSON) (HAS/VERB)) 3)
(EQUAL NUMBER OF FISH TOM (HAS/VERB))
   (TIMES 2 (NUMBER OF GUPPIES
      (MARY/PERSON) (HAS/VERB))))
(THE NUMBER OF FISH TOM HAS IS 6)

The amount of processing necessary to arrive at this solution is considerable, involving the use of token scanners, parsers and other tools. However, for a restricted sub-set of English, the following sequence copes with most input; if it cannot, it reports an error. This is arguably better than a normal command line routine carrying out a mistaken command merely because the syntax is correct.

Analysis of domain-specific natural language input[5]
1. Break the input line into tokens such as 'show', 'all', 'files', 'on', 'b:'.
2. Remove 'chaff': 'a', 'the', 'you'.
3. Reduce redundant terms: 'every', 'all', 'complete' -> 'all'.
4. Look for a command in what remains: 'kill', 'erase', 'zap' -> 'del'.
5. 'Massage' word order so that it fits an acceptable syntax.
6. Issue the command or generate an error.

New programming languages such as Prolog are easing the task of writing such interfaces. The designer need not be concerned with their inner workings, only their usage and effects.

Software psychology
The aspects of HCI we have discussed above should not be regarded as being limited to online interaction. The syntax and usage of programming languages themselves give rise to similar

issues. This aspect of HCI is often ignored because it is assumed that the programmer is not subject to the same constraints or problems as the end user.

12.3.3 Semantic layer

Semantics is the study of meaning, and this layer of communication between human and computer is of central interest to HCI workers. We are concerned here with how the user gets the system to do what he or she *means* it to do, based on a set of high-level concepts. If something is wrong with the mechanics of the interaction, then alternative strategies can generally be found, and any penalty is associated with speed or efficiency. However, errors at the semantic level (which are more correctly termed mistakes) can give rise to far more serious consequences.

Shneiderman[3] has pointed out some useful distinctions between syntactic and semantic knowledge. Syntactic knowledge is:

Unstructured with regard to the task
Device dependent
Acquired by rote
Easily forgotten

While semantic knowledge is:

Structured
Device independent
Acquired by meaningful learning
Stable in memory

Figure 12.7 illustrates the distinction between the two types of knowledge.

Next in this section we will discuss one or two theories of HCI which are useful in exploring communications between human and machine. Interestingly, the first one was developed by psycholinguists developing theories of communication between people and other people rather than machines. It will be evident that there are no semantic 'mechanisms' which can be discussed. Indeed, the meaning of 'meaning' is a subject of much debate between psycholinguists and philosophers. These theories attempt to provide a useful model rather than an emulation of reality.

Channel/agency means/activity nets
These have been described by Maass[6] and are a development of a theoretical construct known as a *Petri net*. Figure 12.8 illustrates

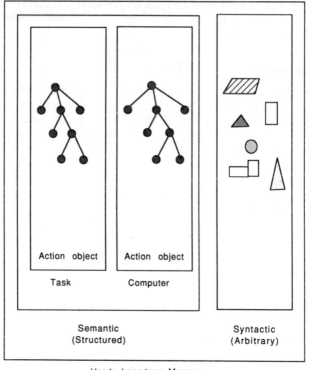

Figure 12.7 Syntax versus semantics (after Shneiderman)

the principle. P1 and P2 have at least three things in common: a number of problem situations, a means of communication (the channel) through which messages are passed, and in addition, some 'private' information and procedures:

CONVENTIONS about how the interaction should proceed;
INTENTIONS about their partner;
A SELF-IMAGE which comprises the individual's orientation to the world;
A PARTNER MODEL;
WORLD KNOWLEDGE which constrains the interaction in various ways;
ACTIONS which produce messages and act upon the world.

The interaction begins by an intention on the part of (say) P1 that P2 should perform some action (generally to the advantage of

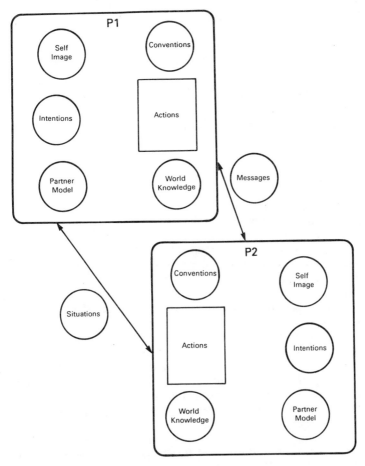

Figure 12.8 Systems transparency (after Maass)

P1). The action is realistic bearing in mind the partner model. An appropriate message is generated and passed via the communications channel. P2 may perform the action or respond with a message. If the response signifies some problem, P1 may have to modify its partner model, or conventions, or world knowledge and generate a new message. A system (or partner) which appears to carry out intentions in a consistent and rational way, irrespective of the low-level implementation details, is said to be *transparent*.

We can now consider the significance of this theory for HCI. Maass[3] has listed the desirable characteristics of a transparent system. It:

Does not hide its functions;
Does not obscure problems;
Is well structured, consistent and comprehensible;
Ensures that its interface conforms with the user's 'picture' of it.

This could be regarded, directly, as a prescription for system designers. Try substituting the word 'usable' for the word 'transparent' above.

Usability and functionality, then, are intimately related: a highly functional system which cannot communicate its abilities in an unambiguous way is effectively unusable. Worse, it may be apparently usable but introduce subtle or unpredictable errors.

The human as a systems component

From a theoretical treatment of how two agents might interact, we turn to practical attempts to explore the relationship between humans and systems. These ideas often come from a tradition of control theory, which treats the user-system as a unified whole (with the user generally being regarded as a slow, noisy transfer function!).

The approach discussed here, developed by Rasmussen[2], differs from the classical in that the user's *cognitive* functions are regarded as being useful, indeed central, to the operation of the system. During normal functioning, the operator is considered to be a slow, somewhat flexible information processor. When the system begins to operate at or near to the limit of its design parameters, the inner mechanisms of the user become apparent.

Rasmussen has proposed two factors that operate within the user:

Conscious – The information processing capacity (perception, motor skills etc.);
Subconscious – The needs, drives, 'process feel', assumptions etc.

This, in turn, enabled Rasmussen to suggest a possible working model of how a user interacts with a complex system. Figure 12.9 indicates how it might operate[2].

Task analysis

From theories of HCI we turn to a more pragmatic treatment of the process. It attempts to analyse the attempts the user makes to structure the overall interaction and to devise and implement strategies for dealing effectively with the perceived task. This

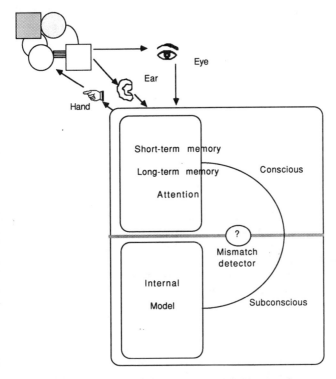

Figure 12.9 User model of a complex system (after Rasmussen)

should be considered in parallel with what we have discussed above.

Task analysis has two components: a methodology for analysing the user's behaviour or ideas with respect to the task and a system for formalizing and representing the resulting information. There are many techniques; we will consider only the basic ideas here.

The process involves an analysis, at the *task* level, of what the user does or should do when 'driving' a target system. A task could be considered as representing a 'unit' of work: a *goal* to achieve, an *operator* (tool) to achieve it, and a *method* (procedure) for using the operator. Tasks are often organized hierachically by incorporating sub-tasks. The *GOMs* approach has been formalized by Wilson, Barnard and Maclean[7].

The task analysis process often starts by considering the frequency of particular 'candidate' tasks and using this as a framework for building up a picture of the system. For example, the frequency of key usage in a word-processing system might look like this:

Most frequent

    Alphanumeric keys – for text entry

    Special keys (<-, ->), INSert, DELete

    Control key chords – for less frequent activities (e.g. text attributes)

    Function keys: Move to command mode, Help, etc.

    Special functions – Installation menus, printer reconfiguration, etc.

Least frequent

In each case, we could describe a goal (for example, 'delete the current line'; an operator (the keyboard); and a method (the CTRL/Y chord). Although this level of analysis seems laborious when applied to a simple task, we have to remember that tasks are rarely straightforward. For example, a well-known word-processing package that runs under a windowing system has four alternative methods and two possible operators for the 'delete line' task: a control key chord, a function key, a mouse click on an icon of the function key, or a mouse 'select, drag and click' operation. In this kind of situation, the GOMs model employs the use of a *rule* to select between operators.

The question has now to be addressed of what constitutes a reasonable profile of tasks for a given application – are there too many, are they too complex, etc. It is evidently a complex matter

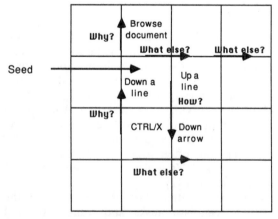

Figure 12.10 Laddering technique (after Johnson)

to establish this, but some methods give a reasonably good idea of how the tasks distribute. We will examine one which is characterized by simplicity and utility: *laddering*, described by Johnson[8].

In the laddering method, an unlabelled two-dimensional matrix is set up. It is possible to navigate in three directions: up, down and sideways. Starting from an arbitrary point somewhere in the middle (the *seed*), we ask one of three questions depending on the task in hand. To go down, we ask 'how do we do this?'; to go up, we ask 'why did we do that?'; and to move laterally we ask 'what else can we do?' To satisfy the constraints of human memory and perception, it is evident that there is an optimum 'shape' to the 'tree' thus generated. A long, spindly one is as bad as a short fat one. Figure 12.10 illustrates the development of a ladder for our simple word-processing system.

12.4 Summary

- HCI represents a broad field of activity, from attention to the physical devices in the system and their ergonomics to the 'psychonomics' of visual shells and natural language interfaces.
- It is arguable that money spent on 'usability' is never wasted. There is enough evidence of expensive systems lying unused because people found them 'unusable', powerful though they may have been.
- What drives HCI research is not the technological possibilities of new kinds of interface, although these are very exciting, but a belief that systems are designed and built for human beings to use. It is the duty of the system designer to work with the HCI expert at all stages to ensure that, in Conran's terms, 'the environment is agreeable'.

References

1 Editorial comment, *Computing*, June (1987)
2 J. Rasmussen, in *Human Interaction with Computers*, edited by H.T.Smith and T.R.G.Green, Academic Press, New York (1981)
3 Ben Shneiderman, *Designing the User Interface – Strategies for Effective Human – Computer Interaction*, Addison-Wesley, Reading, Mass. (1987)
4 Stefik Mark, Foster Gregg and Daniel B. Bobrow, 'Beyond the chalkboard: computer support for collaboration and problem solving in meetings', *Communications of ACM*, January, 32 (1987)
5 Alex Lane, 'Improved command processor', *Byte*, December, 261 (1987)

6 Maass, in *The Psychology of Computer Users*, edited by T.R.G.Green, S.Payne and G.C. van der Veer, Academic Press, New York (1985)

7 M.Wilson, P.Bernard and A.Maclean, 'Approximate modelling of cognitive activity with an expert system: developing an interactive design tool', *Computing Journal*, **31**, No. 5, May (1988)

8 Nancy E. Johnson 'Varieties of representation in eliciting and representing knowledge for IKBS', *International Journal of Systems Research and Information Sciences*, No.1 (1985)

Chapter 13

User participation

Whether you have been reading this book from the beginning or dipping into it, you will have noticed that on many occasions the term 'user' has been referred to. At the start of the discussion on designing information systems (Section 4.2) the user was defined as an information provider and/or and information receiver. This infers that the gap in the middle can be adequately covered by the systems developer, be he a systems analyst or a programmer. We feel that this inference needs more exploration, and this chapter has been devoted to the role of the user in the process of systems development. The term 'user participation' has been used in so many contexts and in so many academic papers that, for the purpose of clarity, the authors feel the need to attempt to define both user and participation as a basis for reading this chapter.

13.1 What is a user?

If we consider the potential number of employees in any organization that would be affected by the systems development process then the problem of categorizing these employees becomes apparent:

1. The instigators of the project could be classified as users. They have a client role in the project and are mainly concerned with economic feasibility. This individual or group could and probably would also fall into the second category.
2. The information receivers within the organization should without doubt be interested parties in the systems development process. They are users in the sense that they receive output from the system to aid planning, control and decision making.
3. The employees who are involved in the primary tasks within the organization (e.g. order processing, stock control) that are in the process of being redesigned are users in the functional sense. They will be running the system on a day-to-day basis.

4. Another user group will be the managers/auditors who will have responsibility for the control of the system and will ensure its efficient running using appropriate measures.
5. Although we have already discussed their role as operators, the employees who prepare and input data to the system should be classified as users (although secondary) in the context of this chapter. Their inclusion has implications that cannot be ignored in discussions of the human–computer interface.
6. People external to the imposed boundaries of the system under development also fall into the category of user in the sense that if they are affected by the system their needs must be considered. These could be either external to or employees of the organization.

Each one of these users has its own needs, requirements, objectives and expectations of the system under development and therefore needs to participate in the process of developing the system.

But what is meant by '*participation*?' If we take the *Chambers Dictionary* definition of the word as 'to have a share, or take part in or have some of the qualities of . . . . . .', the obvious question to be answered is, does every user group 'take part in', have a share of', etc.? We will attempt to answer this question in the following pages.

13.2 The traditional participants of systems development

Over the years, the participants of the systems development process have evolved to include project teams, steering committees, specialist development staff and possibly end-users. Many data-processing departments in organizations have traditionally a hierarchical structure of which that shown in Figure 13.1 is the most common.

Although job titles have changed, merged and been amended, the primary functions and objectives of the department have been the same, essentially that of a servicing department providing computer-based information systems for areas within the organization. Consultants and software houses provide the same kind of service.

These traditional roles are undergoing an evolutionary rather than revolutionary change because of the following shifts in emphasis:

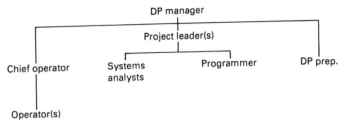

Figure 13.1

1. Distributed computing (rather than one central resource) with its associated microcomputers and software tools. This move has repercussions regarding standardization, privacy, security, etc., but that is another story!
2. A majority of personnel within any organization now have more experience of and education in the potential of computer-based systems and thus have higher expectations of what a computer-based information system could do for them.

These two factors (and many others that we will discuss later) together with well-documented 'failures' of systems development projects have provoked many discussions and arguments as to the roles of the traditional systems developer and the user.

The question is now as Parkin[1] puts it very succinctly, can the user continue to be 'told' or 'sold'? Can we continue to present a *fait accompli* and insist that the system be installed or by selling the benefits and compensations convince the users that it has to be installed?

13.3 Who should be the participants?

Having discussed in a previous section the various categories of user of a system and bearing in mind that these users will have conflicting objectives, surely if the systems developer is aware of the user's requirements, that will suffice? Many systems analysts argue very strongly that they have the user's welfare at heart and do ask the user what he wants on many occasions. By so saying, they imply that it is the user's fault if he cannot define his own objectives and requirements.

So need a user participate in the process of systems development and, if so, in what role and to what degree? Or can the user 'go it alone'?

Consider, initially, the user designing his 'own' application. There are many reasons why this is possible. As discussed in Section 13.2, many organizations have moved away from the concept of a large central computing provision with mainly batch processing to distributing computing with terminal and/or net-worked microcomputers. There is also a proliferation of software on the market to aid in the development of an application. There are fourth-generation languages, application development tools, database software and integrated software (word processing, spreadsheets, database and graphics).

The temptation, therefore, for an end-user (category 1 and/or 2) to take a short cut, as he sees it, is great. He will be the owner of his data and information, and will be able to design his own requirements into the application.

However, this approach has two main drawbacks. First, it is very rare for an end-user, who has access to computing power, to have the technical knowledge necessary to function efficiently. For example, if a terminal 'hangs', is it the line or the software? How does he back-up? What happens if there is a disc error or software is purchased with a different operating system?

Second, and more seriously in the authors' view, is the danger of having many different applications perhaps on different machines written using different software packages. This situation has implications for standardization and data protection. We are all aware of the problems that occur with, for example, Lotus 1, 2, 3 on a Dec, Symphony on an IBM Pc and Visicale on a BBC, all in the same organization probably carrying out very similar functions with, more often than not, inconsistent data. There is an obvious nonsense in running separate payroll and personnel applications but it happens! Users, therefore, have a need for technical support and should adhere to a corporate strategy for designing information systems.

Surely, the system developer should provide the solution to these points. He has the technical knowledge and is aware of the corporate strategy. He will certainly be aware of the value of designing an information system with centralized information meeting the requirements of all users in an organization. We come back to the statement 'requirements of users'. Why is this so difficult to ascertain?

As Floyd and Keil describe in their paper[2], the systems developer is interested in the information-processing aspects of the user's work, whereas users have a wider set of interests and a different perspective. Floyd and Keil classify user requirements into three categories:

1. Functional requirements – describing the desired output to be produced for a given input;
2. Performance requirements – have they the resources available to achieve these functions?;
3. Handling requirements – defining the manner in which the system is to be embedded in the work and communication process of its users.

The performance requirements and the handling requirements, in the user's view, are seen by the systems developer as irrelevant. This would in itself cause resentment, conflict and potentially a rejection of the system when it has been designed.

We will expand these requirements a little and use Maslow's[4] hierarchy of need from lowest to highest priority:

Need	Examples
1. Physiological	Food, clothing, shelter
2. Safety and security	Protection against danger and loss of job
3. Social	Being able to identify with individuals and groups
4. Egotistic	Recognition, status and importance
5. Self-fulfilment	Realizing one's fullest potential in creativity and self-development

We will see that if the systems developer is only concerned with the information processing then many of these needs will not be met and could lead to a dysfunctional user involvement. We are also in grave danger of designing 'incomplete' systems if the user's experience and skill are ignored. As Lawrence[5] suggests in his arguments for user participation, the design of computer systems should become a negotiating process to:

1. Decrease or eliminate the uncertainty of users;
2. Utilize the user's experience and skills;
3. Understand and incorporate the values of users;
4. Minimize loss of power and control from user groups.

To summarize with a quote from Glasson[7]: 'If users were given the opportunity to effectively participate in their systems development projects, perhaps fewer would be driven to seek their own software solutions.' He adds that several roles associated with systems development (e.g. human activity role) are not the sole province of one role (e.g. systems designer). Many papers have been written to extol the advantages of participation between user and systems developer (there is little room to quote all in a chapter of this size) but as Lawrence[6] says: 'Telling somebody to participate does not mean participation will occur.' In the next section we will discuss the possible reasons why this should be.

13.4 Problems of communication

The history of systems development has contributed a good deal to the problems to be found in communication between users and systems developers. Oliver and Langford[2] list a number of myths that have built up over the years about the view systems developers have of users:

1. Users don't know what they want.
2. Users keep changing their minds.
3. Users want everything yesterday.
4. Users react emotionally and illogically.
5. Users are stupid.
6. Users resist change.

They argue that this very negative perception of users results from a basic difference in thinking modes, i.e. logical and analytical thinking being valued above intuitive and holistic problem solving. It is no wonder that problems of communication arise if systems developers perceive users in this way and if indeed users see systems developers as 'machines'.

Furthering this theme of 'machines', a natural communication tool for the systems developer is his methodology (for example, a flowchart, a data flow diagram or a decision table). This, to use a hackneyed phrase, is 'to blind the user with science'. Yet to use these tools and techniques in their proper context (i.e. as a documentation tool), must help the communication process.

In the authors' experience, major problems arise when a data flow diagram, used as an example, is seen as the solution by the systems developer in his narrow-mindedness and the user in his fear and awe of technicality. A user will be able to specify what he wants far more easily if he knows what is possible and clear communication at DFD level should help this process.

Before leaving this area of communication problems, the reader is referred to the paper by Valusek and Fryback[2], which discusses the further obstacles to determining information requirements:

WITHIN individual users
AMONG users
BETWEEN users and systems developers

This paper discusses some interesting research findings in the field of cognitive psychology.

In the following section we will propound some of the solutions to these communication problems given that participation is an unarguable proposition.

13.5 Approaches to user involvement

In the last few years, ideas, approaches and methodologies have abounded in an attempt to increase user commitment and involvement. The authors would wish to categorize these ideas, some theoretical and some that can be applied, into three areas as follows:

1. Evolutionary
2. Experimental
3. Participative

Each of these has its enthusiasts and critics, but we will *report*, not bias!

13.5.1 Evolutionary approach

Floyd and Keil[2] suggest the process-oriented approach to software development. They see this approach as a sequence of development cycles in which the developers and users cooperate. The object of each cycle is to produce a version of the system that can be evaluated (i.e. the systems development evolves).

The structured methodologies such as that put forward in this book and advocated by Gane and Sarson[8] and de Marco[9] are also evolutionary if the user requirements are not paid lip-service only. The user involvement begins with the physical DFD and ends with the DIADS, which document user's 'wish-lists'. They do not, at any stage, purport to address any areas such as job design, etc. but argue that a set of tools and techniques are needed if anything is to be done.

The authors agree with this point of view but put forward a suggestion that a more formal framework for cooperation be included. One such could be Glasson's[7] General Model Framework. Glasson models the systems development process as a series of 'activity sets' which may be related to one of more of the system development roles. The development roles are identified as the people and functions that should participate in the process (for example, project teams, steering committees, users of specialist development staff). This paper makes very interesting reading. Parkin[1] also addresses this area, with user participation classified as 'insider participation' and outsider participation'. In the first instance users would be privy to all design decisions and in the second would act in consultation, partnership or delegation.

13.5.2 Experimental approach

This approach is so called because of the 'trial and error' aspects to the process of systems development. We shall focus attention on the most used of these approaches, i.e. *prototyping*. These are two distinct schools of thought to prototyping, best described by Davies[3] and Capron[10]. Davies gives his definition of a prototype as 'a model or framework for the final system which implies complete not partial design, i.e. its intent is to demonstrate feasibility'. Capron, on the other hand, suggests that a prototype should be a 'limited working system or a subset of a system which is developed quickly, i.e. a working model that can be tinkered and fine-tuned by the user', the implication being that user requirements will be determined by experimenting with a working system. He also points out, correctly in the authors' view, that 'leaping in with a loose test model does not seem to belong to the natural order of things when planning, as in the systems Life Cycle Approach'.

Prototyping has been made possible by the use of *quick-build* software as in the high-level languages and software tools described above, and can either be refined to produce a final system or discarded when its purpose has been satisfied.

There is a vision of a systems developer and user sitting at a terminal, building a system in piecemeal fashion when the word 'prototyping' is used but the approach answers the criticism that the user never knows what he wants!

Finally, Mittermeir *et al.*[2] see problems with prototyping. They suggest that it should be combined with other approaches to reduce the application risk. The alternative approaches are:

1. Objectives Analysis – asking the user about his objectives for the system:
2. Scenario Techniques – relating to the users; how they will react to the potential change to their environment.

The authors refer the reader to this paper for further explanation.

13.5.3 Participative approach

This approach, as described fully and succinctly by Mumford *et al.*[11] addresses the problem areas of task structures and job satisfaction for users. It suggests that users design the system, with systems developers as consultants, within the solution set of a computer-based system. The authors have found that a direct quote from Mumford *et al.* could not be bettered:

The approach is based on four important value judgements:–
a) Financial, Human and Technical factors in systems design can and should be treated compatibly.
b) Everyone affected by a system change can and should be considered in planning it.
c) Employees at all levels can and should design their own work stations and
d) That the overall approach to systems design and development should be based on the principle of reducing uncertainty.

This raises two questions, that of time elements and the technological experience of users. Its critics suggest that the system may be poorly designed and not cost-effective, but who could argue that the best people to design their man/machine interface, for example, are those who will use it, and it does 'involve' the user completely. It could be argued that this is user participation at its ultimate, even if only at the design stage of the systems development process. Three possible approaches have been briefly described in the previous sections, but as Parkin[1] sums up so well: 'The most effective form of participation will be the one that fits the particular system, the particular people and the particular priorities of the moment.'

References

1. A. Parkin, *Systems Analysis,* Edward Arnold, London (1980)
2. R. Galliers (ed.), *Information Analysis – Selected Readings,* Addison-Wesley, Reading, Mass. (1987)
3. W. S. Davis, *Systems Analysis and Design,* Addison-Wesley, Reading, Mass. (1983)
4. M. Leeson, *Systems Analysis and Design,* Science Research Associates Inc., New York (1981)
5. P. Lawrence, 'How to deal with resistance to change', *Harvard Business Review,* January–February, 37–45 (1969)
6. F. Land and R. Hirschheim, Participative Systems Design: its Rationale, Tools and Techniques. In *Information Analysis – Selected Readings* (ed. R. Galliers) Addison-Wesley, Reading, Mass. (1987)
7. B. C. Glasson, A System Development Model for a Changing Environment. In *Information Analysis – Selected Readings* (ed. R. Galliers) Addison-Wesley, Reading, Mass. (1987)
8. T. Sarson and C. Gane, *Structured Systems Analysis: Tools and Techniques,* Prentice-Hall, Englewood Cliffs, NJ (1979)

9. T. De Marco, *Structured Analysis and System Specification*, Prentice-Hall, Englewood Cliffs, NJ (1979)
10. H. L. Capron, *Systems Analysis and Design*, Benjamin/Cummings, New York (1986)
11. E. Mumford., F. Land and J. Hawgood, A Participative Approach to the Design of Computer Systems. In *Information Analysis – Selected Readings* (ed. R. Galliers) Addison-Wesley, Reading, Mass. (1987)

Part 5

Implementation

Chapter 14

Implementation

14.1 Planning

The best way to begin this chapter is with the adage 'Plan the implementation, implement the plan'. This is easily said, so why devote a whole chapter to this topic? Surely, the hard work has already been done? If we consider the systems life-cycle, this is only one phase, but in the authors' experience, a very important phase and one that can make or break a potentially 'successful' system. Many people who have worked in organizations have either been involved in or been spectators of a situation where a system has been designed and very rarely, if ever, used. This could be for reasons discussed in Chapter 13, but blame could fall very firmly on poor planning for the implementation phase. Consider the frustration felt when errors occur in the computerized system and there is nobody there to help, or the loss of interest and motivation when the hardware fails to arrive by the changeover date.

As Daniel and Yeates[1] state, 'Since Information Systems are social systems and most social systems are robust, the informal human component often finds a way of overcoming the failure of a designed system, usually at the cost of some efficiency.' In some cases, this is an understatement, as a failure to implement a system correctly could have cost implications and even deliberate misuse and sabotage as its more damaging consequence.

Consider Leeson's[2] list of prerequisites for a successful conversion, summarized for the purpose of this chapter:

1. Users should have been involved in and informed about the development of the new system.
2. The reaction of employees to the new system should have been carefully evaluated.
3. The complete testing of the new system should have been carried out.
4. The comparative compatibility of the new and old systems should be evaluated.

5. The documentation of the new system should be completed.
6. The careful training of users in recording the initial data, entering the input, operating the system and working with the output should be completed.

These are only some of the project tasks involved: the hardware has to be installed, communication lines considered, etc. The next stage in this discussion should, therefore, be a list of activities to be managed pre-, during and post-implementation.

14.1.1 Pre-implementation

Activity 1 – Software completion or evaluation.
Activity 2 – The evaluation of, tendering for and acquisition of hardware.
Activity 3 – The hiring and training of personnel.
Activity 4 – Testing of equipment, operating procedures and software.
Activity 5 – Decision on changeover procedures.
Activity 6 – Full documentation.

These activities have not been listed in chronological order as each is very dependent on the type of system designed and the size of the organization.

The authors would wish to expand on these activities to a greater or lesser extent and have devoted sections to training (14.2), testing (14.4), changeover (14.5) and documentation (14.3).

Writing the software has been discussed fully in this book. What has been omitted until now is the possibility that an application package has been purchased from an external vendor. Presumably, the evaluation of the application packages available has been carried out according to a set of predefined benchmarking criteria, and a specific package been chosen. This could need certain modifications to fit the organization's requirements and has been promised, with full documentation, by a certain date.

After-sales support and possible amendments and error correction should have been discussed fully at the evaluation stage. On the other hand, with internally developed programs the analyst, programmers and users should agree a fixed but feasible date by which the programs will be ready for a full system test.

The period of time between ordering hardware and its delivery is usually in the region of 3–6 months, so the evaluation of and tendering for hardware should have taken place some time before the agreed date for implementation. The difficulty here is that, very often, evolving software requirements could mean differing hardware characteristics from those initially specified. For example, writing software for a ring network may be too expensive or technically very difficult, and a decision is taken to change to a star network. This would have obvious implications for the hardware purchase. Communication channels should be considered, i.e. are leased lines or private lines required? This would depend on the privacy and security of the data being communicated, and again these communication links must be costed and ordered in advance.

The preparation for the physical site of the hardware is an area which is often overlooked. Environmental and ergonomic considerations are to be considered even if the new system demands only online terminals to be installed. The considerations to be taken into account for full hardware installation should be:

1. The size and position of the room which will house the main computer and console. The security of this room is paramount. It should have limited window access and a digital lock on the door. The lighting and air conditioning should be well designed as a suitable work environment for operators and engineers. A safe for back-up tapes should be purchased and preferably kept away from this room.
2. The electricity supply. There should be a clean power supply to the main machine and telecommunication link points installed. Consideration should also be given to situations where blackouts and brownouts occur.
3. The terminal points. These should be designed for ease of access and if used for data input, furniture of a suitable design should be purchased.

14.1.2 During and post-implementation

The main feature of the implementation phase is the uncertainty of the users. Many users, quite understandably, will revert to the manual system if a problem, however small, occurs. The presence of the system developer or any experienced person during this phase is desirable, if not a necessity.

As Land and Kennedy McGregor state [3]: 'The system is based on a model of the real world and of real world behaviour which is untested and often in error.' It is not until the implementation stage that real-world behaviour emerges, and this must be monitored by the systems developer and users.

Where implementation stops and post-implementation begins is a moot point. However, consider the situation where the system is live and old forms and procedures have been discarded. The temptation for the systems developers to 'walk away' and start a new project is great. However, the whole development process should be evaluated and audited for many reasons. These will be discussed in Section 14.6.

14.2 User involvement and training

The authors have included user involvement in this section as there are many personal issues to be addressed before the training of users can begin. As Hedburg and Jönssen explain[3], social requirements of implementation significantly change the work environment, social interaction or the job design. Yet the organization's personnel strategy must be adhered to, this often designed with certain personnel at certain levels carrying out certain tasks. There is also, with all probability, a policy of no redundancy. Both these factors will lead to the inevitable new tasks being carried out by existing personnel. Therefore the personnel requirements of every new task should be identified and new job descriptions written. More importantly, however, the existing staff should be given every opportunity to discuss fully the potential changes, to decide their level of participation and to have a say in the design of their new environments and jobs. If necessary, trade union negotiations should be undertaken to ensure that users at data input level are at the correct grade. Health and Safety regulations should also be reviewed for operators, VDU typists, etc. Once all these issues have been addressed, training requirements can be considered.

The first question that must be asked is, Why train? If user manuals are provided surely users are capable of learning by reading and practising! But experience and research have shown us that 'Show and Tell', as Capron[4] puts it, is much more valuable as a teaching aid. The confidence of users in the new system is paramount and the psychological aspects of training in promoting this confidence has great import.

There are two features of training that should be addressed.

1. Who does the training?
2. Who do we train?

Present in some organizations are divisions or departments which have responsibility for the training needs of the organization, and although it may be the case that training of this ilk has not been given before, their training expertise should be utilized.

In organizations where this is not the case, then the users and systems project teams should develop and implement the required training programs using such resources as, for example, the hardware manufacturers' external courses or programmed instructor courses. Training could be given to large groups of personnel or individuals, but whoever carries it out or whatever size the courses, it should be efficient, thorough and professional.

The type of training required will vary according to the contact that is to be made with the system by the different types of user. For example, there will be differing training requirements for:

1. User at enquiry/output level;
2. User at input level;
3. User at operator level.

All three will probably need briefing as to the objectives of the new system and possibly will need a computer-awareness course, but similarities will end there.

Consider the users at enquiry/output level, who are probably at management level within the organization. Their requirements will have been ascertained at the investigation and analysis stage, and hopefully, their requirements are now being implemented. Most users will find it difficult to reach the 'happy medium'; they will either access the minimum information or will 'drown' themselves in information. Training at this level should, as Hedburg and Jönsson state[3], either promote curiosity or show how to sift for relevant information.

Users at input level could be clerks or salesmen as well as input operators. For example, training must include the value of filling in the source documents accurately and the procedures for so doing, and for the input operators the importance of typing or punching in the data from this source document correctly. Many systems have suffered from incorrect or incomplete data input, although, arguably, control totals and other validation techniques should catch these errors. Training for these users is usually after the equipment is installed, before implementation takes place, as in-service training is the most effective method.

The best form of training for the computer operators will be at the vendor's schools. The equipment will be available and their instructor's knowledge and experience in both hardware and systems maintenance will be hard to surpass. The computer operators should be fully trained before the equipment is installed as their help in setting up the system will be invaluable. In all three cases, their roles as individuals in the whole process should be stressed. The authors do not wish to give too much space in this chapter to the way in which training should be given, but it must be noted briefly that training material should be of the highest standard and full use made of presentation aids.

One last word on the subject of training: it should be ongoing, both as basic training for new employees and as refresher courses for existing ones.

14.3 Documentation – user and operator manuals

The first draft of the documented system should be available by the time the system is implemented; we say 'should' from experience! The 'most tedious task in systems development is documentation' is the view put forward by many professionals, but is it professional not to document?

Two manuals that are essential before any consideration of implementation dates can be undertaken are the user manual and the operator manual or handbook. These two should be distinct as the training of users and operators is distinct. The *operator* manual should be technical and include areas such as:

1. How to start the computer/system.
2. What to do if the system fails.
3. When to back-up.
4. What data to back-up and how often.
5. Access rights and possibly password generation.
6. How to produce the computer-logging audit trail.
7. References to the relevant technical handbooks that arrive with the equipment.
8. Error codes and their meanings.

The user manuals, however, should act as a reminder of the training courses undertaken, and as a 'trouble-shooter'. Many user manuals are clear on the straightforward procedures but fail to provide cause and effect of errors that could occur.

The content of users' manuals will vary, depending on the type of input and output devices and the objectives of the computer-based information system. A typical user manual could contain:

1. Full description of procedure(s);
2. Description of input form(s); where it originates, who completes it, how the data should be recorded on the form, who authorizes changes to the data or the form;
3. Procedures to be used to correct invalid information;

4. How long the documents/reports are to be retained and how they are to be destroyed;
5. How control totals are worked out;
6. To whom the printout is to be sent;
7. Description of menus and help facilities;
8. Full description of error situations and recovery procedures;
9. Brief summary of straightforward procedure.

There should be a manual for each user and incorporated into the documentation should be pages for notes, by the user, and of error conditions met, for later evaluation (Section 14.6).

Manuals of any description have a notorious reputation for being badly written and difficult to follow and understand: in the authors' view a reputation well deserved. It *is* difficult to produce a manual for the uninitiated when one is fully initiated oneself. It is hard to imagine what users will do when panic situations occur, but however difficult, it should be attempted and rewritten with the user's help. Very often, documentation standards exist within an organization and manuals should be written to these standards. It goes without saying that they should be clear, comprehensive, concise, well written and fully indexed.

Although this section has been dealing only with documentation for users, it must be remembered that full systems documentation should also be available at the implementation phase. This area has been covered in previous chapters.

14.4 Testing the system

A valuable point to make at the begining of this section is that testing has been and should be ongoing. However carefully data combinations have been worked out, experience tells us that there will be a few that have not been tested. Testing, however, should be rigorous and comprehensive and fully monitored.

Although it is difficult to partition testing procedures, as it is the whole system we are concerned with, for the purposes of this section we will do so and consider the following areas:

1. Testing equipment;
2. Testing software;
3. Testing operation procedures.

14.4.1 Testing equipment

Equipment could be anything from a microcomputer to a large mainframe with a full complement of peripherals and a sophisticated communications network. Obviously, it will be easier to test a microcomputer as all are provided with software to carry out a full equipment test. It takes approximately 30 minutes and is relatively straightforward.

Larger and more complicated equipment will be installed by the vendor's engineers and will be technically tested by them. Problems with leased lines, modems and terminals and any degradation of response time will not become apparent until the software test or possibly during live running, when the full volume of data and transactions are present. Thus, all equipment should be covered by a maintenance contract to deal with this eventuality.

14.4.2 Testing software

If the system was written in-house, software testing will have been taking place for some time. This will involve testing individual programs, including every error routine, and a full program link test, until data have passed through the whole suite of programs. In these cases, the data used have probably been test data which, by definition, will be small in volume but high in errors. If the software has been purchased, it should have been tested fully by the vendors but not *in situ*.

Whatever the source, it is at this stage that the software should be tested rigorously with 'real' data preferably or a full complement of 'dummy' data. The software should run on the installed equipment for a period of time which will satisfy most criteria (i.e. month-end statistics, etc.). There should be very careful monitoring at these stages by users and systems developers, with all system peculiarities investigated and corrected. This may involve the software house that the software was purchased from, depending on the maintenance contract.

14.4.3 Testing procedures

The operation procedures are slightly more difficult to test in artificial conditions. However, it is vital that the test be attempted. It would be unfortunate if the system went live and the discovery made, at this stage, that updates could not be punched in until the post arrived, or that the period allocated for backing-up was the busiest time for enquiries. Workflow should be scheduled and timed and adjustments made at this stage. This would involve all users who will be using documents and/or printouts and possibly moving over to the new forms prior to the implementation process.

It must be stressed that implementation should not be attempted until all the participants involved in the testing are satisfied with the results and are confident enough to 'go live'.

14.5 Changeover procedures

It is at this stage of the systems development life cycle that systems developers and users alike are feeling the tendency to rush through the remaining stages and complete the project. Most of the readers will have met the familiar enthusiasm/effort curve, which is self-explanatory (Figure 14.1).

However, unless the preceding phases have been carried out efficiently and effectively, it is at this point that partial or complete failure could occur. Many a system has been 'thrown out' at this stage either for a mismatch of requirements or for user's dysfunctional behaviour or for an incorrect system specification regarding frequencies and volumes of data transactions. Let us assume for the purpose of this section that all participants are interested, and consider the various options for implementation.

Direct
This option is used normally for systems that are either new to the organization or completely different to the system at present being used. A date is set for a changeover, all data converted and the complete system started on that date. This is very much a risk situation, and thus not particularly favoured as a method of changeover unless circumstances dictate it.

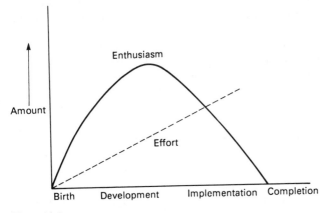

Figure 14.1

Parallel

Parallel changeover is the most favoured option because of its safety. As the name implies, the old system is run in parallel with the new one for a period of time of the order of six months and the output compared. In this instance, the systems must be very similar (for example, a computerization of a manual system).

Parallel running has its disadvantages. It is very costly as, in effect, there is double the staff, double the workload and twice the amount of data for the period of time the systems are running in parallel. However, when this is measured against the confidence of the users and systems developers and the proven integrity of the new system, when the old system is discarded it must be put in perspective.

Pilot

This option is considered in two situations. First, if the organization is not too sure of its willingness to adopt the new system, and second, if the new system has political implications.

Pilot running, in effect, means using a test site which is part of the organization. The system is installed at this test site and a full evaluation of its result carried out before the decision is made to install the system throughout the organization. The advantage of pilot running is that the system is fully tested in a live situation before it is adopted, but the installation is obviously very time consuming.

Phased

Phased implementation, as it its name implies, is a gradual replacement of the old system with the new. For example, in a stock control system it could mean that sales were computerized while purchasing was carried out manually. The other example could be that in an organization with many locations these locations would implement the new system one at a time, until all had implemented the new system. The constraints that evoke a phased implementation are usually financial and force this compromise situation.

In all four options, one of the major tasks at the implementation phase is the conversion of the data. Questions that must be asked are:

How? How much? When? Historical?

There are probably thousands of current records and a similar number of historical records within any organization. It may be the case that all the data on these records are to be converted to some form of magnetic media. It is relatively straightforward to write software to carry out the conversion but the logistic problems of doing so are manifold.

The answer to the question of how much current and historical data are to be converted will depend on the designed system. It must be remembered that planning, control and forecasting cannot be satisfactorily undertaken without historical data, but a decision as to whether these data will be part of the current file or database will be influenced by volumes and present practices. It could well be that a year's transactions will be held on the current file with the previous five years on a historical or archive file. How and when the data are to be converted will again look to the designed system and present procedures.

If a current file is to maintain credibility then it must hold up-to-date transactions. There is no point in taking a month to convert the data when those data will then be a month out of date! It should be carried out quickly and efficiently, usually over a weekend, when few current transactions are taking place. The staff involvement will be high and in many organizations temporary staff are employed. In the authors' view, this is nearly always a mistake, as temporary staff do not have the incentive to ensure that the input data are accurate. If extra staff are needed then these temporary recruits could deal with some of the tasks of the present permanent staff and leave them free to carry out the conversion. The historical data, if on a separate file, could be converted at a more leisurely pace.

The security and integrity of the data is an area that needs obvious consideration. The chances of data corruption by non-fraudulent or fraudulent situations are high and full security of these data is paramount. Procedures should be strictly adhered to, as to how often copies of files and transactions are taken, where these copies are stored and who is responsible.

Whatever the method of changeover there is one important factor which contributes to the success of the implementation and that is the on-site availability of the systems developers: brief period of handholding, as Davis[5] puts it. Capron[4] goes further, and states that the credibility of the system will be greatly enhanced if problems at the implementation phase are handled promptly and that a genuine interest and quick response are incentives that spur users to offer advice and to fully participate. In the authors' experience this statement is fully justified.

14.6 Post-implementation evaluation and audit

To evaluate the success of any project is a difficult task, especially as the person carrying it out has usually been involved in the project from the start. The production of a cost/benefit analysis or an audit is even more difficult, as many of the benefits of a computer-based information system are intangible. These points having been made, the authors will attempt to clarify both areas for two reasons. First, nothing is learnt unless a 'post-mortem' takes place, and second, systems revision or maintenance cannot be effectively pursued unless the result of an evaluation and audit are known.

14.6.1 Evaluation

Testing the system and evaluating it are different in concept. Testing implies the means by which the system is seen to be working, whereas evaluation is measuring the meeting of the original objectives of the system. Floyd and Keil[3] define the purpose of evaluation as 'to establish whether the system fits into all conceivable work tasks in a desirable manner'. They clarify this purpose into three areas:

1. To determine whether the stated requirements have been met;
2. To find errors and misunderstandings in the requirements;
3. Whether priorities stated in the functional specification are in keeping with the actual needs of the work tasks.

As Hirschheim and Smithson state[3], the vehicle for undertaking this evaluation is far from clear, and they put the question of what is being measured and why. They make many very valuable points in their paper and the authors recommend it.

If it is considered that the only criteria by which to measure the effectiveness of the new system are the original aims and objectives of the system, then all parties who would be interested in these objectives should be involved in the evaluation. These parties would be as follows.

The operating personnel
The views of the operators would be functionally based but valuable. Areas that would be considered by them would be how often they have to restart jobs because of poor programming or rerun jobs because of unprocessed records; with what frequency are reports late or *ad hoc* reports requested; and whether the hardware and software are reliable and easy to use.

The user
The user's requirements will have been a fundamental part of the goals of the system, so although their judgements will be

human-centred it is inconceivable that their views be ignored. The main areas that will be considered by the users will be whether the system is providing information in an efficient and timely manner; is it the relevant information; have the reports requested been produced; was training sufficient and effective; are procedures for using the system well documented and are they being followed. Requests for additional features for incorporation into the system should also have been logged.

The system developer
However carefully the systems developer aims for an unbiased judgement, it must be remembered that the system is 'his design'. Therefore basically his evaluation should be factual, based on statistical data from operators, users and systems personnel.

The auditor
The fact that the auditor has not been mentioned up to this point is not an oversight of the authors. Although many academic papers put forward a strong argument for the auditor's involvement in the project team throughout the process of development, most auditors prefer to remain objective. They will have been consulted about the design of controls of the system and will certainly be interested in the evaluation of those controls. They will also wish to evaluate the procedures for physical security and back-up and disaster recovery. To ascertain the effectiveness of designed controls not only of data and information but also of programs, they will use the present documentation, including 'logs' of the running system. They will also note the difference between the informal and formal procedures as described in the documentation.

Readers will have noted that there has been little discussion about the financial aspects of the evaluation process. This is deliberate and will be covered in the following section.

The separation of evalution and audit is for the very good reason that evaluation is ongoing and will occur at periodic intervals throughout the life of the system.

14.6.2 Audit

The systems development project will have been an expensive and costly one, and although the purists would wish to ignore the monetary aspects as it is difficult to quantify 'better' information, management will wish to be assured that the money was well spent. The most well-known project tool for this assurance is

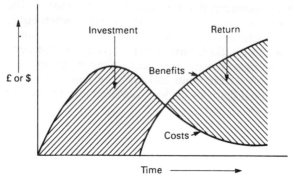

Figure 14.2

cost-benefit analysis. Readers will be aware that in many projects, benefits are slow to emerge and the initial consideration is that of costs. Again, a familiar graph illustrates this point (Figure 14.2).

Very few managers are naive enough to ignore this 'time delay', so attempts should be made to produce a cost-benefit analysis. This will also have the added incentive of satisfying all concerned that the project was well planned and costed.

The costs of a system development project are measurable, and would include those of:

1. Hardware;
2. Software, including manpower;
3. Installation;
4. Maintenance.

Although accounting methods such as discounted cash flow (DCF) may need to be applied to put costs on a comparable basis and to take account of the time value of money, the costs are quantifiable.

What about benefits? There are benefits that can be quantified, and are normally known as *tangible benefits*. These would include, for example, a larger percentage of completed orders, less capital tied up in stock, a better cash flow from a more efficient invoicing system. The benefits that are more difficult to measure are, for example, the improved timeliness or quality of information, a better service to customers and the effect of a new marketing system on orders. However, there are techniques for quantifying such *intangible benefits,* such as *Bayesian analysis, statistical sampling* and *benefit computation.* These are expertly described in a paper by Couger[3].

It rarely happens that costs and benefits balance, as the audit function of a systems evaluation should be concerned, as Daniels and Yeates[1] describe, with cost *effectiveness* rather than cost *justification*. Their definition of cost effectiveness is the 'state of affairs where the cost, in monetary terms, of providing a service is less than the cost of providing it by any other practicable means'.

14.7 Maintenance

Systems maintenance, as distinct from the chargeable maintenance for purchased hardware and software, is ongoing and vital to the continuing functioning of the system. It should include much more than maintaining the *status quo*, as the organization, people and the environment will be constantly changing. As Capron[4] says: 'Some installations devote as much as 80% of their resources to the maintenance function.'

Maintenance, therefore, although the term implies otherwise, should cover constant *evaluation, monitoring* and *modification*. It may also include a fair degree of 'fire-fighting', although this should be avoided if at all possible. As Floyd and Keil[3] aptly summarize, modifications to the system could occur to both the requirement definition and the functional specification. They continue with examples of the possible scenario. The requirement definition may need changes:

1. As a result of the evaluation process;
2. As a result of changes in the user system;
3. As a result of new demands from the data-processing system.

The functional specification may need changes:

1. As a result of changes in the requirement definition;
2. As a result of errors of inadequacies in the present system;
3. According to the plan for systems enhancement,

and back we go to Chapter 5! In other words, the systems life cycle is very aptly named!

One brief point before completion of this chapter is that 'patching-up' a system, without due concern for the systems development process, will end in a system not functioning to its full potential and, after all the hard work, is it worth it?

References

1. A. Daniels and D. Yeates, *Practical Systems Design*, Pitman Publishing Inc., New York (1984)

2. M. Leeson, *Systems Analysis and Design,* Science Research Associates Inc., New York (1981)
3. R. Galliers (ed.), *Information Analysis – Selected Readings,* Addison-Wesley, Reading, Mass. (1987)
4. H. L. Capron, *Systems Analysis and Design,* Benjamin/Cummings, New York (1981)
5. W. S. Davis, *Systems Analysis and Design,* Addison-Wesley, Reading, Mass. (1983)

Answer pointers

Chapter 1 Discussion points

D1.1 *Purposes* must include:

> Supplying bread to the community;
> Making sufficient profit;
> Providing a satisfactory occupation, and income, for *all* the members of the firm; and
> Passing on a family identity.

Components lie within the system boundary. The choice is ultimately arbitrary, but candidates are: active members of the family, inactive members of the family, employees, customers, suppliers, the physical equipment, the premises, and the knowledge of all kinds possessed by members of the firm.

The *boundary* encloses those components we choose to include in the system. Necessarily, if we are modelling less than the entire universe, most entities must be in the environment, outside the system. The choice of what to include within the boundary must depend on the purpose we have in modelling. A model of production capacity would have different components from a manpower planning model.

The most obvious feedback mechanism is *negative feedback* on breadmaking. There is an ideal standard for bread, from which the bakery would not want to deviate. *Positive feedback* could relate to sales of bread. If the firm is seen by its members as successful, then their enthusiasm is reinforced, and the chance of further success increased.

Feedback is a *maintenance* mechanism. Any search for changing tastes by consumers, or different styles of eating by consumers, is an example of an *adaptive* mechanism.

The *environmental information monitored* relates directly to the adaptive mechanisms. Sources of information must include the firm's own sales, and trends in those sales; discussion with customers; and close attention to obvious opinion-forming and monitoring publications.

D1.2 Undoubtedly a village has *parts*: houses, people, church, pub, village store, bus stop, etc. It is difficult to speak of *purpose* unless we treat survival as a sufficient purpose. Necessarily, any view of the village must have a *boundary* somewhere. Most British villages have been in a *steady state* for a long time. This supposes *feedback* which ensures that essential needs are fulfilled. Villages are *open systems* with many flows of people, of material, and of information between the village and the environment.

Changes in the environment will make necessary *adaptive mechanisms* within the village. The entity which survives may be significantly changed by the adaptation.

D1.3 The statement implies that *purpose* subsumes *will, belief,* and *desires*. At present, these are attributes possessed pre-eminently by people. A system which does not have a purpose in that sense can be seen as having a *use*.

D1.4 The family bakery would be a *purposeful* system. The majority of human activity systems come in this category. A *purposive* system can be seen in the terms of our question 3, as a system with a *use*.

D1.5 An information system dispenses information, not decisions. Thus it cannot be seen as having a will.

D1.6 The answers must be subjective. We cannot give an answer pointer!

Chapter 2 Discussion points

D2.1 Discussion must resolve whether there is any difference between *storing* data for subsequent use and *archiving* data for which no future use has presently been predicted. If there is such a difference, is there any gain from using different symbols for storage and for archiving?

The presentation in the chapter suggests that, necessarily, if a data store appears in a data flow diagram then that data store must be accessed by more than one function. This could mean that some data stores are not shown on any data flow diagram. The DFDs then do not exhaustively document the data stores. Is this a bad thing?

D2.2 Once one has reached a function showing a simple conversion, then, necessarily, the steps in the function are executed at the same time or in a single sequence. There is therefore no benefit from further decomposition, so far as relationships with other functions and with data stores are concerned.

If we are looking for a way of defining the function without reference to other functions, then a list of instruction steps is of equal value to a set of connected bubbles. Since the list of steps must occupy less space than a set of bubbles, it is difficult to justify anything more elaborate than a list of instruction steps.

If functional decomposition is stopped before a simple conversion is reached, then it is difficult to preserve the links with other functions.

D2.3 The basic conflict is that we have said that data stores are shown only when they form part of the interface between function bubbles. If the data are all part of an integrated database, then the data store is always *outside* all functions save only the bubble of the context diagram.

It is not correct to see a database *view* as the internal data store within a function. A view is only a representation of an integrated database, and is affected by changes to the database caused by other functions.

D2.4 The most robust approach to modelling is to attempt to represent the real-world entities. Nevertheless, a database actually exists and can itself be modelled. We can have a model of reality and also a model of the database. They may (but need not) be substantially similar. If they differ, then we must have a means of relating the entity types in the real-world model to the data tables in the database model.

Chapter 2 Exercises

E2.1 The sinks and sources (external entities) are: PUBLIC, BANK, SUPPLIERS, and MARKET RESEARCH CON-SULTANTS. Data flows to and from the single bubble of the context diagram are: 'selected goods' (from PUBLIC), 'cash receipts' (to BANK), 'purchase order' (to SUP-PLIERS), 'market research data' (from MARKET RE-SEARCH CONSULTANTS), 'goods received' (from SUP-PLIERS), 'supplier's invoice' (from SUPPLIERS), and 'supplier payment' (to SUPPLIERS).

The functions in the level 0 diagram are: CHECKOUT, ACCOUNTS, PURCHASING, and GOODS-INWARD.

The additional data flows not shown on the context diagram are: 'checkout; cash; (from CHECKOUT to ACCOUNTS), 'point-of-sale data' (from CHECKOUT to PURCHAS-ING), 'copy of purchase order' (from PURCHASING to GOODS-INWARD), 'delivery note' (from GOODS-INWARD to PURCHASING), and 'certified purchase order' (from PURCHASING to ACCOUNTS).

The data stores are not shown on the level 0 diagram because they are all local to a particular function. At level 1, the PENDING PURCHASE ORDER data store appears in the PURCHASING diagram and the SALES LEDGER and PURCHASE LEDGER appear in the ACCOUNTS diagram.

E2.2 The drawing of any data model requires assumptions about relationships, this one no less than any. The following list involves a set of assumptions:

> One CUSTOMER places many CONTRACTs.
> One CONTRACT includes many PANEL TYPEs.
> One PANEL TYPE requires many MOULDs.
> One MOULD produces many PANELs.

and:

> One CONTRACT uses many MACHINEs.
> One MACHINE is used for many CONTRACTs.
> One CONTRACT is worked on by many EMPLOYEEs.
> One EMPLOYEE works on many CONTRACTs.
> One CONTRACT consumes many STOCK ITEMs.
> One STOCK ITEM is consumed by many CONTRACTs.

E2.3 There is no requirement in a supermarket to identify individual customers. The data model is thus largely concerned with the supply side:

> One SUPPLIER receives many PURCHASE ORDERs.
> One PURCHASE ORDER consists of many ORDER LINEs.
> One STOCK ITEM is re-ordered by many ORDER LINEs.

E2.4 The model will depend on the modeller's decision whether or not to have one single model covering both vehicles, and people who own or are licensed to drive those vehicles. We shall assume one single model:

(a) and (b)

One PERSON may be the keeper of many VEHICLEs.
One PERSON may be licensed for many LICENCE CLASSes.
One PERSON may have been given many ENDORSE-MENTs.
One LICENCE CLASS covers many VEHICLEs.
One VEHICLE may have undergone many modifications.

The attributes of PERSON may be:

PERSON (*LicenceNumber*, Name, Address, Dateof-Birth, ExpiryDate), with LicenceNumber as the primary key.

(c)

Possible entry points are PERSON.Name, PERSON.LicenceNumber, PERSON.Address, VEHICLE.RegistrationNumber, VEHICLE.Colour, or VEHICLE.ModelName.

Chapter 3 Discussion points

D3.1 We expect that once a discussion group attempts to construct a world view without control, the hypothesis will be regarded as self-evidently true.

D3.2 If a cake is put in the oven for the prescribed time of 70 minutes and then removed, we have an example of *open-loop* control. If a knife is pushed into the cake and then examined to see whether any cake-mix adheres to the knife, we have *closed-loop* control.

D3.3 If the faculty board passes resolutions that a certain person is going to carry out some task; or that certain guidelines for recruiting students will be adopted; *but they never afterwards check whether the task has been carried out or whether the guidelines have been used* then we have open-loop control. If the faculty board minutes record the name of the person delegated to carry out a task and those minutes are read and commented on at the next meeting then we have closed-loop control.

D3.4 (a) For the inputs to the system, the information system should monitor the quality of the raw material purchased and the timekeeping and state of training of the employees. For the environment, the activities of competitors, the trade press, the prices of competing raw materials and the going pay rates of the various trades should be monitored. ,

(b) For the inputs to the system, the information system should monitor the qualifications of new students, the qualifications and experience of recruited staff, the state of training of existing staff and the quality of existing library and other facilities. For the environment, the expressed desires of the learned professions and of employers of graduating students, the activities of other educational activities, and the utterances of both national and local government should be monitored.

D3.5 The levels differ according to the differing lengths of the transactions they handle. A *technical core* transaction is completed using the facilities which are readily available. A *strategic-level* transaction could require setting up a complete capacity to produce and sell in a different market.

D3.6 The three levels are not immutable. The division could be into two, or four or five levels. It happens, however, that there are short-term decisions which depend on available facilities; there are the strategic decisions; and there are decisions between those limits which depend on the strategic purposes, and supply the framework within which the technical core operates.

D3.7 No! Except in a completely rigid organization, there must always be the need to cope with the unexpected. If it is unexpected, it cannot be dealt with by a formal system.

D3.8 To an extent, this is true! If information is available to a decision maker it will tend to be used. If information about what a decision maker does is available to other people, the decision maker will try to make that information reflect credit on himself.

D3.9 The prescription describes rather precisely the activities of most national government. The characteristics of a computer system would include the 'What if?' ('What would happen if we did this?'), and also a fuzziness in prediction: 'There is a chance of outcome A, but also a chance of B, C, or D.' It would be nice if the information system were able to attach some probability estimate for outcomes A, B, C and D.

Chapter 4 Discussion points

D4.1 This may be true. Designers are anxious to see their designs implemented. Ideally, they are designing systems which help achieve the purposes of the system, but who should specify what those purposes are?

D4.2 The statement has a lot going for it! It must surely be true that the commitment of the potential users of the system must be won. The Chief Accountant's list includes everything from employee participation to employee coercion.

D4.3 We cannot add any explanation to this. The statement demands some introspection from students.

D4.4 The difficulty is that we tend to portray systems on two-dimensional pieces of paper. We may stretch our portrayal to three dimensions. More than that is very difficult.

A data flow diagram presents an overall view of what the system does. It is bad at showing how decisions are made; it cannot show the relationship between one data object and another data object. A data model does show what a data object is and what relationships affect it. The data model is static; it shows what the system remembers but it doesn't portray the time-dependent changes in the system.

D4.5 There are several relevant points here. One of them is that 'users' often have urgent immediate problems. If a hard-pressed user takes time off to talk to an analyst about something which may or may not happen in six months' time, the immediate problems don't go away!

Another point is that the user is probably coping with the world as he experiences it, with the tools he has learnt to use. It is difficult to contemplate using tools whose purpose he doesn't fully understand in an environment he has never experienced.

D4.6 Vested interests become very powerful. Once a project has gathered steam, the line of least resistance is always to allow it to continue. The earlier in a project life the decision to abort is made, the less the inertia to overcome, and the less the cost of wasted resources. The feasibility document is designed to provide the information on which this early decision can be made.

Additionally, since time spent on an aborted project is wasted time, the earlier the abort decision is made, the better. The knowledge that time will have been wasted often (wrongly) inhibits a decision maker from making a desirable decision to abort.

D4.7 What the system does, what it remembers and how it behaves do summarize the information requirements specification for any system. The three-part specification needs to be supplemented by a statement of purpose, or what the system is for. We contend that the procedures set out in the following chapters do meet the specification need.

D4.8 The production controller was taking the risk of bringing the steel works to a stop. It is understandable why he was willing to take this risk. It isn't reasonable to ask people to keep two information systems to the same degree of accuracy. They will take care to update the system which they intend to use. Perhaps a separate cadre of people could update the new system. This could have disastrous effects on the morale of the existing staff.

The changeover decision will always be a difficult one.

Chapter 5 Discussion points

D5.1 Yes, there could easily be such circumstances. If the physical solution relates exactly to an ideal logical solution, then we could have the same names and symbols on both diagrams. What the logical diagram should not tell us is how the functions are to be implemented; are they to be human or computer functions? It follows from this that we cannot specify the medium of the data flows on a logical diagram. The label 'Accounting' in the Sellmore logical DFD has to be interpreted as 'the function which converts all the input data flows shown on the diagram to all the output data flows from the same function!' The difficulty about any further development of the Sellmore system is that we have already declared what the 'Accounting' function is. If we subsequently decide that 'Accounting' includes something else, then we have egg on our faces.

D5.2 It is irrelevant that 'identify requirement' is carried out by the Department Buyer. It appears on the data flow diagram as a *function*, with input data flows which are required for that function. The Department Buyer as an external entity is a different matter entirely. It shows that he receives data *in his own right*. In that diagram we do not need to show what he is going to do with those data.

D5.3 There exists a phenomenon known as '*deadlock*'. If transaction 1 locks data object A and then demands a lock on data object B while transaction 2 has simultaneously locked object B and demanded a lock on object A, then both transactions are stuck.

If we can always specify the sequence in which transactions will seek locks on data tables then we can go a long way towards eliminating deadlocks.

Chapter 6 Discussion points

D6.1 Essentially, the models in this chapter describe a set of actions which occur at one time and in one context. In some cases the actions must occur in a particular sequence. The set of actions is not easy to relate to other sets of actions specified elsewhere, except through the medium of a common set of data, which is modified by the various sets of actions.

There is no real difference in the expressiveness of procedural or of non-procedural specification. Procedural specification does unnecessarily constrain the method of implementation. It introduces sequential actions in situations where it isn't required.

D6.2 Every implementation includes these constructs. They allow specification of any task in which we are likely to be interested.

D6.3 If an audit trail is required then the audit trail record is appropriately completed *after* the insertion of new data or the update of existing data. If a query is directed to a particular data table, then a *post-query* transition rule can ensure that additional data are attached to the retrieved data.

For example, a post-query rule can ensure that a customer's name and address is always added to the selection list whenever customer order data are retrieved.

Chapter 6 Exercises

E6.1 The appropriate rules relate to the local data model shown in Figure 5.10.

Rcd 1 :Pre-Update CD SUPPLIER ORDER
For All :cd_merchandise_line
Exists CD MERCHANDISE LINE within 'includes'
where CD MERCHANDISE LINE.Merchandise-Number = :cd_merchandise_line.merchandisenumber

and CD_MERCHANDISE-LINE.OrderQuantity = :cd_merchandise-line.orderquantity;

Rcd 2 :Pre-Update CD_SUPPLIER_ORDER (2)
Exists CD_MERCHANDISE_LINE within 'includes'
where CD MERCHANDISE LINE.Merchandise-Number = Any (:cd_merchandise_ line.merchandisenumber);

Rcd 3 :Update CD SUPPLIER ORDER Set Received= 'Y'
where OrderNumber = :cd_supplier_order.ono;

E6.2 Using a procedural format for the 'prepare program' functions:

Insert SPORTS subject to 'logistic details';
For each SCHEDULED RACE entry within 'includes'
  Assign :racenumber;
  Assign :eventname;
  Assign :estimatedstartime;
  For each CONTESTANT entry within 'has'
    Select :scheduled_race.racenumber into :contestant-.racenumber;
    Assign :cubscoutname;

Using a non-procedural format for the 'prepare program' function:

Rpp1. Insert SPORTS;
Rpp2. Insert SCHEDULED RACE within 'includes';
Rpp3. Insert Contestant within 'has' with default values;

Using a procedural format for the 'order to supplier' function:

For each SUPPLIER ORDER entry within 'places'
  Update MAXNUMBER set Seq No = Seq No + 1;
  Select MAXNUMBER.Seq No into :ordernumber;
  Assign the value for :suppliername at the keyboard;
  Select SystemDate + 14 into :duedate;
  For each MERCHANDISE LINE entry within 'includes'
    Select :supplier_order.ordernumber
                          into :merchandise_line.ordernumber;
    Assign the value for :merchandisenumber at the
                                            keyboard;
    Assign the value for :orderquantity at the keyboard;
Commit all changes and release locks;

The procedure does assume that referential integrity is enforced.

Using a non-procedural format for the 'order to supplier' function:

Ros 1: Pre-insert SUPPLIER ORDER
Update MAXNUMBER set NewSeqNo = SeqNo
+ 1:

Ros 2: Insert SUPPLIER ORDER into 'places' with default values;

Ros 3: Insert MERCHANDISE_LINE into 'includes' and into 'is re-ordered by' with default values;

Chapter 7 Discussion points

D7.1 There is not an answer to this dilemma. There are two different and conflicting goals. On the one hand, there is the goal of recording on one diagram the static integrity rules which should protect any database. This is of value both for the sake of understanding by the designer and for communicating that understanding to other people. The conflicting goal is the simplicity of the straightforward ERA model. With the simple model the essential outlines of the data structure is communicated. The complexities can be, and indeed must be, written down on a separate set of rules.

D7.2 The situation can be illustrated by Exercise E7.1 below. With the exception of the profit record, the entity types and the relationships between the entity types are static, and are therefore perfectly adequately represented by a static model. The profit record is *time related*. There is no sense of precedence in a data model, and the yearly sequencing of profit to time. The injection of a time sense into a data model never follows naturally from the way the model is constructed as it does with a JSD (Jackson System Development) structure diagram.

D7.3 It depends on the assumptions made. Two analysts who agree on the entity types about which information is required should arrive at similar models.

D7.4 Primarily, a data model seeks to represent reality. If the design of the database, for whatever reason, does not adopt a one-to-one relationship between real-world entity types and database data tables, then the model of the database will differ in some degree from the model of the real world.

Database management systems exist in which the relationships between data in two different tables are implemented by a series of physical pointers in the database. Since the relationship lines on the data model then display the navigational routes through the database, the data model *does* map the access paths to data.

Chapter 7 Exercises

E7.1 The entity types which clearly emerge are:

PERSON (*Name*. AddressCode)
ADDRESS (*AddressCode*, PostalAddress)
BUSINESS (*BusinessName*, BusinessSize)
PROFITABILITY (*Year*, YearlyProfit)
INTEREST (*InterestName*)

with relationships between the entity types:

One ADDRESS may accommodate many PEOPLE.
One PERSON may be employed by many BUSINESSes.
One BUSINESS may employ many PEOPLE.
One BUSINESS must report many PROFITABILITies.
One PERSON may pursue many INTERESTs.
One INTEREST may be pursued by many PEOPLE
One PERSON may be the father of many PEOPLE.
One PERSON may be the mother of many PEOPLE.

The 'employ'/'is employed by' relationship has an attribute which can be called 'Job'. This is an attribute of the relationship.

E7.2   One PERSON is associated with many TOURs.
One TOUR associates many PEOPLE.
One AIRLINE transports many TOURs.
One HOTEL accommodates many TOURs.
One TOUR is accommodated at many HOTELs.
One RESORT is the site of many HOTELs.
One COUNTRY has many RESORTs.
One BUS OPERATOR provides transport for many TOURs.

Again, 'may be' can be added to these relationship predicates as appropriate.

Chapter 8 Discussion points

D8.1 It will always be appropriate if two conditions are met. First, there must be periods during which the system can be closed to any interrogation; second, when the system is open for interrogation, the timeliness represented by the previous update must be suitable for the users' purposes.

D8.2 True! We have to ask what role the people have. Efficiency is meaningless unless it serves the purpose of a significant number of people. In some circumstances 'a sufficient number' could be just one person.

D8.3 During update, as many back-up copies as desired may be taken. Therefore there really is no problem about obtaining back-up copies of the database.

D8.4 The problems are those of any file with an index. A telephone directory is a good example of an indexed file. If new data are inserted, then the entire index may have to be re-formed. From this, we can say that an inverted file is very useful for static data, with a wide variety of entry points.

D8.5 A hashed data table does not have a systematic tendency for data to be grouped according to the age of the data. It is therefore very suitable where *volatile* data are being handled.

Chapter 9 Discussion points

D9.1 No! We may have tendencies towards either of these models; but if a person is faced with the possibility of a loss which he or she believes cannot be afforded then that person will be a pessimistic decision maker at that particular time.

D9.2 There is an element of truth here. If we always try to identify the worst possible outcome then very many actions can be seen to have the potential for disaster.

D9.3 There are at least two considerations which support the industrialist's point of view. One is that some predictions of a future are necessarily imprecise: it is foolish to use a technique which assumes greater precision than actually exists. The second point is that if it is difficult to decide whether something is worth doing, the difference in the pay-off between doing it or not doing it is probably small. If this is so, it is wiser to look for an alternative action with more obvious benefits.

D9.4 The large, early, negative cash flows are only discounted to a small degree. The later, positive cash flows are heavily discounted.

D9.5 The first two strategies assume that a market price is charged for the development. If the criterion for performance by the client departments is profitability, then we must assume that a 'correct' allocation of company resources is achieved. If external contractors are *not* allowed to compete with the internal software development department, then that department is in a monopoly position, and optimum resource allocation will not be achieved.

If the criteria for performance by the client department are anything other than profitability, then the 'market forces' argument cannot be expected to achieve an optimal allocation. This is particularly relevant to client departments which cannot possibly be profit centres (for example, treasurers, public relations, and personnel).

If the internal software development department is a cost centre rather than a profit centre then they will seek to recover their costs from the client department. The charge made will depend entirely on the extent to which the development department attempts to recover its overheads. This, in turn, depends on the amount of work in hand. If it is fully loaded it is likely to charge for any work done at the average cost per person doing the work.

If the development department is seen as an organizational service (like the treasurer's department), then presumably any charge made would be at the straight cost of doing the work.

D9.6 If an assumption about the world is found not to be very significant so far as the decision about what action should be taken is concerned, then it doesn't much matter which assumption is made. Only if the decision is very sensitive to the assumption do we need to worry about the assumption. Sensitivity analysis therefore concentrates the minds of the decision makers onto the variables which actually matter.

D9.7 Apart from purposes which are quite unrelated to money, there are others which, while we know that they affect profitability, are not predictable in their effects. There is a danger that excessive emphasis on simplistic monetary profitability will be harmful.

D9.8 Very few decisions that we make are driven entirely by our own monetary profit. 'Utility' is a synonym for satisfaction.

Chapter 10 Discussion points

D10.1 'Do we know what training courses our employees have attended?' and 'How many database tables contain personal data about students?' are the only two questions for which you would consult a data dictionary.

D10.2 It depends on the use you make of the table. If the structural data are intended to drive an *active* data dictionary, then it will be segregated. Both context data and administrative data are primarily of use during the design process.

D10.3 The advantages of normalization are primarily that control of duplication helps to maintain the integrity of the database and that reduction of the database to the smallest practicable discrete fragments gives great flexibility in meeting different search requests. If two tables really do belong together as a complex data object, such as a customer order header table and all the attendent item lines, then there is little advantage for control of duplication in separating them. It may be that by removing the need for foreign keys the redundancy is actually reduced.

Again, if the data selection and update needs are fairly static, the advantages of flexibility in meeting search requests are small.

The cost of normalization is that many computer-processing power-hungry 'joins' may be required for quite modest queries and updates. If a complex data object is always handled as an entity, these joins may be unnecessary.

We believe that the onus should be on the database designers to show why data *should not* be normalized.

D10.4 It can ensure that foreign keys are defined identically to the primary keys to which they point. It can also be of value for carrying identities through hierarchies of data, from the root to the leaves.

D10.5 We believe that there are advantages from writing integrity rules in a format which is recognizably similar to the way those rules are going to be implemented in the database management system. The expression of rules as entries in tables also allows specification of constraints such as legal domain values and default values, which have no conventions allowing them to be displayed on a data model diagram.

D10.6 Consistent enforcement of consistent rules.
D10.7 The process of design is difficult, if not impossible, unless consistent data object definitions are available to the designer.

Chapter 10 Exercises

E10.1 Table entries must include SUPPLIER, SUPPLIER ORDER, MERCANDISE LINE, and MERCHANDISE. There may be other 'view' tables, in particular, views relating to management information. We suppose that the highest supplier order number is stored in a table called MAX. 'Number' has been abbreviated to 'Num' in the following display.

The column description table should include:

TableName	ColumnName	Status	DomainName	Null?	Default
SUPPLIER	SupplierName	K	name	No	No default
SUPPLIER ORDER	OrderNum	K	num	No	MAX.NewSeqNo
SUPPLIER ORDER	SupplierName	F	Name	No	No default
SUPPLIER ORDER	DueDate	–	date		SystemDate + 14
MERCHANDISE LINE	OrderNum	FKa	num	No	:supplier.ordernum
MERCHANDISE LINE	MerchandiseNum	FKa	num	No	No default
MAX	SeqNum	–	num	No	No insertion

The relationship owner table description should include:

RelationshipName	OwnerTable	DegreeOfMembers	OwnerDeletion
places	SUPPLIER	None or more	Inhibit if members
includes	SUPPLIER ORDER	One or more	Delete members
is re-ordered by	MERCHANDISE	None or more	Inhibit if members

And the relationship member table:

RelationshipName	MemberTable	ForeignKey	Maybe/Mustbe
places	SUPPLIER ORDER	SupplierName	Mustbe
includes	MERCHANDISE LINE	OrderNum	Mustbe
is re-ordered by	MERCHANDISE LINE	MerchandiseNum	Mustbe

E10.2 If virtual columns are either not allowed, or are allowed to be defined on only one base table column, then there would be a fairly straightforward many-to-many relationship between TABLE DESCRIPTION, and COLUMN DESCRIPTION:

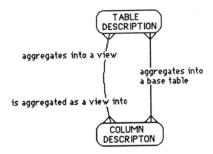

If the view includes several table columns, and perhaps also a complex expression combining these base table columns, then the text of the column description should be included:

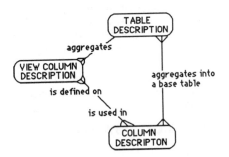

E10.3 We contemplate that where feasible, integrity rules are expressed within the tabular form that we have presented. There must however be transition rules whose structure we are not able to accommodate within an existing data dictionary table format. These rules can be related to a particular function which has to be performed. We propose to handle these by simply listing the rules:

    Rule order entry 1: --,
    Rule order entry 2: --;

Since rules relate to functions, they will have a many-to-many relationship with individual tables, as shown in Figure 10.11.

Chapter 11 Discussion points

D11.1 'Purpose' could be interpreted in two ways. If the artefact is unsuited to its ultimate purpose, then that discrepancy will become increasingly obvious as time progresses, and acceptance of *something* becomes more and more imminent. In a different sense, an artefact must also be designed in a way that facilitates its construction. If the artefact fails either of these counts then corrective action is needed. That corrective action will cost time and extra resources.

D11.2 If the system being built is one seamless whole, then it is true that the construction of that whole entity would necessarily take more than a fortnight. The construction of a 6000-foot concrete-lined mine shaft on the Witwatersrand is a good example. The point of 'do it in a fortnight!' is to avoid unnecessary difficulties in how much of the task is finished. There isn't any difficulty about measuring how much of a mine shaft has been finished!

Generally, complex systems will have many parts. The existence of those parts provides scope for intelligent partitioning of the total system to form sensibly sized packages.

D11.3 It is only in the case of tree data structures, and entity sub-types, that an entity inherits any identity from a higher-echelon type name, e.g.:

SHIP, FREIGHT-SHIP, CONTAINER-FREIGHT-SHIP

Little would be gained by this, since an entity type does not represent a work package, which has to be included in larger work packages.

D11.4 What the manager *cannot* do is to throw more resources at the project. It would be more effective to stand back, take more time over the planning of the job and decide whether further controlled partitioning is possible.

D11.5 Software designing and building is intellectual work. Our natural inclinations would make a sensible session the period between two meals or half a day. If management tries to monitor more closely than this, the irritation produced would probably be counterproductive.

D11.6 In de Marco's words, an estimate is not a negotiation. If your boss insists on his figure, then it's his estimate, not yours.

D11.7 It probably isn't meaningful to use probability estimates unless a similar job has been done several times before. One-off estimates are notoriously difficult to attach probabilities to.

If the estimate is genuinely a 'best estimate', then it's a swings and roundabouts situation. Some of the estimates will be too short and some too long. With experience, you should get somewhere in the right ball park!

D11.8 After the Second World War the Nuremberg trials established quite clearly, if there was ever any doubt, that everyone is responsible for what he or she does. If you join an unethical activity, you too are tainted.

D11.9 Yes! It is the only way to ensure proper discharge of work assignments.

D11.10 There is no firm answer to this. We believe that such a stage does come, and that designers should get on and build whatever has been currently specified. Unless this is done, building would never start. Occasionally, it must be necessary to abort started work because it has become obvious that it is going in the wrong direction.

Index